The
Wore Black than Purple

Interviews

compiled and edited by
Jerry Bloom

First published in Great Britain in 2007
by Wymer Publishing
PO Box 155, Bedford, MK40 2YX
www.wymerpublishing.co.uk
Tel: 01234 326691

ISBN 978-0-9557542-0-3

Typeset by Wymer UK
Printed and bound by
Lightning Source.

Cover design by Wymer UK:
Front cover photo © Neil Davies
Back cover photo montage, Wymer UK

Contents

Introduction

Whether or not artists love them or loathe them, interviews are something of a necessary requirement in the entertainment industry. While some musicians relish in talking about themselves, others dread the thought. But sometimes even the most reluctant can end up providing the interviewer with enlightened anecdotes and often hilarious stories. Indeed the music business is renowned for the many amusing tales that have been passed down through the years.

Irrespective that this book is essentially a compilation of the many interviews published within the Ritchie Blackmore magazine, *More Black than Purple*, and the obvious angles therein, hopefully it will offer some chuckles along the way.

Since *More Black than Purple* was launched in 1996 it has published many interviews with musicians who have been linked to the world of Deep Purple, Rainbow, Blackmore's Night and beyond. In some cases, parts of the interviews that were felt not applicable for the magazine have until now remained unpublished. In addition other interviews, previously unpublished in their entirety have also been included.

For anyone interested in Deep Purple and the family of bands that have become embroiled in the history of arguably Britain's finest ever hard rock outfit, then hopefully the interviews included within this tome will be of great interest. I hope that the interviews go some way to giving a greater insight into not just the bands in question, but also the career ups and downs of the individual musicians featured.

Some may question in this day and age of the Internet, why a book like this exists in the first place, however many of those who subscribe to *More Black than Purple* appear not to use the Internet. Besides, that medium has yet to convince me just how well it will archive data that is posted on it. Furthermore, there is something more substantial about a book, and although, this particular tome is designed to be delved in and out of rather than reading in one sitting, such activity is still best done in traditional book form.

For each interview I have also included a pre-amble, some of which explain the background behind the interviews in question. Rounding the book off is a selection of photos, many previously unreleased. If this book is well-received there is the possibility of a second volume, but until that point, enjoy what is within.

Jerry Bloom
Bedford, September 2007

GLENN HUGHES

The first interview I conducted was actually done a couple of years before *More Black than Purple* was launched. After Purple's dissolvement in 1976, Glenn Hughes recorded the excellent 'Play Me Out' along with help from his former Trapeze buddies, Mel Galley and Dave Holland. Despite another fine album five years later; the joint collaboration with former Pat Travers guitarist, Pat Thrall, Hughes career went off the rails due to serious drug abuse.

What followed was a period of stop-start projects including involvement with established artists such as Gary Moore and Tony Iommi (under the guise of Black Sabbath) as well as performing with The KLF on their hit single 'What Time Is Love?'

By 1994, Hughes had cleaned himself up and re-activated his career. Now straightened out he was working full on. Not only had Trapeze reactivated as an on-off project but a full solo career was blossoming. Following the album simply called 'Blues', his first solo release since 'Play Me Out', Hughes was touring again and promoting his then current and excellent album 'From Now On.'

I can't recall exactly just how the interview had been set up but I think I had spoken to Glenn at an earlier gig on the tour and he had agreed to be interviewed once a suitable moment was found. That moment turned out to be early evening before the gig at the Woughton Centre in Milton Keynes. The interview was jointly conducted with my erstwhile colleague and namesake, Jerry Witherstone.

Unsure whether or not it would be at the venue or Hotel, we chose the latter first, and hung around in the lobby mid-afternoon. I shall never forget the two receptionists, regularly looking over at us as we sat waiting for Hughes to emerge from his room. Clearly they were aware that a rock band was staying there, but obviously had no idea as to who they actually were. Hughes band at the time also included former members of Purple influenced, Swedish rockers, Europe, who for a while became the darlings of many female rockers after their excellent, and massive hit, 'The Final Countdown.' Eventually one of the receptionists started to gingerly walk towards us and then confronted us with pen and paper. "Could we have your autographs please," she tentatively asked! I didn't know where to look or what to say. I felt embarrassed, and even more so for her. I didn't want to make the receptionist feel even more stupid, but nor could I carry the charade through and had to let her down gently, explaining that we were not the band but were actually there to interview the star of the show.

When Hughes finally emerged he suggested we did the interview at the venue but along with his assistant was unsure exactly how to get there. Consequently it was arranged that they would follow our car. It was a somewhat strange feeling to have Glenn Hughes following in the car behind, and also brought home to me how the mighty had fallen since his glory days with Deep Purple. This was the first major tour of his homeland since those heady days of the seventies. No longer were there chauffeur driven limousines, but instead Hughes sat in the passenger seat of and old Ford Sierra!

This interview has remained under wraps until now. It went surprisingly well and Hughes was very frank and open about his career and the personal experiences that had dogged him for a decade. Before the tape was rolling, we had started talking about his unexpected friendship with Ian Gillan, which continued as the tape started rolling...

Ian's not frightened of me like most singers are. We don't sound the same we've different voices. We jammed three years ago. Just sitting around at a friend of mine's house. I started playing a song. And Ian wanted to compose something. I noticed he was very spontaneous in the way he writes, which I didn't think he was. No that's wrong. I didn't really know about the way he wrote but Ian has a definite thirst for writing.

Where did your first paths cross then?
He was with Mark Nauseef, and Tony whatshisface...

Ashton?
No, it was the Ian Gillan Band with Ray Fenwick and I went to see them in Birmingham; he came out and he was very nice. Then we did the Butterfly Ball together. Ian and I really became real friends about four years ago. I didn't realise what a great guy Ian was. You see a lot of really well known singers... I scare them off or they get weird around me but Ian said that he really thought I captured... that I was the best British soul singer, which coming from him I thought that was really great. Because I basically took his place in Deep Purple, I sang. And that was very big off him to say that and that was really nice.

Didn't David Bowie once say that of you as well?
He said I was his favourite white singer. Stevie Wonder said the same. A lot of great singers... Paul Rodgers has said I'm his favourite white singer and that's the greatest compliment of all. See once again, singing to me is like tying a shoelace and if the crowd are behind me you can expect miraculous things. And that's a pretty heavy statement.

Like last night.
Yeah for anyone who was taping last night they must have got one hell of a bootleg. (laughs)

We weren't unfortunately.
(He mishears what I say) *You were taping?*

No.
Well you guys will find a tape. We videotape everything. Anders (Tegner, Hughes assistant at the time) *will make a videotape; may take a couple of months.*

So you record all the shows.
He tapes everything.

You said on stage last night that it was your first proper gig since leaving Purple and that you weren't nervous.
No not at all.

But considering it was your first gig weren't you a little apprehensive at all?
No and let me explain why. When God shone his light on me in recovery. When he said to me very specifically I have work for you to do... his work consists of me singing to the best of my ability and writing songs and being there and suiting up and showing up and doing my performance. But also his job is for me... you see a lot of people when you mention the name Glenn Hughes they go "Aaah that's the guy that does drugs" or "that's the guy that's recovering from drugs." It's always a drug thing. I want to be known not only as the guy who kicked drugs but came back from it and kicked serious arse. It's going to take a few years. I don't want it to happen right away because I want this to slowly ease into it. So the reason I said that it was a very emotional evening for me, like tonight will be: I came like Montgomery, I came to kick arse. I came on this tour to really show the British public and all those other people who are flying in that I'm the best singer that we have in England and I think I am. I am because God has given me that privilege. It's not Glenn Hughes the egotistic. I've got an ego but I'm not like... I don't hear anybody else doing what I'm doing nobody else can do what I do.

Do you think there's a part inside of you then that's really gnawing at the bit to all the people that have been quick enough to put you down in the past. Glenn Hughes is dead and buried...
To some extent: Those people didn't understand the disease of alcoholism. They thought that I was some guy who really wanted to screw up and I didn't. I didn't want to grow up to be a drug addict, but unfortunately I became very sick. I relate it to having cancer. If you don't cure it you'll die. If you don't go to the dentist you will have toothache. That's it for me.

So was that like a continuous thing for years or were there any times when you were coherent?
No, once you're an addict you're an addict. In Black Sabbath I did try to curb it and in Gary Moore I tried to curb it but it's always looming, sitting on your shoulder going, 'just one more drink.' Until you surrender you'll never get cured. By the way I'll never be cured, I'll always be in recovery.

Are you completely dry now then?
Oh yeah, I don't drink anything. I don't even brush my teeth with alcohol in the toothpaste, or mouth wash. I don't eat meat or fat. I don't eat a lot of dairy products. I don't put anything into my body... I won't take an aspirin either unless a doctor prescribes it. I won't put anything into my system that will make me in anyway chemically dependent. What you have now is a Glenn Hughes who is cleaner than anybody you will ever meet. What you used to have was the most fucked up addict that has to have as much alcohol and drugs in his system at all times, to escape. And we addicts and alcoholics are not happy with our lives. We try and escape into another

dimension because we can't handle reality. The reality for me was that when I was in Deep Purple, I was so rich and so fucking famous and so unhappy because I wasn't really singing lead vocals, I was taking second seat, that I escaped into a world of drugs.

So didn't you enjoy your time with Purple then?
I enjoyed every minute musically but... when I say musically I did enjoy it but I wish I had been singing all the vocals. I am a vocalist. I can't really think of any other band in history that has had a better singer bass player than the original singer. David will tell you I'm a better singer it's just that he happened to get the gig.

If you read all the history it says there was a load of friction. Was that between you and David or with the rest of the band?
David would sometimes walk off the stage in my solo spots and go (through clenched teeth), *"God listen to him" and I would be carrying on doing my thing. And that was the thing I told them when I joined the band. I will be doing my thing and if you don't want me to do it I won't join.*

Looking back you certainly changed the sound of Deep Purple. Knowing your background maybe they shouldn't have employed you. I don't mean that disrespectfully but with your black music background...
I totally agree. Ritchie loved it. He loved the fact that I was doing what I was doing but then he didn't realise the kind of writer I was. I wrote Mistreated with him; it wasn't David. That turned out to be really good. I wrote a lot of songs on Burn.

How come you weren't credited?
Because I was signed to another company and I was hiding my publishing rights because I was signed with a company that would take the lot. Burn by the way has kept me going all these years. It's sold over four and a half million copies.

And you are still getting royalties from it?
Yes thank God for that, it's the album that keeps me going.

Talking of 'Burn', why did you do 'Burn' on this latest album?
'Burn' was something the record company chose. I recorded it as a bonus track originally for Japan, and then they got greedy and said, "we'll put it out." I said, "okay." It's not really relevant to what I'm doing now. But I do it live. The reason why I am doing all these Purple songs now is, wouldn't it be a travesty if I came, like tonight and there are all these Purple fans, a lot of them around, and I didn't play any Purple songs? It was like Robert Plant when he started, he didn't play any Zeppelin. Why not give the fans what they want? Why not sing 'This Time Around' when I sing it like an angel? Why not do it? The songs that people have waited twenty years to hear.

They're nice to hear but don't you think it's a millstone around your neck. I mean you've somehow eventually got to get away from it.
Absolutely it is but I've got to do it on this tour.

And from then on more of your own material?
Eventually in the next two or three years you will see me lean less on these songs because I'm getting the fans singing at the same volume for the new songs as they are for the old songs.

Can I ask you about Tommy Bolin, your memories?
Tommy was a sweet loving kind humble man who... he and I got on famously but we were sick

though. We both had the same views on music and life. We stretched boundaries; we really were out there musically. But Tommy and I were sick; we weren't good bedfellows we shouldn't have been together. When he passed away it didn't really stop me from using unfortunately.

Did it come as a surprise to you his passing?
Yes it did, absolutely.

There was talk that you were going to get a band together with him when Purple split.
Yeah, we hadn't actually done anything but we did some tapes at my house just fucking around. Tommy wanted me to do the whole of the album 'Teaser' but I said no I thought he should sing it. But I did a bit on the end of 'Dreamer.' Tommy Bolin, I miss him just as much as a friend but I miss him as a musician too.

What's your favourite thing of Tommy's musically?
I like 'People, People' without a doubt.

My favourite is the 'Private Eyes' album I really like that album.
Oh me too.

I think the acoustic solo on 'Gypsy Soul' is really beautiful.
It's really nice to see a lot of Purple fans that got into Tommy. We have a lot of Glenn Hughes fans that are Tommy Bolin fans.

The solo album you recorded for Warner Bros that was never released- are there any plans for it?
I hope not... yes, it's out (as a bootleg). *It's called 'White Soul Rockin Black.' It came out on a very dodgy cassette that someone copied off a cassette of a cassette and it's horrible.*

There are some good songs on it though.
The songs are great but they sound awful.

But wouldn't you want to see another record company release that?
No. Here's a thing you got to know about me. When I've done something last year it's old. Hughes Thrall still sounds good fourteen years later but 'From Now On' to me is old, let's get the next one done.

And the direction for the next one will be in a very similar vein?
No, I've got to get to the real Glenn Hughes issues, which are funk, soul and rock together. That wonderful element of those three together: Trapeze of the 1995 if you want.

Do you find that as a dilemma at all- that artistic and commercial balance? Doing something that isn't commercially successful to your fans, because you have always had that image as a rock musician, but I get the impression you would be happier doing an album of James Brown covers.
Yes, you know that but you know something, some of you folks would like it. But as much as I would be jerking myself off and enjoying it...

I'd love to hear you tackle 'It's A Man's, Man's, Man's World' (James Brown song).
Funnily enough I'm doing that with Mick Mars of Motley Crue. He's doing a solo album with a full orchestra. He asked me to do that with him two years ago.

You took the bass for 'Gettin' Tighter' last night. Why not choose to take the bass and sing on all the songs?

The true answer is I felt on this tour I had to play bass on one song. I think anybody... Sting when he first formed his band he played guitar I think. It's something, a phase we go through. I may not be doing this lead front man thing forever. It's something I want to go through. Doing the Trapeze thing in March and April convinced me I should be playing bass full time.

You looked comfortable, but I remember when you were in Black Sabbath, you didn't know what to do with your arms.

Awful experience.

Do you feel comfortable now?

Not from day one, I've been performing as a front man since last June and it took probably until May this year. Japan sorted that out.

How did that go, were you playing bigger venues there?

Their Purple connection is very strong there. A lot of the fans from my generation have now born their generation who have insisted they listen to Glenn Hughes. So I'm like this twenty-year-old kid who has gone to Japan. I have a lot of 12-18 year old fans of Glenn Hughes now. For Christ sake I'm forty-two years old.

I have a couple of tapes from Japan of the radio things you did acoustically, such as 'You Keep On Moving.' Do you have any plans to do something like that on a grander scale?

I'd love to. What I have to do, and I will be exclusively honest with you. I have to hone in on my... I write so many songs I have to really, really develop more. I write very quickly and I just record things and I don't pay much attention to it. Tell you the truth, the last three months I have been at home in the studio writing I think the best songs ever, because I'm taking more time lyrically, melodically and groove. Really just honing in on these gems now. I really believe these songs are my children. I really want to make them that bit more special. The next album is going to be a lot stronger than the last one.

I've read that you want to go more diverse.

The next one will be more diverse. It will definitely be more funky and I will be happy to talk to you in a year's time and go, "that's much better."

More in the direction of 'Play Me Out' then?
I'd love it to be. The record company I'm with right now won't let that happen but they say the next one after that will be, but I may not stay with that record company.

Is that frustrating?
They are throwing enormous amounts of money at me to make me happy, but I'm not happy. I'm okay financially now, but musically, I've got to be honest with you, I'm not happy.

So you enjoyed the 'Play Me Out' album then?
Immensely. I listen back to it and it's like genius. When I say genius it's God's genius through me. I'm just channelled. I just sit at the keyboard and I write my shit.

Were there any other songs from that session that are unreleased apart from 'Smile'?
What you are going to get. I'm going to deliver two demos I did last year that will be on the next 'Play Me Out' (re-issue). Songs I did at home that I think the Purple fans will dig. Very soulful, very Glenn, very Glenn on his own with nobody else because when I'm left alone you get 'Play Me Out.'

What about Trapeze, any unreleased stuff that is still to come out?
Yes, you are going to get a live album next Spring from Dallas 72 that somebody recorded on a reel to reel. We got a DAT of it and I improved it, it's amazing. It has four encores.

Who is going to be releasing that?
Polygram will probably be releasing it in America. I don't know. I'm on top of it right now.

Is Trapeze still in your mind?
Yes and the reason why is, it spiritually progresses me. I feel good playing in that band. You can't really say like Ian is with the Javelins, that's Ian's hobby. Trapeze for me is like something I have to do. It won't make me millions of dollars.

Will it be purely a live thing?
At the moment it will be. We've recorded one new song and I wrote another new song that I will record around Christmas time that will be on a compilation plus two songs Polygram will release next Spring.

Mel (Galley) was at the gig last night.
Oh yeah. Dave (Holland) is coming tonight.

I read today in a magazine you have done two new sessions. One of Purple covers and one of Cream.
Yeah I did 'Stormbringer' and 'Born Under A Bad Sign.'

The old Booker T number.
You should hear me sing that. Kick arse. I had a cold when I did that but it still sounds good.

So can we expect to hear you tackle more stuff like that in the future?
What you will probably get from me over the next few years is another 'Play Me Out' type album where it's obviously Glenn left alone in the studio writing those spacey numbers.

So that won't involve different musicians?
I like to work alone. I really do. I'm not sure if I want to have a "band" band around all the time: Like Prince does it. He does his thing and has people come in now and again. I like to work alone in the studio. Like I can program the drums, and I can play bass and guitar and keyboards. Then I can get people to play over that if they can. That's how 'Play Me Out' was done. I was in there alone played all the instruments and then had Mel and Dave garnish it.

I wanted to also ask about bands before Trapeze.
Finders Keepers, 1968, The News 1967, The In Pack, 1966. Before that 1965-66 was my very first band The Intruders and the band before that, we changed the name, was the Hooker Lees, as in John Lee Hooker.

So you were playing blues?
Sort of, we were playing Rolling Stones.

When we were talking earlier about the 'Blues' album, I know you said you try and forget it now, but I'm surprised when it came out: I was expecting something more like Negro Blues.
Once again the label president wouldn't allow me to do it.

Did you want to do something like Muddy Waters, Howlin' Wolf Stuff?
Well it would have been but he wanted an "LA metal type blues" album, which I thought sucked but I did the best I could for the tools I had to do it with.

Again, I'm surprised that you only played bass on a few tracks.
I hired Tony Franklin to do it because I wanted fretless and I am still learning fretless bass. I didn't really want to play something I wasn't in control of so I got somebody to play fretless. I'll always give somebody a chance of helping me, or if I don't think I can do something well. I'll never get somebody to sing for me though! (laughs)

Which albums did you enjoy most with Purple. What had the happiest memories?
'Burn' was a great experience; because it was the first album and it was a really good time we had making the album. 'Stormbringer' was bloody awful because Ritchie was on the way out. 'Come Taste The Band' was a drug-crazed trip in Germany. Burn was the best.

Do you think the songs are the strongest ones then?
As a classic rock album, yeah.

I think 'Come Taste The Band' is a very strong album.
I love it.

It's very popular amongst Purple fans, it was nice to hear some of those songs last night. The way you did 'This Time Around' and dedicating it to Tommy was quite emotive.
Well that's the way I feel about Tommy, it's a genuine love for him and his family. I genuinely am

moved. I don't have any brothers or sisters; he was like the first one.
Were you familiar with his music before he joined Purple?
Only the week before, I started listening up. Joe Walsh of course is a good friend of mine; we spoke last week actually about Tommy.

What's your view on some of this unreleased stuff of his that is supposed to be coming out?
I think it's great for collectors.

Some people just want to forget about the past they don't want things released from the past. You don't feel that way you are happy to see it released?
I don't mind, it doesn't bother me, you're gonna get it anyway.

Like you sanctioned the release of 'Play Me Out 'and 'Four On The Floor' to be re-released. That was fun.
Strange combination.

Can't be any stranger than the KLF though?
Aaah that was great.

It looked on the video as if you were having a lot of fun
A lot of fun, great guys.

Do you plan to do anything with them again?
Oh absolutely. I don't know if they will get back together but I'm sure we will. Right chums, I'm off to get some grub.

****

RITCHIE BLACKMORE

The first major interview published in *More Black than Purple* came to us more by accident than design. Noted journalist Neil Jeffries interviewed Blackmore in Long Island, New York on Saturday, September 9th, 1995, several months before the magazine was launched. In fact the main reason for starting the magazine was because Blackmore was getting very little press after his departure from Deep Purple. Despite his years in the business, Jeffries was also up against it and having travelled to New York for his chat with Blackmore, failed to find a magazine that would do justice to his mammoth interview.

Mojo did publish a few quotes from it, but eventually a year and a half later, and in conjunction with an MBTP subscriber, Rob Walton, Jeffries agreed that the interview should find its logical home in a magazine devoted to its subject matter. The interview was both lengthy and highly fascinating. Jeffries knowledge of Blackmore's career brought out some worthy responses from the man, and for the most part, Blackmore was honest and straightforward with his answers. Jeffries also provided an entertaining preamble...

In the shadowy, candlelit corner of a restaurant about an hour's drive north of New York City, a dark figure sits alone. Through the restaurant's window the figure looks like he may be up to no good. Through the window of the house opposite, a disgruntled Long Islander will confirm this, having seen the red dot of the man's laser torch bouncing around his sitting room walls all too often. Tonight, the laser is directed inward and around a restaurant packed with people. Packed, that is, but for one corner where the villain of our piece sits alone. Around the restaurant, curious diners crane their necks and peer into the candlelight to catch a glimpse of him. Directly across from where he sits, an ancient black statue - a life-size wooden carving of a knight - does the same. Decades ago, according to old photographs, this knight used to gaze over his opposite shoulder at the fireplace. Now, he looks to the corner where Richard Hugh Blackmore always sits. I know this to be true. Richard Hugh Blackmore told me so.

Between now and 3.30 tomorrow morning, Ritchie Blackmore will tell me many things, the wooden knight's changing pose by no means the strangest among them. Pretty weird too is his account of a seance he held here a couple of months ago, when the spirit of a young woman contacted the table and revealed the name of the man who had murdered her - a name known to others in the restaurant! Indeed, someone who lives not far down the road...

"We'll have to do something about that guy. I'm not sure what, but we'll think of something," intones Ritchie matter-of-factly, as he recommends the chef's chicken and orders an evil-sounding cocktail from a waitress. "Er, no, on second thoughts, forget the measure of Tabasco. I was only kidding." But we are here to discuss matters of even darker intrigue and feuding, of blood and thunder. Of Deep Purple. And of family trees. It was back on July 8th when many *Darker Than Blue* readers, doubtless with a dewy eye cast over to a dog-eared copy of 'Machine Head', or perhaps upwards to the loft where an ex-RAF greatcoat now rots, sat in front of BBC2 to watch the 'Deep Purple People' episode in Pete Frame's excellent 'Rock Family Trees' series. The story which unfolded had grown bizarre with time. It was the story of a band seemingly hell-bent on destruction, supremely adept at snatching defeat from the beckoning jaws of victory. Of men who simply could not get on with each other, no matter how many millions of listeners their music united. Hanging over proceedings like a spectre was the absence of Ritchie Blackmore.

Grown men like Ian Gillan, Jon Lord, Roger Glover, Ian Paice, Glenn Hughes and David Coverdale spoke of their erstwhile guitarist (and tormentor) as if he had died. Each of them struggled to come to terms with their loss; trying not very hard at all to speak ill of the dead. This analogy amuses Mr. Blackmore very much...

Have you seen the BBC 'Rock Family Trees'? (He misunderstands me and thinks I am asking about the video made of his final UK tour with Deep Purple, filmed against his will in Birmingham.)
I don't tend to watch things that I'm in. I'm very self-conscious.

But you weren't in it.
I know. (laughs) I shy away from anything that's related to myself. I find it too boring - I hear everything I want to hear without watching television, and I can imagine what they would have done on that show; the fuss that I made about not doing that show.

That still doesn't explain to me why you didn't do it...
It was way back in Germany. When we first went on tour, the whole point was: "Let's get a video out very quickly to push the record" ('The Battle Rages On' album, in 1993). We had 'Anya' out (as a single) and we started to work in Bavaria, in Southern Germany, and I said: "Let's get the video out now to push that particular song." But the guy from the record company said: "No, no, we're gonna do it in England.' I said: "What is the point of doing it in England? That is six weeks down the road. That is really stupid. Let's do it in two days' time. Let's do it before Ian Gillan loses his voice, which is the manner of ... it happens every time, within the week. "No, no, can't do that." "Why not?" "Well" ... bullshit reasons. Anyway, that's what started the ball rolling for me to be pissed off with the whole thing. They said: "We're gonna do it in England." And I said: "Well, I'm not doing it then, it's just too late. It's too stupid." (laughs) So I told them to count me out. But I said if you're going to do it, I really don't want cameras in front of the audience. I have a thing about that. It's not fair to these kids who have paid their money to sit and watch the back of some guy's head with a camera. So I just got all uppity about it. I thought it was completely

futile to do it that late on the tour. What is it going to promote? Nothing - the tour's over two or three weeks later. (it was over for Blackmore, who declined to accompany the band on the next leg in Japan.) *Sure enough, Gillan's voice was crap, it had just gone! And they said: "We can overdub Gillan's voice." But I said: "Why overdub when you can record in two days' time?" But they couldn't see that logic. So when we got to Birmingham I said it would be okay to film, as long as the cameras were off stage and not around me. Take the rest of the band, whatever. Then, just before I went on stage, I started playing 'Highway Star' and was told that the cameras were off stage. Colin Hart* (tour manager) *had told me: "Yeah, the cameras are nowhere near you." I said: "That's good - don't include me - keep me out of it." I didn't want to pull the rest of them down. That was just my personal opinion, how I felt...*

At this point had you made the decision to leave the band?
Oh yeah. There was a big letter that went down. I'd sent them a letter, within two weeks of getting on the tour, that I was leaving. But I went to walk on stage and someone said: "The camera's not gone, it's still on stage." So I thought: "What the hell's that doing there?" So I turned around, went back down the steps. I told someone: "Get rid of the cameras and I'll go back on." A minute later, they're still playing der-der-der.... (laughs) *Colin Hart comes over to me: "They're off, they're gone." Great! So I go back on and the guy is still right there! So I'm like: "What the fuck is this?" And I turn around again and walk off. I've been on twice now and the audience is going: "Yeah!" Then ....* (creases his eyebrows). *They didn't know what was going on. It's not their fault. Great audience. But I was so angry because they were pushing, thinking that because they had started playing that I was just going to go along with it. Ritchie won't do anything because we've started playing. Oh yeah? Do you wanna see what I'll do? I told you, all of you, that I didn't want any cameras near me on stage. This is what's gonna happen. The night before, at Brixton, I'd sprained my ankle - a bad sprain so I was all taped up - the doctor said I shouldn't go on. I said: "I can't just not go on" I remember him saying: "Well, I admire your stoicism." So I immediately looked the word up .... So if I'd wanted to be really nasty I'd just have said: "No, I'm not playing because of my ankle."*

You'd slipped on the monitors, hadn't you?
That's right. It was a combination of being drunk and not being able to see. I miscalculated because I had these silly boots. The heels were this wide instead of a normal heel. It was a girl's shoe... Anyway, the next night in Birmingham I walked off stage and got a glass of water. Then I ran around to the guy with the camera and threw the water - or the beer - and threw it in the camera lens so then I knew he had to back off. And, sure enough, he did. But then, of course, some of the beer went over some of the "royalty" that was backstage, namely peoples' wives. They thought I'd done it purposefully, so I got the finger from all the wives. But if I'd wanted to throw beer on the wives I would have gone over and thrown it at them, but that was not my intention. I came back on stage and tried to play, but I was so angry because the whole thing was such a fiasco. Why lie about where the cameras are? Don't just start playing, get it worked out beforehand. Don't take it out on the audience. The audience shouldn't be put into this position of wondering: "Who is this guy walking on and off?" But I wasn't going to play until they moved these guys, which could all have been done in five minutes, two minutes... But no, they had to go on and start without me.

When you do that, you upset people in the audience who have paid their money to see you.
I know that it'll only be for a couple of minutes while I go round there and throw beer over someone. Plus - it's rock 'n' roll! I don't want to be comfortable in a wheelchair or an armchair like the rest of them. This is just rock 'n' roll. I'm throwing beer over a cameraman - so what? That's what rock 'n' roll is all about. I could go on there and say: "Give me your money," and

*"Birmingham - do you wanna rock 'n' roll?" - not that I would say that - but I could go through the cliche. But I think if I saw an artist I would want to see him.... it's like Ian Anderson told me a story once. I went to see Jethro Tull in Hamburg, and afterwards I asked him: "What did you do to that guy in the front row? It looked very strange. You kind of jumped down into the front row, something happened, then you jumped back on to the stage." He said: "Oh! That guy! He fell asleep - fell asleep at **my** show! So I jumped down there and smacked him!" I thought that was brilliant. Talk about inspiration - that's perfect, that's great; it's all part of it. As long as you don't just play, or not turn up, you can always add a little bit of spice in there. Really - it wasn't the band's fault - it was Colin Hart's fault. He should never have told me the cameraman was off the stage. Paicey doesn't know that I'm not going on.*

But Pete Frame's "Rock Family Trees" programme?
Yes, I've heard of him.

He must have approached you to do it?
I think he has, apparently. I can't really remember. I think he's a bit like Simon Robinson: the head of the Deep Purple fan club, but he doesn't really like them. Which is brilliant! He doesn't like the band, or anything they do, and he's the president of the fan club!

I think he does...
Does he? He has a very strange way of showing it. I don't follow it, but every now and then people bring things to me and tell me things, and I say: "Well, who said that?" "Oh! Simon Robinson." Who is this bloke? He's like a nightmare!

But Pete Frame?
I think I did receive a letter saying: "Can you help us?" - I vaguely remember - but I forgot all about it. I'm very bad at returning calls.

It was a big series that was very well received; and all the people that I have spoken to thought that the Deep Purple programme was probably the best of the series. Everyone was there - apart from you! They had Nick Simper...
They got Nick? I tend to remove myself from anything I've done, most of the time. But Nick? That guy used to bellyache all the time. He was like the fifth Beatle that was aimed out. He was such a nice guy, but he couldn't play. And he couldn't sing! So it was like, sorry Nick, but you've got to go. He just never got over it. Very sour...

Also on there was Jon Lord, Ian Paice, Roger Glover, Ian Gillan, David Coverdale, Glenn Hughes, Cozy Powell, Tony Ashton...
You know, they might have asked me to do it but the old management might not have told me.

Well, let's do it now. Let's fill in the gaps. My girlfriend watched it with me and said: "Everyone talks about Ritchie like he is dead." *(laughs)* You were this spectre hanging over the whole thing... *(laughs)* Jon Lord said, at one point: "This guy's been a part of my life for a quarter of a century and I'm still steamed at some of the things he's done." And you were made out to be this driving force behind the band that kept splitting up for no obvious reason. It was very funny - but probably unintentionally funny.
I wouldn't watch it.

Why not?
If I'm involved with something I'll very rarely watch it. It just doesn't interest me. Seems a strange thing to do. You know, some people, they make films but never watch their own films? I'm kind of like that with music; but especially with film stuff. We did something the other day that my girlfriend says I must watch because it's very funny. But it's like: Maybe one day, when I'm drunk." I get very self-conscious if I watch my own stuff. Even football games; watching myself kicking a ball...

Are you unhappy with the way you look?
It's just a kind of strange... I can't relate to people looking at me either. (laughs) *I don't feel comfortable watching myself at all. Or listening to myself!*

Do you not listen to your music either?
I listen to what I play, because I think I'm quite good at what I do playing wise; but when it comes to talking, being in a video it tends to make me go... (winces) *"Is that me?"*

Is it shyness?
Shyness to the extreme!

Okay then... Jon said Chris Curtis came up with the idea for Roundabout, but the idea was kicking around for a year before you committed. Why?
*Nothing happened. I was waiting to join but nothing happened. I was in Hamburg, and had played with The Searchers in '63, and remained friends with Chris Curtis. When he wanted to put a band together he sent me all these telegrams in Hamburg and called me over. I came over and it was - all very Monty Python - he was very animated and very theatrical; a bit like Hitler! I asked him: "Who's in the band? What's the deal?" And he would go: "The **best** guitarist in the world is **you**. You're in the band. You'll be playing second guitar?" "So you'll be playing lead, right? Who will be playing drums?" "I'll be playing drums." "Jon Lord?" "Jon Lord will be playing organ!" It was going to be called The Light. And then he said: "And I will be playing bass and vocals!" So he was playing lead guitar, drums, bass and vocals! So, when I saw Jon, I said: "What's going on? Is he a bit ... !" (Makes circular motion by his temple with his index finger). So, after a while, we were playing together at this little house where Deep Purple started in - Cadogan Gardens, that's it, in South Kensington and just off Sloane Street, a short walk from Sloane Square and the Kings Road. One of those nondescript areas. But Chris was saying such ridiculous things it was... it was like Hitler. He was so ludicrous with what he wanted to do. We were gonna be called The Light, initially, and whoever the biggest band was at the time - I think it was Clapton and The Cream - they were going to be opening for us. He was nuts! The second time I went there the house looked like it had actually been hit by a bomb. There was rubble - no more furniture and carpets - just rubble! Someone had gone in with a pneumatic drill and drilled up everything. Plaster was down everywhere; then I saw some of the plaster move. It was Chris, who was sleeping on the floor. "Ah, Ritchie, come on in. The band's great, it's all happening." He was just full of bullshit.*

And that's why you never joined Chris Curtis?
Funnily enough it did take off about a week later. I met Jon - thank goodness we kept each others' numbers - and he asked me: "What do you feel about Chris?" "Urn, bit of a strange guy, isn't he?" "Eccentric? Mad?" Fucking mad! So we got together and thought what are we going to do with him? We had these backers that were going to push the band; and that was when we started to go: Maybe we should just get him out." So we spoke to our backers - Edwards and Coletta. They were excited about the band but thought that Chris, being a name with The Searchers... Is he still alive? (Curtis was still alive when this interview was conducted but died in 2005)

I really don't know.
He's a strange guy, but he's so eccentric he's a really good bloke. Great guy. I remember him in the good days in the Star Club (in Hamburg) *in '63. He would be standing up playing the drums, a really forceful character. A genuine rock 'n' roll character. He wasn't a showbiz character; he wasn't manufactured - and I can relate to that. I think he got into drugs and he started to get silly, unfortunately, for he did get everyone together. It was his band., for what it was worth. A very important person; without Chris Curtis it would not have happened.*

Your record company biography mentions that you were in The Outlaws, but says Jimmy Page was in the band too.
No. I was in a group called Neil Christian And The Crusaders. Pagey was in The Crusaders. Albert Lee was in The Crusaders. Jeff Beck was in The Crusaders. (Laughs) *All these guys!*

Did you ever play with Jimmy, then?
Er, I played on the same bill, and I did a record with Jeff Beck once, that Jimmy Page was producing, back in '64 or '65. I can't remember who for. But that was interesting. It was the first time I met Jeff Beck. I always remember him playing a solo - it was a great solo - and I asked him: "What's your name?" "Jeff Beck." "Who do you play for?" "The Tridents." And I made a kind

of back-handed compliment like: "I've never heard of you." But what I meant to say was: "I've never heard of you, but you're so good and you should be a name." It kind of stuck in his head, because when I saw him again in '67 or '68 I said: "Hi! I'm Ritchie" and he went: "Ritchie? Ritchie? Sorry, I've never heard of you." (Laughs) But I didn't mean it that way, and he knew I didn't - bastard! But in '64 he was a great guitar player. It was "Who's Jeff Beck? Where's he come from?" I knew Pagey and all the other guys.

Page and yourself went for lessons with 'Big' Jim Sullivan. Who was there first?
I didn't know he went to 'Big' Jim. I knew he played with 'Big' Jim at a lot of sessions. But I went to Jim for lessons. I used to go sit on his doorstep, when I was thirteen, and he was in Marty Wilde And The Wildcats. Jim was God, because he had this Gibson and he could really play. Unbelievable. When you're thirteen or fourteen... (1958 / 59). In those days I used to listen to Marty Wilde on the radio and it was pure rock 'n' roll. Actually I was fifteen, because I remember this show - and I'd love to get to the radio archives because there was some great guitar playing on it. The first wah-wah pedal came out - way before it's time, This would have been in '60 / '61. Way before Hendrix. He did 'The Cryin' Game - although Page tells everybody he did 'The Cryin' Game'. Even, I've noticed with The Kinks too. Dave Davies did the solo on 'You Really Got Me', but Pagey always tells people that it was him. Even Ray Davies says I don't know why people would want to tell people it was him: it was my brother. But Page is a bit like that. He likes to say: I did this, I did that. What I think... the way he used to do it is that people would ask him if he played on something and he'd say yes, but he omits to say that he's playing rhythm guitar. Maybe that's how it got screwed up. Because Ray Davies should know who played on his own songs, more so than maybe Jimmy Page.

Your memories of those days seem pretty clear.
Of those days, yes. My memory gets hazy around '71. When it got into the big stuff and over the top. Whereas in the '60s everything was very small and you tended to get very excited about things. In the 70s it had all been done and it wasn't so surprising any more. I like the old way back days. But then again, I can look back on those days because I've been lucky enough to go on. And there are quite a few players that I used to play with back in the '60s that are not so happy to talk about the old days because they have just stayed stagnant.

Jimmy Page, of course, just claims that he doesn't remember what happened.
Every time I talk to Pagey about Neil Christian, he just looks at me blankly - I don't know why. It's like, come on Jim, you made it as a big superstar, you can admit that you were in a small band. What's the problem? "No, don't remember." He does, he just doesn't want to know about that.

Do you speak to him very often?
No, I haven't spoken to him in years.

You didn't see the Page Plant reunion?
I didn't go to see them, but I saw a bit on television...

The name Deep Purple, according to Jon, came from your grandmother's favourite song. True?
Close. It was a song my grandmother used to play on the piano. I once saw it in print that it was the last song she ever played - but I don't think it was.

Was your grandmother a professional musician?
No - she just tinkered around on the piano - but she used to play 'Deep Purple.'

Where did the name Rainbow come from?
It came from the Hollywood Bar and Grill (on LA's Sunset Strip). *I was in there with Ronnie (James Dio) getting drunk as usual and said: "What shall we call the band?" Just pointed to the sign.*

It was lucky you weren't in the Pheasant and Firkin...
Or the Bull and Bush. Or all the other transvestite bars we used to go to!

It was your idea to split the first line-up, Deep Purple Mark I. But Jon said Mick Underwood recommended lan Gillan.
That's right. I said to Mick: "We're looking for a singer. Do you know anybody?" And he said: "Well, we have a singer; you can use our singer if you like." "Why aren't you using him?" "We're breaking up." "Okay so you don't mind if we look at your singer?' "No.." That's how we got lan Gillan. Gillan could scream. We said: "Can you scream?" "Well, yeah." "Okay, you're in." But he had a really good voice then.

Nick said in the programme that he was very upset about being told he was out of the band second hand. None of you ever told him to his face.
I think whenever anybody gets fired, nobody wants to jump on the phone and go: "Hey! You're fired!" And, you know, I've often wondered what managers get paid to do. One of the things they should be doing is to fire a person, or to put it their way. I don't believe in going: "You're out! We never want to speak to you again." But I believe in the management going: "The boys have had a meeting and they don't think you're quite working out. Now you can speak to the rest of the guys But of course they don't want to, because they've just been pushed out." But that, really, to me, is management's job. They don't do fucking much! I think the least they can do is to try and buffer the band from each other if there's a problem. Usually, I've found with managers, that the last thing they want to do is spread the bad news. They want all the good news - and to be paid commission on it - but they don't want to do the hard work.

The Concerto: Jon said you got upset because it diverted the focus of attention in the band to him from you.
That's true. What I got upset about was... We'd done the orchestra thing for about a year, two years, and we were a rock band. I couldn't understand why we kept playing with orchestras. It started to get up my nose because we did the first thing - it was a novelty, a band playing with an orchestra; I didn't think it was particularly good but we pulled it off. It was just a novelty. Then he wrote another one ('The Gemini Suite') - and they wanted us to do it again, and I went: "No, no, I'm not getting involved again. I'm in a rock 'n' roll band." In fact, I said: "Jon, we should make a rock 'n' roll record for people in parties. It should be nonstop, hard-hitting rock 'n' roll." I was impressed with what Zeppelin did, and said, "I wanted to do that kind of stuff," and if it doesn't take off we'll go and play with orchestras the rest of our lives. I remember saying that. So we did it and it was 'Deep Purple In Rock' which, luckily, took off. It's funny, because someone spoke to me about six months later and said: "I always hear that record at parties." We'd purposefully made it so it hammered along every song. There was no lull. There was no showcase of the band, which always loses that party feel. Different tempos, but the energy level was high. So it worked - and I was very pleased with 'Deep Purple In Rock', because I never wanted to work with an orchestra ever again. But then 'The Gemini Suite' came out and it was like, oh no! The nightmare's back again. So I said: "No, count me out, Jon," and I think he got Albert Lee. And Albert, being the brilliant, wonderful person he is, brilliant guitar player: "Yeah, I'll do it. Where am I?" (Ritchie's memory fails him here because he did, perform 'The Gemini Suite' once at the Royal Festival Hall on September 17th 1970 before the studio version was released.) *But I really don't care to play with orchestras.*

Which is odd, because you are very influenced by the classics. You've used strings on 'Stargazer', you've just reworked 'Hall Of The Mountain King'...

Which I was very pleased with, incidentally. That was very exciting. I thought that came across very well. Because when I first thought of the idea, I thought: "Nah, could be a bit corny." But the more I got into it, playing with the band, I thought this could sound really good if it's done properly. And I'm very pleased with that, There are certain things that stand out. I was very pleased with 'Stargazer', and I'm very pleased with 'Hall Of The Mountain King." There's no startling guitar stuff, it just... works. I'm so often disappointed with what I do - that's why I won't listen to my stuff very often - but that one I could always listen to. If I hear it I really get into it because I saw, and maybe I'm digressing here, but I saw 'Peer Gynt' when I was nine years old, on the television on the BBC, the whole four hour play and Peter Ustinov was in it. As a nine year old kid I was watching witches and 'In The Hall Of The Mountain King', and it really had an effect on me then. So I've always wanted to do it, and I did it in 1964, actually, as a small single. But I thought I'll do it again because I love the tune. It's funny, because I was playing it and somebody said: "Why don't you do that?" I said, I can't, it's a bit corny." And they said: "No, you can do anything you want, if you like it, you get off on it And I thought: "That's fucking right!" Because previously, the last six or seven years with the other lot, everything had to be tempered down. What I wanted was a side issue, it was what the committee wanted. The committee rules. But a committee never got anything done. Should it be black, should it be white? I want white. I want black. In the end, I was going: "I don't care any more. I don't care if it's pink." "Pink? Okay, I'll take pink. That's how things were done. Because you had five outspoken egotistical maniacs going: I want it this way!" "No, I want it this way!" Now there's just one egotistical maniac. There's a couple budding, right behind me (laughs). *But when you're trying to get a band and get decisions made, it just doesn't work. You've got to have a leader, someone who says we've got to do this - blame me if it doesn't work. If it doesn't they do, but if it does work it's: "We thought of this." It always becomes "we." The old management was like that. "Well lads, we've sold it out tonight. Great! "Well lads, you haven't done so well tonight, it's only half full."*

In the seventies, were you keen to be seen as the leader?

Not so much keen to be seen, I just had my own set ideas. It was passion. I didn't want to be awkward. I just really felt it should work. I was like: "C'mon lads!" But I felt the rest of the band weren't so passionate. A bit armchair stuff.

That's why I felt it was odd that you didn't want to be involved in this programme.

But it was a passion that fell by the wayside. I have other passions now. To talk about Deep Purple - I'm very thankful that I can live a certain way now, but I don't think the band towards the end was very truthful. I don't think they were in it for the right reason, so for someone to say: "Would you like to say something on behalf of Deep Purple?" It was: "Not really, because I think I'll let the side down. It's probably better that I say nothing." To be thought a fool, than to speak up and remove all doubt, as they say. The less said the better. Small point. Won't mention it again. More than my job's worth (laughs).

Roger mentioned how you wrote 'Black Night', how you came back from the pub drunk, having been told to write a single.

That's right. Very true. That's a very nice memory. We went down the pub next to Kingsway in Holborn. The management came in - it was like 'Leggy Thing' from The Rutles - "Lads! You need a hit!" We need a hit? God, I didn't know that. You know how these people come up to you and say: "You need a hit, you need to be in the hit parade, you need to be on the television..."? And you go: "Fucking hell! I never thought of that! That's brilliant!" So, we were drinking, then we went back. I knocked out the Ricky Nelson 'Summertime' bass riff which went bom-bom ba-bom-

bom; we did that as a shuffle. Because the top line to Ricky Nelson's 'Summertime' was 'Hey Joe' before 'Hey Joe' came along. 'Summertime' came along in about 1962. Then Jimi came along in '68 and used the top line. So I thought if he can use the top line, we'll take the bass line. We just added a couple of bits that worked very well, and all of a sudden it was number one or two. Poor old Ricky Nelson, or whoever arranged it - the bass player and the guitarist. I hear certain songs and - I used to be very friendly with Bonzo from Led Zeppelin. We'd be sitting in the Rainbow and he'd be really up and drunk or really depressed, but we'd be sitting there drinking and he'd be looking at the table. And he used to say to me: It must be really hard to stand there and go der-der-derr, der-der, de-derr ('Smoke On The Water')." "Yeah, it's nearly as difficult as going duh-der duh-der dum ('Whole Lotta Love') At least we don't copy anybody!" "What are you talking about? That's bullshit! I know exactly where you got duh-der duh-der dum from; you got it from 'Hey Joe', you just put it to a rhythm." And he's thinking. "And 'Immigrant Song' was 'Little Miss Lover'." "What are you talking about?" Bom-bobba-didom ba-bom bobbadidom... He was not a happy man, but he started it. We then went upstairs to the toilet. We're both there, weeing away, and he says: "Rich, did you mean all that?" "No, not really, I was just having a go back at you." "Oh. I didn't mean it either. There's room at the top for everybody." So we carried on weeing, then went back downstairs and started drinking again. But he loved it, he was the kind of guy who liked confrontation, and I would always give it to him. But I always remember when he said that, thinking how we'd taken bits and pieces from people, so I told him where he got his stuff from. It was interesting to see how his mind was going: "Pagey, you bastard, now I know!" They were good days. I had some very funny times with John Bonham and Keith Moon.

Were you living in LA at the time?
Yeah. Keith used to come up to the house all the time. I used to supply the people, and he would supply the goods.

You worked with him on one of the 'Screaming Lord Sutch And Heavy Friends' records.
Mmmm. Keith was a great drummer. I remember talking to Keith and asking him: "Keith, how's it going with The Who?" And Keith had two accents - the upper class one and the Cockney. That night he was in upper class mood and he went: "I don't know, Richard, they haven't called me in two years." Wonderful. Only Keith Moon would have come out with a statement like that. Everybody else was: "Cool man, everything's happening..." That was why Keith Moon was the funniest man I ever met in rock 'n' roll, aside from Freddie Starr.

Was Freddie Starr in rock 'n' roll?
Just about. He's a good singer. I used to back him on record in '67... '66 (he actually backed Starr on several recordings in 1963 / 64). *Freddie Starr And The Midnighters. Apparently, so rumour has it, he went on stage and upstaged the Beatles! Because he's a hard act to follow when he's on. I have some very funny stories. Freddie, when we were in the studio doing a session, and Joe Meek - who wrote 'Telstar', met a tragic end, shot himself - and we're there getting it down. The band was basically The Outlaws. We had Chas Hodges on bass* (later of Chas and Dave) *and Chas would always arrive late. If the session was due to start at ten it would start at twelve because... His story at one time was: "Er Joe, I was on my way here and I saw this poor little bird, picked it up and took it back home, nursed it back to health. All bullshit. But he always came up with these ridiculous excuses and would always wear his pyjamas under his jeans. Anyway, I was playing my solo in the control room and Freddie came up to me and undid his flies and put his knob in my ear, while I was playing. Joe Meek wasn't entirely impressed. Another time when I went somewhere on a train with Freddie, he sat on one side of the aisle facing a young girl and I sat on the other side of the aisle facing a man in a suit, reading a newspaper. Suddenly Freddie, who had a dose of some anti-social disease, was talking very loudly to me in an upper class accent:*

"Richard, what am I to do? I've got all this white stuff coming out of the end of my thing! What is it Richard? What should I do?" And he's waving it around while the horrified girl tries not to look, the guy hides behind his paper, and I'm trying desperately to pretend I have never met him before in my life.

Ian Gillan was clearly the guy you wanted in 1969. You asked him again in 1980 to join Rainbow. You worked with him again in 1984 when Deep Purple Mark II reformed. Yet the pair of you cannot tolerate each other! Is this the ultimate love/ hate relationship? What went wrong? Do you feel he let you down?

No, he hasn't let me down. I used to call him Oliver Rude, because he is very similar to Oliver Reed. He's a very brash individual. It wasn't just the voice. I found him very disquieting to be around. I always found myself going: "I've got to get out of here." We used to get reports in the band, in '72 I suppose, a roadie would call us up and say: "If you're thinking about going for a drink in the hotel, I just thought I'd tell you: Gillan's in the bar." I'd say: Is it hunched shoulders?" If he said: 'Yes, very hunched shoulders" that meant that Ian had been in there all day and night, and just wanted to blow off steam to someone. That used to bother me. Why was this guy so overbearing? Sure enough, you'd walk past and you'd look into the bar and there would be this hunched shouldered figure, looking into his beer. Of course, if you walked in and he saw you, he'd sit up and go: "Hey!" But I'd be like (slumps into depression): *"Yes, Ian, all right? But, er, I've got to go now."*

Was he not like that at the beginning, though? Didn't Mick Underwood warn you and say he's a great singer, but ...?

No. He did say he was very annoyed at Gillan. I remember him saying he didn't like him as a person, and I asked why. He said because he'd said he'd lost his voice and couldn't carry on the band - but the next thing we know he's got a band together with you lot. Because you've got to know Ian to figure out what his personality is. And it takes quite a while because he's a very astute man, very clever, he's got this very strange psyche. He's got this very strange side to him which is another side I don't like, the obnoxious side, and that doesn't often come out until you've been around him quite often. Because he's got the flattering side, the very charming side that some people see. He knows how to put the charm on; he's an intellect in his own way. He's an intelligent man. People often say that Jon Lord is the most intelligent one of us, but no - Gillan is the most intelligent. But he just used to be so coarse. I didn't like to be around the guy because I felt that he was doing things for shock value, to be talked about, for the hell of it. Stories wouldn't come around naturally with Ian; he would manufacture a story, invariably, of course, with no clothes on. There was always the no clothes story. The first ten times it was funny, but after that...

But what was the difference between Ian Gillan being coarse and Freddie Starr putting his dick in your ear?

Freddie, I suppose you can leave; I wasn't backing Freddie Starr too often (laughs). *But it's something, when people ask me about certain people, I have to go: "Wait a minute, let me think what this person's all about." And I think the bottom line with Gillan was it really bothered my psyche to be around him. And of course on tour the big thing was... if someone loses their voice, I don't care - that happens to most singers, fair enough. But when he would go on stage and just not care - he would sing two songs without remembering more than two lines in both songs. I would start getting really pissed off!*

What tour are you referring to here?

This was lately, the last tour I did with him. I wrote a big letter to the band. I spoke to Jon Lord first and said: "What do you think about Ian just grunting his way through the fourth or fifth number? Why do you think he does that? The poor kids in the audience are mouthing all the words, but he doesn't remember the lyrics at all!" Jon's like: "Hmmm, I see what you mean. I'll have a diplomatic chat with him." "Okay, good, if you can talk to him, great, because I'm really pissed off! I don't think this is very professional, backing some guy who is just grunting, laughing and spitting and throwing up" - because he was drinking and throwing up! Which is great, that's rock 'n' roll, but not when you forget two songs. That's not right for the audience. That's what started the rot. I thought, this guy is a joke. He's lost his voice, he doesn't care that he's lost it; he's so fucking smug he's even grunting on stage and doesn't give a shit whether he remembers the lyrics or not. I even got Rob (Fodder, Ritchie's P.A at the time) *to write out the lyrics one night and pin them on the stage by the microphone. But when Gillan walked out he saw them, picked them up, ripped them up and threw them away, and proceeded to grunt over those two songs. By that time it was too late anyway. It became a standing joke.*

But this is 1993. What about in 1973?
I couldn't relate to his style of singing.

So what had changed since 1970?
On 'In Rock' it was good for what he was doing, but I wanted to progress, to have certain phrasing, and he was still just singing the same type of thing. He wasn't actually singing a melody, and his phrasing I thought was very dated. Plus, I think if you fall out with a singer for his singing is one thing - I completely lost respect for his singing - but as a person we didn't see eye-to-eye in every way, because he was just a very strange guy. So we never got on.

The very reason you reformed in 1984, surely, was that the vast majority of Deep Purple fans thought that Gillan was the ultimate voice of the band. But now you're suggesting that actually it only worked for 'In Rock', 'Fireball' and 'Machine Head'?
Yes, I thought it only worked on... 'Machine Head' he was good on, 'In Rock' and 'Perfect Strangers.'

Why don't you like 'Fireball'? Ian likes 'Fireball.'
I know he does.

Is that why?
No. I just don't see anything on 'Fireball' that's worth even thinking about; that's a personal thing. I would never play it. It's like 'Who Do We Think We Are'; the same. Just a non-nondescript piece of nothing. You have that, when you're worked to death by the management and they say you've got to record too. And you say: "How can we record when we've got one week off between these tours?" I always felt that 'In Rock', 'Machine Head', then a jump to 'Burn', and 'Perfect Strangers.'

A friend of mine, after watching the Rock Family Trees programme, said he thought Jon Lord came across as totally spineless He spent most of it regretting what he hadn't done and said at the time.
That's a very interesting word. I've heard somebody else - not me - use that same word for Jon. But if you're going to make a mistake, you've got to stick with it. Yeah, I agree with that observation. There's a lot more to that than... 'cause I know my side of the Jon Lord stories. And Jon Lord is no angel. Jon would always be the bearer of good news, but if there was any bad news he would just not be around. He didn't want to hear it, which was very strange. I know that Ian Gillan doesn't like Jon. He calls him spineless. I've heard him use that same word, funnily enough.

Jon said when Gillan and Glover were going to leave, the first he knew of it was when you told him you wanted a bluesier singer and a bassist that could sing harmonies.

That's true. That's what did happen. (Long pause) *I'm a good little devil* (laughs). *But I hadn't "decided"; I had gone: "Come on, we've got to do something." And it was always like: "Okay, you're right - what?" I remember with Roger; I didn't want to get rid of him, I wanted to leave. I said: "Paicey, we're leaving!" 'Cause I wanted to form this thing with Phil Lynott* (a three piece called Baby Face). *I said I wanted to leave, and he said: 'Well, could anything persuade you to stay, because we're on to such a good thing. Why mess it up?" I said: "No, I want to get together with Phil; myself, you and Phil will be a great band. I want to do a bluesier thing." I felt that Purple was getting into that armchair thing, that security thing. But Paicey was reluctant to leave: "Phil's good, but don't you think we should try... ?" I said: "No, I can't handle Gillan." 'What else is the problem?" "There's just too many changes I would make and that's not fair for me to say", "Well, what are the changes?" That doesn't matter; I remember being hesitant about it, because Roger was Mr. Nice Guy. But the next day Paicey asked: "What exactly are the changes you would make to stay in the band?" So I went* (sighs): *"Get rid of Roger... But I don't want to. He's the anchor of the band, such a nice guy, he's done nothing wrong. I would want another bass player who's bluesy. But I can't ask for that. That's why I want to leave, get out and do my own thing and hopefully you'll come with me - if not I'll get someone else." He's going if you want to get rid of Roger, we'll get rid of Roger." No that's not really fair, he's done nothing wrong." I had no regrets about Gillan, we were both hating each other and that was it. But Roger didn't hurt anybody. Why should he get sacked? But then it was: "Okay, if you can do that I might stay, 'cause this changes everything." I had my thing with Gillan but I wasn't going to force Roger out of the band. it was time for me to leave. But Paicey talked me into it. Jon didn't know anything about it. He was reading a book somewhere as we used to joke.*

So you went for a fresh start rather than Baby Face?

Yeah, but I also had hesitations - and I think Phil did too because he was doing kind of well. We wanted to play together but he's just had a hit ('Whiskey In The Jar').

But you did record, didn't you?

Yeah we did a couple of songs, two or three.

Who has the tapes?

I have no idea.

Phil told me in 1983, that you had them.

No I don't have them, they were only half-finished anyway. The management would have them. I think they were produced by Derek Lawrence.

It is strange they have never surfaced, isn't it?

Yeah it is strange because they were... with respect (laughs) *they would sell anything that was going to make money. And they've done it twenty-five hundred times with Deep Purple. How many times can you reissue? I've never seen anything like it in my life. Rob showed me in London, all these albums, and I'm going: "People actually buy this?" 'Deep Purple In Rock' has just been re-released for the fifteenth time and one of the tracks is two seconds longer. Absolute crap! But the tapes must be lost because Derek Lawrence would have released them. He released that 'Green Bullfrog' thing and that was not too clever.*

Roger said that the only words you spoke to him on the final Japanese tour in 1973 was: "it's not

personal, it's business."
I could have said that, yeah.

He also said he resented Ian Paice and Jon Lord more for their cowardice.
I'll tell you one thing, Paicey does tend to shy away, but Jon is very, um... he'll back off. He won't say anything that's negative.

On to the silly stuff, the Coverdale stuff.
It's no more silly than the other stuff.

He was calling you Riccardo on camera. Did he ever call you Riccardo to your face?
No he used to call me Blackers. One of my favourite stories about David Coverdale - because he's now acquired a very posh upper class English accent although he's from... where's he from? (Saltburn by the Sea, North Yorkshire) *and you know how they speak up there. One day he was in some restaurant and did his "Waiter! bring me your best Brandy!" And the guy turned round and said, "Would sir prefer the 1912 so-and-so, the 1915 such-and-such or the whatever?" And Coverdale was like* (freezes in panic): *"Er, oh yes, that'll do!" That just about sums him up.*

He told a funny story about his first gig in Europe, where he was very nervous, and so he went off in another room to compose himself. He said he thought the management believed he was so nervous he had actually done a runner. Do you remember that?
No I don't, but I never mixed with them, anyway. I just saw them on stage.

You weren't talking to them even then?
Well, it wasn't that I wasn't talking to them. It's just that at a show I very rarely talk to the rest of the band. Sometimes I do, but it's not as if I'm not talking to them, it's because I'm trying to focus myself and don't need the backstage bullshit. If you go into their dressing room it would be the same old thing: Jon was playing the Benny Hill Theme, Glenn would be doing his Stevie Wonder impressions, and usually David would be going (soprano): *"Baby, baby, baby!"* (bass) *"Baby, baby, baby!" So I was in my own room with the candles going, trying to centre. We were talking and we saw each other, but I wouldn't go out of my way to go into the room. I've always hated that.*

So there was four of them in one room, and you in another?
Yeah, always. For tuning up purposes: and I usually have the room just lit with candles, just to mellow out. It's a great way of relaxing before you go on. You can't relax when you've got four other guys yelling and screaming. And they'd always bought their liggers with them who'd want to talk and shout.

They had a brief clip from the California Jam where you seemed to be watching Coverdale very closely indeed. You looked like you were either expecting him to fuck up any minute or were wondering "just what on earth is he doing?"
If I saw it I would remember exactly what I was thinking, but I don't recall much from then. I tend to put thoughts out of my head about a lot of things that went down. Just people coming and going in the band.

'Burn', the album you were promoting at the time, remains one of your best.
It's a very good album. It was such a relief that we had some new blood.

It showed, Purple had a track record for making a good album and then slipping a bit, but from 'Burn' to 'Stormbringer' was a massive slump in a very short time.

Yeah, that's true. 'Cause we did 'Burn' and it was a rock 'n' roll band having a great time and playing well. By the time we got to 'Stormbringer' Glenn was really pushing for the R 'n' B bit, and David had become much more into it too. So those two were really into R 'n' B and were taking Jon with them, because they could use funky organ, and of course paicey was in there ' cause he could play funky too. Everybody except for me. I was like: "I hate this fucking shit! What is this Stevie Wonder crap? I'm not a Stevie Wonder fan."

How did it happen that you lost interest so quickly?

because they started to go for this funky music.

Were you just outnumbered?

Outnumbered, yeah. Maybe I had times when I was not pushing and would tend to hold back and watch. So they got into the Deep Purple R 'n' B show.

On 'Burn' David and Glenn were the new guys and did what they were told, but after that they wanted their own way?

That's right, exactly.

Jon also said that in the studio you would play stuff that they would compliment, then you would explain that it was not for the band but your solo album.

Yeah, because I got really tired of it, I had to get away. It got really - from what I saw, everybody was into buying houses in Malibu and putting things up their noses. it was all getting very corporate, and the guys just got carried away with themselves. At the end of the 'Burn' tour and into that 'Stormbringer' period it all got very showbizzy.

Was 'Stormbringer' written in the studio?

More or less. 'Burn' was done a little bit more at rehearsals, because we had the break to write it. But when we came to 'Stormbringer' we didn't have any time.

Was that the first time drugs became a part of the Purple story?

Yes, I think so. I never saw them doing drugs but I heard later: "Oh I don't do that anymore." I never knew they were doing that!

You're well known for liking a drink, but drugs have never been a thing for you then?

I'm proud of the fact that I've never touched cocaine in my life. I must be the only person in rock 'n' roll, but... I mean I'll drink like the next guy, but the cocaine thing? I don't need to do that shit. I see all these people putting things up their noses and.. I'm like Frank Zappa in that way. He always said: "Anybody who puts something up their nose has no respect. It's so stupid to put something up your nose." But I heard they all got into that, I just wasn't aware of it.

Glenn quoted you as saying: "I didn't want to play any of that shoeshine music."

Very true.

That sounds kind of racist.

Yeah, I'm a racist. (laughs)

Are you against black music or black people?

I don't like... from the point of view that Jimi Hendrix taught me an awful lot, and black blues

players. But I don't like black R 'n' B music, I don't like disco. But Glenn was not being himself.
He wanted to be Stevie Wonder.

Have you spoken to Glenn recently?
I think the last time was a couple of years ago, on the phone. I said: "Are you coming out for a
drink, Glenn?" And he said: "No, no, I can't come out. I weigh over 200 pounds. I don't go out."
He had a hang-up about his weight, but why that would stop a guy going out for a drink I don't
know

He's actually turned it all around now; he's dried out, lost the weight, cut all his hair off and is
singing better than ever.
He is a natural musician. I always liked him as a person; he was a very nice guy. But I always
preferred Coverdale's voice. I didn't like the high range that Glenn had.

He re-recorded 'Burn' and sang the whole lot, probably better than Coverdale did.
Really? I heard he'd done it. He is a talented singer.

When you left Deep Purple Mark III, Coverdale said he wrote a short-list of replacements: Jeff
Beck, Rory Gallagher and Tommy Bolin - but most other stories say it was you who
recommended Purple contact Tommy. Which is true?
I didn't recommend Tommy Bolin. I was aware of him because I saw him in 'Spectrum' and I think
someone asked me about him and I said: "Oh, he's really good." But like this last time, when I
wanted to leave, I didn't just want to go and sink their ship. I wanted them to have time to find
someone else. But I don't think I recommended him, I think it was Coverdale who found him.

Did you ever see the band with Tommy?
No.

Jon said: "We went around the world, unravelling Deep Purple's reputation wherever we went".
Again, perhaps, another indication of Jon speaking up too late?
I've got enough negatives towards Jon and positives - he was a great dinner guest, my favourite
dinner company. In the band he was great, he could emulate very well. But I don't know why, to
this day, he doesn't come up with any ideas. I still find that awesome, that he still doesn't come up
with one idea. It's very odd. You'd think someone would have an idea over a period of ten, fifteen,
twenty, twenty-five years. I've always wondered why is that guy so proficient but... I remember
complaining to him once, on stage, I walked over to him while I was playing and said something
like: "The sound is really awful tonight" or "the lights are really bad", and he just kept playing
and said: "Another day, another dollar!"

Rainbow came out of your disenchantment with Mark III, and initially you used the band that had
supported Purple on the 'Bum' tour, the American band Elf. Did you ever play on Elf's third
album "Trying To Burn The Sun'?
No.

Was that guy just very good at apeing you, then?
Steve Edwards? Yeah. He was good. But I definitely didn't do it.

Did you ever intend to tour with that band? (All of Elf except Edwards played on his first Rainbow
album "Ritchie Blackmore's Rainbow').
I did... until we got to rehearsals and I realised how bad it would be. In the studio, they made it -

except for Gary (Driscoll) *the drummer. Bonzo really liked that guy as a drummer; it's a compliment that one of John Bonham's favourite songs was what he used to call "Love On The Silver Mountain." Although it was "Man On The Silver Mountain." He used to come to the house and say: "Play "Love On The Silver Mountain." "John, it's called Man On The Silver Mountain." "Fucking play "Love On The Silver Mountain"!" "But I'd like to play some classical stuff, because there are a lot of people here, I don't want to just play that." I want fucking "Love On The Silver Mountain"." "Okay, I'll put it on." We nearly had a fight over that. We had a stand-off in the house. He'd already been beaten up and had a big patch on the top of his head where he'd got stitches, and he's looking at me, going: "I'm the fucking guest I think he was in love with one of the fills, but it was done purely by mistake. Gary Driscoll had a tendency of losing the tempo, then catching up. Any drummer hearing that would think: "Wow! That guy's so clever." He could pull back and go forward. But Gary was going: "Are we still playing? Oh..." He would have periods of pure genius, but I remember in the studio when we were doing that first LP, he had trouble with his headphones. We'd go: "Okay, ready?" And we just see him* (gazes off into space). *"Hello! Gary? Gary! Put your headphones on and turn them up!" "Oh yeah, right, right, right!" So we'd start playing and I'd watch him - 'cause I'd be in the control room and his headphones would slowly slide off and he'd slowly lose the tempo. So after four takes we would have to tape them to his head. I remember once counting in: one, two... And he just went: "Er, what? Oh... three, four, yeah!" He was so nervous. Once he counted one, two, three, four, and everybody came in - except for him!* (laughs) *Another time he just stopped half way through and Martin* (Birch, producer) *is yelling at him: 'What are you doing? Did somebody say stop?' I*

thought I heard someone say stop. But he was such a nice guy. I used to think, this is much better than The Troggs... I've got this thing with drummers if they can't keep time. I can't understand why they should be in a band.

Perhaps you've been spoilt with Ian Paice?
Yeah, he's a great drummer.

'Rainbow Rising' is, most people think, the best album Rainbow made.
At that point, yeah.

But not now?
Oh no, no. The best Rainbow album I have made, without a doubt, is this one. Without a doubt. Now people will say: "Oh, but he would say that. But not me - I wouldn't. But I am saying it now. The best one I've made is this one. I liked a couple of others: 'Straight Between The Eyes', and 'Difficult To Cure' in there too; 'Stargazer' was very good, but the rest of the album was very extremely average. That's my opinion, anyway.

Jimmy Bain - did you really set fire to his bed while he was still in it?
Yeah. But I told him.

You mean you woke him up?
No - he had some girl on the bed with him. I walked in and he's: "Hey Ritchie! Do you want a drink?" "No, I'm away to my bed, I'll see you tomorrow." But I... let's see... I set fire to something and put it by his bed, and it started catching the bedclothes. And I thought he would see it, pick it up and put it out. But he didn't see it. So I'm there watching these flames, going: "Er, Jimmy, er "Yeah, right, see ya later Um Jimmy?' "Fucking hell! The bed's on fire!" And I thought, yes, that's more like it, and then I could leave. 'Cause I couldn't leave him in a bed that was on fire without telling him!

That would really be like getting caught inflagrante.
Of course. So he grabbed the bedclothes and threw them out of the window. That was all he could do by that stage. But when it hit the ground it hit the Astroturf and set that ablaze too. The hotel wasn't too happy. But the whole point was like when you set fire to someone's newspaper. They're supposed to put it out. But Jimmy was too engrossed in this girl...

Why did you put out 'On Stage', a double live album, after only two studio LPs, and why was it so short?
I have no idea. Blame the management.

'Long Live Rock 'N' Roll' was the last album you made with Dio. Was it a happy album to make? Did you fall out with Ronnie afterwards or before?
I was always very close to Ronnie until, to be quite honest, he met up with Wendy (his future wife and manager), then it got very strained after that. She was a nice enough woman, but we didn't really click. I remember being at the Chateau (studio in France where Elton John's Honky Chateau was recorded) when we were trying to sort out a song. Cozy and Ronnie were across the courtyard, I thought, and I was playing an effect, trying to get the song down, and in both of them walked and one of them said: 'We want to talk to you". I got prodded in the back. I was kneeling down at the time, so Ronnie could reach me. "I've just heard from Wendy that you're on the front page of Circus and we're not." "Really? I had no idea." The three of us had done the photo session, but the photographer did a couple of me on my own, and one of these got on the cover.

*And Cozy or Ronnie said: If we're gonna be your fucking sidekicks then we'll act accordingly."
That really pissed me off, 'cause that was nothing to do with me. After that, it went downhill,
'cause I had no respect for either of them after that - how petty can you be?*

And he used to eat all the cheese?
What?

Cozy; you once said that he ate all the cheese on the rider.
*Cozy could be your best friend or your worst nightmare, depending how he wanted to be. But I
don't remember saying that about Cozy.*

You're actually quite reticent to badmouth people you used to work with?
Urn, sometimes... Eat all the cheese? No. He took all the milk.

Well, I knew it was some dairy product.
*Right. He had some woman who came with him called Mrs. King - it's a very long and boring
story. I wrote a whole diary during the making of 'Down To Earth.' It's in the Michael Palin vein,
like Tompkinson's Schooldays. Day one: nobody shows up. Day three: got to the castle, made a
fire, went to bed. Day four: made another fire, had a few drinks, got drunk, went to bed. Day six:
Don Airey shows up... he is given the chapel room. It was a castle where we recorded 'Down To
Earth.' Of course, I got there first and being the leader of the band I got the best room, which was
great. But as it went down the band, the rooms became (laughs) really bad. So there's this Gothic
castle in Germany and Don was the last one to arrive, so he got the last room, which was the
converted chapel room. Now this room never got above 32 degrees (Fahrenheit), no matter what
you did to it. You could light a big fire there, but the fire always went out and the smoke came into
the room through the cracked chimney, and you'd be back to 32 degrees. It was freezing in this
room! Cozy gets a really good room, 'cause he's second there, and he brings the chef with him,
this woman. Don arrives last. He's going: "Where's my room?" I pointed to these steps: "Down
there!" It was like being in a Vincent Price Hammer horror film. The door creaked open and Don
looked in there: "Fucking hell, its cold in here!" The rest of the castle was warm, so it was
obvious there was some bad stuff in there. And it was so obvious that the bed was right where the
altar used to be. It had little railings around it. And he's going: "Hmmm, I don't know about this
room". "No! Not a bad room, Don." So we go back to the main room and Cozy gets up to go for
a bath. But Cozy, being Mr. Spiderman, got out of the bathroom wearing this little rubber suit. He
went down the drainpipe, across the courtyard, up another drainpipe and into Don's room. From
the main room, Don can see his room, down the staircase, and we're all standing there drinking
by the roaring fire. But Don's still standing there going: "Oh dear, I really don't like my room".
And as he looks back at it, he suddenly sees this hooded figure in it look up and close the door.
'Fucking hell! What was that?" Because everybody that's in this gigantic castle is in the room,
and Cozy - you can hear his bath running. Don's gone berserk: "What was that?" So we all ran
down the stairs and burst through the door. "No one here, Don!" I saw this ghastly hooded figure.
It looked like... it was a demon! I'm not staying here!" So Colin has a look around, throws back
a curtain and goes: "See, nobody here!" But Cozy's standing there! So Colin does a double take
and quickly throws the curtain back before anyone else sees him. Don misses this too 'cause he's
still standing there going "It's a demon! It's a demon! I'm not sleeping here." We all go back to
the big fire and continue drinking, but Don's just standing there and shaking: I saw that face! I'll
never forget that face!" So I said: "What was it like?" And at the time I hadn't known it was
Cozy... A lot of stuff went on there: David Bowie went there, but nobody would stay in that room
because too many people had seen Chopin in the mirror above the bed. We were all so scared to
go to bed at night we would often sit around the big roaring fire, drinking away in the middle of*

winter. Then I'd go: "Right; I'm going up, retiring... anybody else? (mimics terrified looks) Nope? Right! Well I'll have another beer too." It would be four in the morning. I didn't realise what was going on at first because I'd be getting drunk and wondering why nobody was going to their room. It was because everyone was so shit scared! They were all waiting for the dawn to break; as soon as it did they would go: "Ah, well, I think I'll go to bed now. They were so petrified. Everybody went in twos everywhere. Great place!

So you just got disillusioned with Ronnie after that episode and that album?
Yeah that didn't do any favours for me. I didn't like that. Because he was so nasty about it. "We're not on the front cover with you!" Is that my fault? I lost a lot of respect. But I still talk to the guy and we still get on well; I always remember the good times. It was just that one thing that turned me right off. Great singer and a very funny man. He makes me crack up! A great sense of humour that guy's got.

For the next Rainbow album, 'Down To Earth', you asked Roger back...
As a producer, yeah. But we didn't have a bass player, so he started playing the bass.

Roger said in the programme that he thought that was your way of admitting that you were wrong in 1973.
Really? (laughs) I never thought of it quite like that. But on the other hand the manager talked to me and said: "Roger's a good producer; he did this..." And I said: "Yeah, let's get him on... But I never thought of him as a bass player. It was just that it suddenly happened that we had no bass player. Don heard him play and said: "Roger plays really well!" I went: "He's all right." Then all of a sudden he's on bass. But it wasn't something that was worked out.

But it can't be something that just happened by accident; it was your band!
Yeah, but the bass player we had - Jack Green - wasn't working out, so Roger goes: "I'll play bass for the time being." Okay, but there's Don going: "Roger's a really good bass player." I'm going: "Yeah, but he's a producer; I'm not looking for a bass player."

Why didn't Jack work out?
Jack was disliked by the others. I loved him.

You did a couple of tracks on his solo album "Humanesque.'
Yeah; Jack was great. A really nice guy. But he was hated by the rest of the band. For once it wasn't my fault! (Laughs)

Cozy said something like: when he first joined the band he thought you were driven, and had a point to prove, but after a while he watched you go cold and lose your ambition, your anger. Is that true, not just of Rainbow, but of your whole career? Looking back, there are peaks and troughs.
Yeah; you can't be angry all the time or you'd go nuts.

But you seem to be fired up whenever you get a new line-up, and do your best work when you've just had a change.
That's right; when I get the new blood. Like a vampire, it's the new blood; that's what it is. It's a lot of that, plus what's happened before.

The first Deep Purple album with Mark I, then 'In Rock'... "Machine Head' kind of shoots the theory down. Why was that such a peak?
That, to me, is my favourite LP with Purple. But it does. It came after 'Fireball', which I thought was a complete flop, disastrous.

Why was 'Fireball' so bad then? Were you not really involved with it?
Yeah, I was. There was just nothing on it worthwhile talking about.

Purely because you were so tired from touring?
Yeah. And if you look at the songs - I can't even remember any of the songs.

'Demon's Eye', 'No No No'...
'Demon's Eye' was like a riff. 'Farmer's Daughter?' - 'Anyone's Daughter?' - was a spoof on Country and Western. 'No No No' was just... that to me was bordering on banal. People liked the track 'Fireball' but that was just fast with a double bass drum - and an air-conditioning unit.

Back to Christmas 1981. You asked Ian Gillan to join Rainbow, didn't you?
I think I did. I went round his house and knocked on the door. Ian!" "Fucking hell! Come in!" We were like the best of friends, you know? So I went in - his girlfriend was there - and said: "I came round to see if you wanted to join Rainbow?" "Come and have a drink." And we started drinking a full bottle of vodka. But before I got half-way through the bottle I was thinking to myself: "I'm not so sure this is a good idea." He's going: "Rich, I'm so glad, I'm so fucking happy you are here." 'Cause he's like that; he's got two sides to him. But I'm thinking: "Fucking hell! What am I doing?"

How long was it since you'd seen him last?
About seven years... eight, nine? But I suddenly realised that maybe I shouldn't have asked him. That's what I'm thinking as I'm sat there. Then at the end of it he goes: "I dunno Rich, I don't know if I can join." But by the time we'd finished the Vodka I was like (puts his hands together in prayer) *I hope... he doesn't... say yes! So he says: "Rich, I don't know if I can; I'm going to have to let you know." "Yeah, okay Ian, great seeing you again." Phew! Let's get out of here!*

What made you do it, though?
I don't know. I'd just forgotten what he was like. But when I met up with him again I thought: "Oh, it's all coming back." But he turned it down, so it lies with him. Had he said yes I would've gone: "Oh, shit! Now what am I going to do?"

So, he stayed with Gillan, you and Roger with Rainbow, and Coverdale, Paice and Lord with Whitesnake. The programme suggested there was a big rivalry between the bands. Were you aware of that?
No. I had a lot of faith in David Coverdale when he first came to the band. Paicey discovered him; he played me his tape and I said: "This guy is great, who is he?" It's David Coverdale." Okay, let's get him down." Coverdale was the guy that I always went towards in the band, more so than Glenn. I always found Glenn a really nice guy, but I didn't like his vocals. I was always very pro-David Coverdale until I left, got my own thing together; and for some reason he took it so personally. It's almost like I'd slept with his mother or something. He got this really nasty shit with me, for years! "Oh, Ritchie, slag slag slag Everything was slagging me off. I thought: 'What did I do?" Just because I left the band, went off with Ronnie, did the Rainbow thing? He has Deep Purple; what was the problem with him? I could never understand what his problem was.

He told this story about how, when both your bands were touring Germany at the same time, the promoter invited him backstage to a Rainbow gig, and you threw him out!

What happened was the girl came up to me and said: "You know David's in town?" And I'd had it with him knocking me; I'd had about four years of this fucking shit in the press. He'd be asked: David, what's your new LP like?" He'd say: It's better than Rainbow's." It was always like that! Out of the blue; for no reason. So I used to read this stuff and wonder: "What's wrong with this guy? Why's he always picking on me?" So I started getting antsy (phonetic) *towards him. So, this girl said: "Oh, David might come tonight." David who?" "David Coverdale." So I was like: "Just keep him away from me. If David Coverdale wants to come and see the show I want him to pay and be in the audience, I don't want him back here." So I told that to the girl who was running the show, and she said: "Of course." I said: Don't you even think about bringing him backstage, because I'll lose it if I see him" - after all this bullshit that he'd been saying about me. Sure enough, what happens? I come offstage and go into the dressing room, really uptight. It was a really good show. I'm there, coming down, and Cozy comes in: "Hey! Seen who's out there?" Out where?" Cozy was brilliant at stirring. "Coverdale! He's in the corridor!" "Coverdale is in the corridor? Why?' "He's backstage, drinking our Scotch, and he's putting the show down." 'He's putting the show down?" "He just said what kind of pantomime was that? quote." Cozy knew that was enough to get me going. So I'm going: "Where is he?" Sure enough, he was in the corridor, up against the wall talking to some girl, doing his grandee pose* (affects Coverdale's upper crust accent): *"Of course, I usually drink only the very best brandy." So pompous! I went up to him and said: "What the fuck are you doing here? Roadies! Get this guy out. I don't want him here sipping our drinks going "What kind of shit was that"?" With that, I grabbed him by the collar - he's quite tall - and went: Out!" He lunged at me, missed, and we fell to the floor, wrestling - at the feet of the guys in Queen. The drummer Roger Taylor and the bass player were there, drinking away, but looking straight ahead while we're grovelling away on the floor.... "You fucking..." fucking..." ..."Fuck you. I'm looking up to see Roger Taylor just casually talking to his girlfriend, very nonchalant. So my plan was - if I'd wanted to whack him, I would've wacked him - but I wanted him thrown out. Then he started throwing punches at me and I thought, okay, we're into fighting. So they pulled us apart and the promoter Erik Thomsen is going: "Calm down! Calm down! Are you okay?" But as soon as they let us go I went, wham! Hit him straight in the fucking head! With that, Coverdale ran back to get his own back - but punched Eric in the face. So I didn't get anything, and that was that. But the whole point was that could have all been stopped had this girl listened to me.*

The story that before Coverdale joined, you were going to get Paul Rodgers to sing with Deep Purple. How advanced was that plan?

Paul Rodgers said yes, it was interesting, he'd give it some thought. So I was like: "Great! Fantastic! Best singer there is!" The rest of the band was into it, but all of a sudden it's in Melody Maker that Paul Rodgers had joined Deep Purple. I thought: "Oh no! What's this shit?", and called up Paul to say: "I'm sorry about that; I don't know who told the paper'. And he said: "I'm sorry, I've thought about it, and I can't really help you out". And I can't believe that Melody Maker fucked it up. They pushed him into saying no!

That was before you'd got Glenn?

Oh yes! Paul Rodgers was my all-time favourite singer. Amazing singer! Fucking amazing! Just his presence. That guy had it down. I think if Paul had been interested in joining, he would have. But I think when he saw that in Melody Maker he went: "What kind of morons are these, saying I've joined their band, when I haven't even made my mind up!' I don't know who put it in the paper, but I have a good idea. It was one of the band. He couldn't stop himself - he had to tell someone!

Jon said...
Funny you should mention Jon... (laughs)

Thank you for answering the question that I should have asked. Jon said that Ian Gillan leaving Deep Purple was the greatest shame in rock 'n' roll, ever.
In rock 'n' roll?

I thought maybe John Lennon getting shot was...
I thought Adam Ant! (pauses) *Was Jon standing next to Ian at the time he said that?*

No.
Really? There were a lot of delusions of grandeur within the Purple camp. I really do think that. That's another reason I wanted to get out.

Was 'Down To Earth' your best selling album?
'Since You Been Gone' did very well because it was written by Russ Ballard. There's an interesting story there - and now I'm bashing Cozy. I remember when 'Since You Been Gone' came up, the management said: "What do you think of that?" I said: It's a great idea, let's do it.' It had just been done by another band called Clout. But when we went to do it, Cozy was going: I don't like this song." We did it once, then when we went to do it again his famous quote was: I am going to play this but one more time!" He hated the song! So we did it, and Roger went: "Yeah, that was good, but let's do one more take." And Cozy went: "Nope!" Roger's going: "Oh, come on, just a few little fills" 'cause he'd been a bit rigid. And he said: "No! I fucking hate that song! It's bullshit! I don't want anything to do with it!" So Roger said he thought he could manipulate it with effects, and he did. So, to cut a long story short, when it was like number two or three in the charts, I heard from someone who went up to Cozy and said: "Oh, I love that 'Since You Been Gone' Cozy had said: "Yeah, 'yeah, that's one of my favourite tracks." Isn't that interesting?

So what happened with Graham Bonnet? Why did he leave? Was it the whistling and Percy Thrower impersonations?
Urn... Graham... fucking hell, Graham... Roger always had a good thing for him, although Roger used to say: "God said I will give you a wonderful voice - but I will take away everything else." Roger used to tell every interviewer everything else! Graham was a nice enough guy; just completely... lost! One day - it's easy to pick on peoples' faults, but I remember this going down - I said to him: "How are you feeling?" "Oh, not too good." "What's wrong?" I don't know, I just feel odd!" Colin said to him: "What do you mean?" I feel kind of fuzzy." "Have you eaten- That's it - I'm fucking hungry!" Colin actually turned him around and smacked him across the head, and marched him off to the restaurant. He had literally forgotten to eat for ages! And all these singers used to say I was a mental case...

That thing Chris Curtis had planned for Roundabout - that people would get on to it and walk off again - really worked for your band. Wasn't it you who once described that band as 'like a revolving door'?
I remember, harking back to him, being in the Speakeasy one night with Chris, when he went up to Clapton. He said: 'Eric, meet the world's best guitar player - after me ...... Eric's like: "Who?' It was so embarrassing!

When Deep Purple reformed in 1984, you made a video that showed the band getting together for the first time in Vermont. Was that footage staged or real?
It depends...

The bit I'm referring to in particular is when you walk in and shake hands with the guys and hold your hand out to Ian last, and pretend to withdraw it at the last moment.
Do I? I've had some good times with Gillan, too. I often blame myself for him - he tells this story too. We were in the Rock 'N' Roll Circus in France, a club, in 1970. He was a very shy reserved guy until I did this maybe it was my fault. But we were in this big club and... for some reason I retain this very childish love of pranks - I love practical jokes - he went to sit down, and I saw he was a bit drunk, so I pulled the chair away so he would miss. But what I didn't realise was that behind us was a big drop of about fifteen feet, and he fell down this drop and crunched his head. I heard his head go (thumps the table hard for emphasis) on the stone floor. I'm going: "Oh no! He's split his head open." After that, he was never the same. He did change.

So it was the blow on the head, rather than the fact that he resented you for doing that to him?
No, no, that was all right. It was the blow. I thought he was out cold - and he was a strong guy. I thought it was all over. I thought he was dead. But then he got back up, and I go: "Are you all right?" and he goes: "Yeah, I just hurt my head a bit." But he hit his head on the concrete and he seemed to change as a person. Incidentally, there's a brilliant story there! We were in this Rock 'n' Roll Circus, a very pretentious place, and in came this woman to dance on the dance floor; and she had this hair all piled up, looked like Brigitte Bardot, Marilyn Monroe, very 50s. She'd obviously been in the hairdresser's for hours, and she thought she was the cat's whiskers, dancing with this guy. Gillan was in his usual mood, looking around. We were having champagne at the time, given to us by the guy that owned the club, but the champagne had gone and the ice in the bucket had melted to water. So Gillan looks at this woman, looks at the bucket of water, goes over to her and sticks the bucket upside down on her head! Her hair's ruined! She went berserk, completely lost it! I was laughing my head off because I really didn't think he'd do that. She went somewhere to dry off, then came back half-an-hour later. Another bottle of champagne has been drunk and he's looking at her again. I'm thinking: "He won't do that again... he can't do that again". But sure enough, he goes up behind her and does it again! This time she comes over to Ian and slaps him across his face. Then her boyfriend comes over, furious, and goes: "You do that one more time and I will... At which point Ian stood up, and showed how much bigger he was. "... leave!"

But you're changing the subject. Are you really saying that feud between you and Ian is all because of a blow to his head, that you caused?
That's right!

Amazing! I don't know how to follow that. So I'll be boring and ask you about your set lists - sorry! Why did they change so little until Joe Lynn Turner joined? Why did you never do 'Flight Of The Rat' or 'Pictures Of Home?'
We tried 'Pictures Of Home' - which I liked a lot on the record - but it never seemed to work out on stage. It was that six-eight fill. But I liked it a lot, really liked that tune. (He sings the tune). But we did it and I was watching the audience. They were like: "Yawn." Flight Of The Rat - I think we did that once or twice. Same thing, it didn't go down too well. I can't remember it now. Probably haven't heard it in twenty years. Because you have to get rid of things, move on. I like to look this way (points forward).

But that was the good thing about Joe. Although I never liked him as the Deep Purple singer' - I thought he was wrong for the band - he did at least make you uncover a few gems in your catalogue.
I disagree. I think Joe was the best singer we had in the band, in Rainbow, without a doubt. Him singing things like: 'Can't Let You Go', 'Street Of Dreams', he was brilliant. On his ballads no

one could touch him, and his was the voice I was looking for. And when we broke up and I had to do the Purple thing - I shouldn't have really done that but I did it because it was basically easy money. The money was dangled in front of me and I thought: "Well, the Rainbow thing's going well but, shit, okay." Gillan came along and talked us into it. I thought we'd do maybe one LP, but then it got to be more than one. But looking back, I probably shouldn't have made that move. I should have stayed with Rainbow because Joe was singing really well. He pissed me off on stage because he was like Judy Garland! I could not stop his little twee movements. "Joe! Don't do that crap!" I threatened him backstage at Leeds. I grabbed him and said: If you do any more of those pansy movements I'm gonna fucking nail you! You can't do that in England!"

I remember he used to do split jumps off the drum riser.
Yes, because some little girl would go: "Joe, I love your little jumps." And I'd be right back to square one. But when I think back, Joe did, more for Rainbow than any other vocalist by far. Ten times more! I don't go around waving a banner but I do resent it when I hear people going: "Well, I thought Ronnie Dio..."

But surely he was wrong for Deep Purple?
Then again, one of my favourite LPs was 'Slaves And Masters.' He sang so well.

Still, a lot of Purple fans thought that was a travesty.
Sometimes, whatever you do - I'm a big Bob Dylan fan and I'm reading his biography. Everything he did somebody would say it was a travesty. "How can you do that? How can you play with electrical instruments? You've sold out!" Meanwhile, 'Blonde On Blonde' comes along, and it's one of the best LPs ever made. But people always want it to be the same as the last time. As soon as you digress a little bit and do something new, they go: "This is rubbish." I didn't like the way that Joe got to be the brunt. Even Doogie (White) said that the other day. He said: "Joe was the worst singer in Rainbow." And I said: "No, no, no, he was the best." When he was on, he was great. Now, forget it! We had to get rid of him because his voice was shot. But what a voice he had! Sometimes, on a ballad, a power ballad, he was brilliant!

What are your favourite tracks off the very first Rainbow album?
'Man On The Silver Mountain'. 'Sixteenth Century Greensleeves' was great. The way he sang that was perfect for what I wanted. I didn't tell him - he just sang it. 'Stargazer' too, great. 'Long Live Rock 'N' Roll'... I started finding out that he couldn't do a power ballad ('Rainbow Eyes'). He started going into a little girlie voice, and that used to bug me!

Some of your best tracks have been those on which, at least in part, you have used an acoustic guitar: "Catch The Rainbow, 'Temple Of The King', 'Sixteenth Century Greensleeves', 'Soldier Of Fortune' - yet you've not used one very often. Is it harder to play?
No, not at all. Easier actually. But it doesn't translate to live because you're relying on some guy to bring you up, and those monitors are crazy. But my next LP will be all acoustic - although that's a different type of music. I have eight songs that I'm doing in a medieval folk-type vein. That's with my girlfriend singing. We play it to our friends in the bar at home. I'll see how the Rainbow thing goes, depending on whether people want to hear any more Rainbow. I'll leave it up to the audience. If they don't want to hear any more I'll go, hey, and knock it on the head. Because this next project I'm very excited about because it's a big change. It's completely different from the hard rock thing.

You've been talking about that for a long time, haven't you?
Yes; but I have to move gradually. I like to know exactly what I'm doing before I get into a thing.

People say: "Play the acoustic; do this, do that... But I'm like: "Not yet, I'm not ready." But now I'm ready to change. I think this might be my last LP as an out-and-out rock player. I might come back to it in a few years - it depends. But I'm finding it harder and harder to be inspired by just playing loud. I'd rather just sit down with a guitar and play. This whole "you've got to hit with a big riff" thing is beginning to wear off. It's been thirty years, you know.

This sounds a bit negative. Your new Rainbow LP is not even released yet, and here you are saying it won't last.
I am an extremely negative person. I dwell on the negative in any situation. (Laughs) I'm British to the core!

'Burn', you said, was exactly how you wanted Deep Purple to sound. The ultimate Deep Purple track.
That's true. It was done very quickly, too. In about five takes.

What is it about that track that makes it so special to you?
Coverdale's voice, the song, the content. Some of the solos hit... the solo's okay. I played with Jon, and Jon's part is very good. I thought the riff was very good. It's 'Fascinating Rhythm.' Although I didn't know it until Jon Lord told me. (Laughs)

What can you do with Rainbow now that you couldn't do with Deep Purple last time?
I can sing a lot of Olde English acoustic folk songs with Doogie. We have a set, which is about half-an-hour long, of all acoustic stuff like 'Lincolnshire Poacher', 'I Belong To Glasgow', 'Lights Of Aberdeen'... really! He is brilliant at that stuff. He is so funny, he cracks me up! I could never have done that with Gillan or Coverdale - they were all too serious. 'We're not going to sing 'The Lights Of Aberdeen'."

But seriously, will you be doing a "best of Rainbow" set?
Yeah; the set will be about three or four of the really old ones, probably nothing from the Joe Lynn albums.

That's odd, because Doogie can sing like that. He also - as the album shows - can sing like Ronnie Dio, and I know he can sing like Paul Rodgers too.
Yeah, he's very good.

Did you always intend this to be a Rainbow album, or was it ever the roots of another Purple record?
No, it was always done for Rainbow.

Do you listen to much music these days, because this record sounds as if it could have been made on the back of the last Rainbow album 'Bent Out Of Shape', in 1983? You've picked up where you left off rather than taken it forward very much.
What Is taking something forward?

Rainbow still sounds very much as it did twelve years ago. Musically, it hasn't followed what has happened over that time.
I don't follow fashions. I stick to my own thing. It sounds corny, but I think it's very apparent. I would never follow today's music. If I thought it was any good, I might. But instead, I've gone

back five hundred years! That's where I really feel at home - five hundred years ago! As far as I'm concerned, I'm going to stay back there and have a good time. I really don't want to be involved in grunge. I don't want anything to do with any music I don't like.

What was the last thing you heard that moved you?
Abba. And I heard some German friends of mine playing 1600s music on mandolins and old instruments. But recently: nothing. I don't live today, I really don't. I don't want to know about what's going on. (Laughs) I'd rather be a painter than be involved in it.

Where do you think Ritchie Blackmore stands in the great parade of guitarists?
As a guitar player? Um, I think I'm very good, when I'm at home, but I don't really put too much down on tape. But there are very many great guitar players out there, technically better than I am. I do have a "stamp", and I'm very happy now not to be among the top guns. In the Eighties I felt like I had to be the fastest gun.

When you were winning so many of the polls?
Yeah. Then it was Eddie Van Halen, and I noticed that eventually Eddie couldn't stand it any longer, and started playing the organ! But that fast style of guitar playing is not for me any more. I don't listen to it. I mean, I wouldn't buy an LP anyway, but when I hear something on the radio I think: "Wow, that guy's fast." Like Joe Satriani - this guy really knows how to run around. But then I hear people like BB King and think: "This guy plays from the heart" but I think "I wish he'd play more than those three notes, and a bit faster." (Laughs)

Do you think your playing abilities have been generally appreciated? People often talk about Page, Clapton and Beck, but your name is not usually mentioned in that company.
Jeff Beck is always my favourite. He doesn't have to run around. He plays a note and I think: "where did he find that? It's not on my guitar!" I've always loved Jeff, and I love his attitude: "Am I a guitar player? No, I'd rather fix a car." And that's true. He doesn't jump up and down, he doesn't show off the latest fashion. He just stays as he is. He always looks the same, wears the same T-shirt; doesn't pander to fashion, wear shorts, or long shorts, doesn't spit. He's just always there, and has been since '64.

But don't you think you deserve to be mentioned in that kind of company?
I hear that a lot. But Jeff's done a helluva lot. Page has done an awful lot. He got very famous with Led Zeppelin - he wouldn't be spoken about so highly if it wasn't for Led Zeppelin.

But that's fair if he created them.
Yeah. I wasn't a fan of theirs particularly, but I did respect them, what they did in the 60s. It wouldn't happen today. What the fuck is this grunge thing? Why are record companies signing this stuff? I think they are being intimidated.

What's your biggest regret?
I'd have to really think about that... Um, I don't really have any regrets.

How would you like to be remembered, then?
I'm not really interested in being remembered. When I go, hopefully I'll go on to other things. I won't be looking back. My hobby is a living. I have to tell myself that sometimes, because I get a little bitter about what sells today. I have to remind myself, just keep playing the guitar, don't knock it. I just get so angry, because I know how many good musicians there are out there. Music is so derivative: everything I do has been done before.

Roger Glover said that he thought you were one of the people that God had pointed a finger at...
He has a lot of stories about God.

... and given you something that nobody else would have. But that you can't deal with that talent.
I practice a lot. But only about ten per cent of what I have done is me; ninety per cent of it is very contrived. Only about ten per cent is pure. It's like when you hear a joke: it only works once. If you're told a joke you can't then ask to hear it again and say: "Could you do it slower, and this time would you walk over to the door when you say the punchline?" I always play my stuff before I come to put it on tape. You can't turn it on or off. And that's why I get so angry if people around me aren't doing their job while I am. If the sound guy is getting it wrong, or the singer, or whatever. And that always comes across as me being moody!

But aren't you your own worst critic? Like when you upset people because you choose not to play an encore?
If I don't play an encore, it's usually for one of two reasons: either because I feel that I haven't played well, or I think the audience wasn't into it. They just stand there and go (claps apathetically): "Now come back and do 'Smoke On The Water'." So I don't. But I can't just turn it on. Roger used to say that: 'Well, why don't you just play it live?" And I'd say: "I can't play live if you're going to record the drums twenty times. I agree, but just do one take; I can't do it twenty times just so you can get a perfect paradiddle." By then I've lost it. Live has to be one take, I can handle that. Paicey couldn't. He was always going: "Let's do it again, do it again." Jon and I would just walk out and go to dinner. 'We've done it fifteen times, and we're not doing it anymore despite what Ian Paice says!"

(His dinner guest Artie recounts tales of his goosebump-inducing wee small hours jam sessions, rock 'n' roll, medieval and classical style...)
But that's all done in one take. I couldn't do it again. I almost resent people hearing that. I've got this deep-down resentment that says: "This is my private music; that's really me." But I don't want that to get out. It just flows out of me,' when you're in the right company at the right time. It's not music, it's just 'flow.' It's music as far as its got notes but... Like sometimes when you're on tour someone will say: "Right lads, it's eight o'clock, ready to go?" and you have to switch on. You get yourself hyped up, and what comes out, some nights, is great, but often it just doesn't happen. If you're trying to pull something from your soul you can't always do it.

Okay, last question. What do you want on your tombstone?
(long pause) There must be some funny answer I can come up with...

That was the plan, yes.
(Another pause before an earnest reply) "This man has gone to his grave still wondering what the hell it was all about..." Because I would - I would go to my grave thinking: "Why has this happened? What the hell was that?" Because I get into philosophy and religions and I'm... I get into these events that I can't even explain. I've heard things and witnessed things that are so strange. (Laughs) And the joke is, you try and tell someone else and they won't believe you. They'll go: "No, that didn't happen." And, in a way, maybe it didn't happen because we're not ready to understand it. I don't understand it but I'm ready for it. I can't do it justice; I can't explain what just happened. I know something just happened that is unbelievable. But it's almost like, well, you're one of the chosen few because you try and tell someone what you've just witnessed and they won't believe you. The thing about séances is that people are so afraid of them, that they just say they are evil. But it's just communication. It strikes me that it's just like being back five hundred years. Imagine if, in the days of King Henry VIII, in his court, he suddenly picked up a phone and went: "Hello George." They'd all be going: "The devil! The devil is speaking to him

on that apparatus." But imagine, five thousand years from now, five million years from now, we are going to look back and go: "Can you actually believe, in the days of the electric guitar, they actually didn't believe in..." Timing is so weird. If you take away time and space, all you're left with is complete chaos. No facts, no logic is going to work, because time was invented by man. So what's going on? It's now been proved that you can go backwards as well as forwards. What does that mean? That we're running parallel with another life, other lives, billions of lives? People say they believe in reincarnation, but have you ever thought that reincarnation could be ahead of you and that we're going back? Start building up logic and inverting it and they're coming up with black holes that suck anything in. "I can't understand it", all the scientists are going, "Well, what is it?" "This doesn't exist." But it's still in our universe. Logic, I don't think exists. It does if we want it to, because we have to have a sense of order. Take that away and we're really confused. I can't explain it. I' m still toying with the idea in my head. Certain séances I do ask certain questions, and the answers I get mean another realm, another part of my brain, can start opening up. A part that has been dormant. I ask: "Have you ever lived before?" And the answer is: "No, I haven't lived in the way that you would know it." Okay, so we're talking about other realms here. It's really weird. You just have to go out and look at the stars and think: "Where does it end and where does it begin? What's on the other side?"

How often do you have séances?
I haven't had one for a couple of months now. There was a time when I was compiling a book, keeping a log - I'd been doing it for years. Very interesting stuff. A particular spirit - or whatever you'd like to call it - that we were in touch with was incredibly articulate and very intelligent, and some of the answers were so profound it was unbelievable. The things that he would come back with you had to keep going back over, because they were so heavy, so deep, so profound, that you can't comprehend it when you go through it. But after a while you came to realise that it, makes perfect sense. It's not the way we live here, it's obviously the way ahead. But it's amazing, communication with other... I'm a great believer in: this is not it, this is too shallow. The hurt that goes down: we're killing things to live. There's something wrong with that - but I still eat meat. That can't be right. Or living for money, power... It's like, I love music because it's so pure, until it becomes a fashion and it's on MTV. A minstrel on the back of a hay truck: that music I think is the best. You can't fuss that up. Like Frank Zappa said: music came across as making a big industry about thirty years ago. People thought: this could be big bucks, let's get involved - and that's ruined music. It's too shallow. And it's all redundant. Nobody is going to get away with it. Everybody's putting off the terminal disease whatever it is going to be: heart attack, cancer, or something. It's just a matter of time. So what does that mean? That's when I start to go: "Hmmm. I'm gonna get drunk tonight. I can't take this fucking heavy -stuff." We're all living to die. Dying to live and living to die. That's why I think everybody is so fascinated by the man with the gift of the gab, the court jester, who makes us laugh - because he is the one who is least afraid of dying. It's inherent in all human beings. We're so petrified of dying that anyone that can just throw that to the wind and go: "Have you heard the one about ... ?" that we all go: "Hey! This guy is great!" He's like a shaman. He might know the answer. And if you'll believe that you'll believe anything. People that can make you laugh can make you forget what's coming.

Late night TV programming reflects that. Comedy before you go to sleep.
That's great! That's very therapeutic. You can't go to bed reading a letter that tells you, you owe X amount on your taxes. Go to bed laughing, you're going to get a good night's sleep.

Footnote: ... Ritchie later told me the following (paraphrased story) which he said could be printed, because he would have said it had the tape still been rolling....

After "Fireball" had been recorded, we were told to go back and write a single (January 1971), so we booked some studio time and arranged to meet. When I got there we were all there but Jon. I phoned the office and said: "Look, the four of us are here and ready but there's no sign of Jon". "Oh, he's here", they said. "What's he doing in London, he should be here to write and record? Put him on. "I, er, I had some things to do. Carry on without me, you don't need me to be there." So we did. We sat around and came up with "Strange Kind Of Woman', and after we'd recorded it I remember Paicey coming over to me and saying: "You don't think Jon is going to expect his name on the writing credits for that, is he?" And I said: "I'll bet he does, why not ask him?" Sure enough, he did - he insisted on it! I couldn't really take him seriously after that.

Ritchie's memory failed him with the last comment as 'Strange Kind Of Woman' was written before most of the 'Fireball' album. Neil missed out the story of when he asked Ritchie directions to the toilet. Ritchie sent him through the kitchen door where Neil, quite pissed by now, crashed into the pots and pans, came out the other side, finally got into the cubical, where he heard Ritchie in the next one say quietly: "Found it alright, then?"

****

COZY POWELL

The interview I conducted with Cozy Powell was one of those unforeseen occasions, when the whole thing was utterly spontaneous. I had decided to go to the Esbjerg Festival in Denmark when news that Rainbow would headline on the Saturday evening was sprung upon me at short notice.

With the possibility that it was going to be Rainbow's only European show for the foreseeable future I booked a flight. As it was, the gig turned out to be Rainbow's last ever concert.

Also on the bill was Peter Green's Splinter Group, which at the time included Neil Murray and of course Cozy Powell. Flying out the day before the gig I happened to be on the same plane as Peter Green's entourage. At the check-in desk I recognised a couple of the band, and it instantly occurred to me that Cozy would be around somewhere. I'd never met him but as the legendary drummer had been such a major part of early Rainbow, the possibility of having a quick chat with him at the airport soon dawned on me.

Cozy was the last of the entourage to turn up at the check-in and when he arrived, clutching a motor cycle magazine, he seemed more interested in talking to his fellow band members about a bike he had just been reading about, rather than concerning his self with the forthcoming flight. He immediately struck me as a very approachable guy. Thinking there may be an opportunity to arrange an interview I introduced myself, gave him a copy of *More Black than Purple*, and asked if it would be possible to do an interview sometime over the weekend in conjunction with the 'Rainbow Rising' retrospective that MBTP was in the process of publishing. Without batting an eyelid Cozy immediately responded positively and was happy to oblige. I was amazed that he was so willing there and then to commit himself to giving up some of his time before we had even arrived in Denmark. He seemed genuinely keen to do it and during the flight, read the magazine with great interest. I think it helped encourage him to look forward to the interview. After reading the Neil Jeffries interview he talked of some inaccuracies in Blackmore's comments that he wanted the opportunity to address.

Having agreed to set up the interview for the Saturday evening, I actually turned up at the Hotel much later than arranged. Cozy was sitting in the lobby and didn't seem at all bothered that I had made him wait for ages. On top of that, because many fans were aware that I was doing an interview, there was a small army of people with me. Once again Cozy wasn't bothered by the entourage. We chatted for about an hour and he came across as a very honest, sincere and regular guy. There was none of the 'Rock Star' bullshit that accompanies some people. There was nothing pretentious about him and no heirs and graces. As you will read, Cozy was someone who would speak candidly and to hell with the consequences, a quality I admire in anyone.

Ideally I would have preferred to have done the interview at a later date, to have given me time to prepare better questions, but the opportunity of doing it there and then was too good to miss. As a result it turned out to be more of an informal chat than an interview: A very amusing one at that, with occasional interjections from my Danish friend Rasmus Heide and Cozy's band mate Neil Murray.

As we sat down to begin the interview, Cozy started by talking about his conversations with Ritchie the night before...

You'll be pleased to know that Ritchie and I had a very interesting evenings chat yesterday. Very constructive. Very positive He's probably mellowed a little bit since we...we're talking twenty years ago when we worked together.

There are some good stories about Erik Thomsen (Danish tour promoter).
I saw Erik, I was there this morning... In fact the second thing Ritchie said to me after hello was, "will you agree not to do my room, if I agree not to do yours!" So we both agreed we wouldn't do each others room! Then we started working out which windows we could get in to do everybody else's.

As we left last night, Andy Scott (Sweet guitarist) was still down there. He'd heard a rumour that you were going to do his room.
Well we were going to try to but the problem is he's on the second floor. If he'd been on the top

floor it would have been easy, 'cos I could have gone over the roof. Had he been on this floor we could have climbed up, but as he's on the next floor up and there was somebody above him I couldn't get out of one window and down and then in, so it was a bit of a problem. At that time I'd probably had just a couple and I thought... well.

Ritchie was saying how he still doesn't understand how you did the thing about sixteen floors up.
Well, I use to kind of do... I was very good at tree climbing when I was younger and I could get up any drainpipe of any building, get into any room. I was just good at it. I don't know why. Crazy things to do but... this is so easy this hotel. I could get into any of these rooms, pretty much. But the one that I did the tour manager was in Gelsenkirchen, and it was about twenty two floors and the floor I needed to get to was the thirteenth and because I was a bit drunk I got out all right, got across to the room but unfortunately got the floor wrong. Got the room right but the floor wrong. Got the poor guy in the room above instead of the one I needed. Very expensive little practical joke that was. Cost me about a thousand pounds to pay the hotel to have the room completely...

So okay, first thing. This interview that Ritchie did with Neil Jeffries. You've read it and you said there's a few inaccuracies.
There's a couple of pointers that in the mist of time are slightly inaccurate. The first one is the 'Since You Been Gone' single. I remember well when the first time I ever heard it, Bruce Payne played it to me in the office in New York and he said "what do you think about this track?" I said great. It sounds really good. It was done by a girl band. Forgotten the name now. Cradle?

Clout. Was it Clout?
Yeah Clout that's it, and then he said well we're thinking of doing it for Rainbow. I said you must be kidding. No way is this a Rainbow track, it's a pop song. Anyway it went backwards and forwards and Roger liked it and he wanted to do it. Maybe perhaps Ritchie wasn't even sure that he liked it or whether he didn't, but he agreed to do it and I just said this is ridiculous. We should never be doing these kind of songs. We are Rainbow, we are the leaders in this kind of field of music. In the end I said I'll play it but I'll play it once and that's all. So I did play it and yes it did come out, but I mean I didn't...It wasn't that I didn't like the song, I didn't like it for Rainbow. I thought we were going to far over. I thought the fans would say "What's this?" It's obviously a very commercial song and as it happened it turned out to be a big hit. And at that time that was one of the reasons why I decided that if Ritchie was going to go along... ah sod.
(at this point Cozy suddenly got soaked in water from three floors above!)

There's Candice. (leaning out of the window filming it with her camcorder)
(looking up to the appropriate window) *Right that's it.*

Somewhat unperturbed by the soaking ...
So I thought if he's going to go along... It's probably better if I move off and go and do something else so that was basically it. After about another six months and whatever. (Cozy looks up again, convinced something else is about to happen)

I think you're okay. They've shut the window now. He's about ready to go now.
Okay.

So the other thing you were saying was the situation with Ronnie.
Yeah, the Ronnie situation was a bit unfortunate because at that time I think Ronnie and Wendy were kind of starting to be really... well I don't know it was much more of a sort of power struggle

between Bruce Payne and Ronnie and Wendy and all the rest of it, so it had got to the point where it was getting a bit heated. I think Ronnie then started to get, because it was just me, him and Ritchie that he decided that he should make a bit of a point and he started trying to get me on his side and "Cozy and I think this, and Cozy and I think that" and it's absolute bollocks. I may have agreed with him on a couple of things, but at the end of the day I ended up staying with Ritchie, and Ronnie was booted out. That shows where my loyalties were. I think in actual fact he asked me to do some recording on his new album and I said no. I can't do that I'm working with Ritchie. I'll stay with Ritchie and that's it and he didn't really like the fact that I wasn't going to do that, so he's never really been a great fan of mine since then. But he did try and twist it around a bit. Sometimes it's nice to put the record straight. I keep seeing things about what I've supposed to have said or what I've supposed to have done, or what somebody has supposed to have said about me so it's nice to actually say, well this is the issue at the time.

Which album was this you were suppose to be working on at the time?
We were working on 'Long Live Rock 'n' Roll' at the time.

But Ronnie's solo you mentioned.
I don't know. I think it was the first Dio album whatever that was.

Holy Diver.
Yeah. Was it Holy Diver, I think it was. Didn't Jimmy play on that?

Jimmy Bain, yeah.
I think the idea was, that Ronnie's very clever at manipulating things to his own advantage if he thinks he can. He comes across as a very nice guy, but underneath it there is a little bit of... you know like we all have a little bit of something and his idea was if he could get most of Rainbow to play on his solo album it would take away from Rainbow and so the fans at that time would buy his album and they would forget Ritchie's. So at that time, although I was being quoted with saying this, that and the other, at the end of the day I stayed with Ritchie. So at the end of the day it was just Ritchie and me, and then we got a whole new band in and went from there. (Cozy's memory of this is slightly inaccurate as Ronnie joined Black Sabbath after leaving Rainbow. His first solo album was not until 1983, by which time Cozy was in Whitesnake.)

So they're the only two points in that interview.
In the article, yeah. I mean Ritchie says another interesting thing that "Cozy's either your best friend or your worst nightmare." He's going to find out what his worst nightmare is... later !

You seemed to get on okay last night didn't you?
Yeah

First time you've seen him for quite a while?
Yeah, I haven't seen Ritchie for ten years, maybe more. Ritchie's Ritchie, you take him as he is. I suppose he's just like me, he's a boy who's never grown up and he likes to do stupid things, but I can get along with that, that's fine.

Like the radio in the fire.
Ah, the radio in the fire, we were talking about it last night, I mean it's so funny. Some of the things we got up to were just amazing, I mean really were outrageous. So in that respect we share quite a lot in common. I mean I've calmed down a fair bit since all that. I don't go setting fire to people anymore, blowing up hotel rooms but I might tonight. Later!

(During the recording of Long Live Rock 'n' Roll in a French Chateau, Cozy and Ritchie took it upon themselves to throw a vintage radio that belonged to the Chateau's owner into the large fire, before dashing out of the room. Colin Hart (Rainbow's tour manager) sensing something was afoot ran into the room, and tried to retrieve it, at which point the owner walked in to see Colin with his hands on the radio in the fire!)

If we can take you back a bit further to when you actually joined the band. How did you get into it?
I got a phone call from Fergie actually, who's Ritchie's guitar tech at the time who new me vaguely and he said "we've had about eighty different drummers come down for Ritchie's band. Would you like to be number eighty one?" What happened was my tour manager phoned up and said "look I've had a phone call from the States Ritchie's looking for a..." (At this point in the proceedings Rasmus Heide starts to shuffle his chair away from Cozy) *Why are you moving away. Has he got another glass? If you see him with a glass of water you tell me all right.*

(Heide) I will.
I got this phone call out of the blue really saying can you come to the States. Would you like to come and audition for Ritchie's band. Simple as that. I wasn't doing anything at the time. I was just in the middle of doing some motor racing actually. I thought, yeah okay. Literally got on the next plane the next day. Flew to Los Angeles went to where the auditions were being held. There were like hundreds of people in there, and the band and like goodness knows half of Hollywood seemed to be there. Got the drum kit together and just started playing. Ritchie said "can you play a shuffle," so I said you want a shuffle, bang, I played this shuffle and about twenty minutes later he said you've got the job.

So presumably that was the first time you had met him.
I think I'd met him a couple of times before. He'd come to see me when I was with Jeff Beck at the Roundhouse. Which is what kind of alerted him to what I could do, and he's a big fan of Jeff's. He said to me afterwards I remember you from the Roundhouse show and I think he had auditioned so many people and not really got the kind of playing that he wanted from any of the Americans. Most of them were American drummers I think. I think Ritchie, maybe not now but obviously with Ian Paice and various other people he liked the English style of drumming so that's probably why I got the call.

So, as I mentioned yesterday the main reason for doing this is that we are doing a retrospective on 'Rainbow Rising' for the next issue, as it's twenty one years ago.
Right.

So what are you recollections of that?
I remember it was done very quickly. It was done in the winter of '76, was it January '76?

February '76.
Yeah it was wasn't it. I think the actual recordings were done in a week. Backing tracks. Very very quickly. We used Musicland Studios in Munich. To get the drum sound we actually went into the corridor and built a kind of shed if you like, for me to play in. It was the corridor that goes down to the cellars, and a concrete staircase, and concrete is always very good for drum sound. It's very ambient. So instead of using the actual studio which I thought was a good studio, but it didn't have a very good room for drums, we actually built this kind of alcove I could actually play in inside the corridor. From what I can remember we ran through the stuff in a disused club outside Munich just to run through the ideas for the songs. Ritchie kind of let me get on with it as far as the drum

tracks were concerned. Once I knew the format, we'd worked out 'A Light In The Black' which was sort of fifteen minutes of mayhem or however long it was. 'Stargazer' was kind of worked out. We got the basic track worked out but we hadn't got the beginning so I kind of just worked out a drum fill for the beginning of that. The other tracks were pretty straightforward. (Once again, Cozy's memory has failed him slightly. They may well have run through the stuff in a club, though three tracks, 'A Light In The Black', 'Stargazer' and 'Do You Close Your Eyes' had already been performed on stage in November '75.)

Were there any outtakes at all from there?
There are probably outtakes, though I honestly can't remember.
(At this point Neil Murray appears.)

So there weren't any alternative songs as such?
I can't remember how many songs we rehearsed. I expect that all the tracks we recorded were the ones that were written. There may have been an outtake but it's such a long time ago I can't remember whether there were anymore.

(Heide) Alternative takes?
Yeah may have been. I think the idea was to try and capture it as quickly as we could. I think I was there for a week, ten days and then once all the drum tracks were done then Ronnie did the vocals which took for ever and a day. Ritchie and Ronnie used to go through quite a lot of grief trying to get that sorted out and Wendy was of course on tour with him as well, so as soon as I'd finished my stuff I got out of there and let them get on with it. I remember it was done very quickly. It wasn't a sort of manufactured record. It was done spontaneously and the musicians input is the way you here it. Which is possibly why it's one of the better albums that we did.

I think it's generally regarded by the fans as the classic.
I'm certainly very proud of it. I think it was a real milestone at that time. I mean we were competing with the likes of Zeppelin and obviously the Purple sort of thing. We had to come out with something that was seriously contender stuff. Ronnie was singing really well, the band was gelling pretty well. (At this juncture Cozy takes another look up to the third floor window to see if Ritchie is still there.)

I think he's gone. (Cozy then puts Neil Murray in the picture about what had happened a few minutes previously)
He's chucked a bottle of water out of the window. That was his first mistake!

Then of course there was the tour to follow, which again I think a lot of the fans regard as a great tour.
Yeah. I can't remember much about the tour to be honest. Things stick in your mind. It seemed that the tour that followed went on for ever. I can't even remember where we started. Was that when we had the rainbow?

That's right, yeah.
You probably know better than I do.

You started the tour in Canada?
Canada? Oh yeah that's right, Toronto with Argent. Yeah I do remember now. It was nothing but grief. The rainbow either broke down or something happened or the lighting truss collapsed on various people and it was fraught with all sorts of... (It was the first dates in November '75 where Toronto was the first gig. The '76 tour actually started in Idaho, USA)

But from a musical point of view I think Ritchie was playing some of his best, and the whole band was just...
It was an exciting time, yeah. It was one of those kind of line ups that just worked. At the time it was really good. It was only sort of after the first tour that the various problems with individual members started coming to the surface. First person to suffer I think was Tony Carey.

Well, it's funny you mention him because Ritch was saying last night that the last time he ever saw him was...was it at Le Chateau?
Yeah, well the last time I ever saw him he was running down the road with his suitcases in his hands after we'd tried to kill him!

Ritch told us that last night, it was incredibly funny. He was there with the Javelin smashing all the windows.
I'd forgotten about how funny some of the things were. They obviously weren't very funny to him, but if you think about everybody in the band and crew are all trying to make your life a misery it

must have been hell for him. Poor bloke really! We really put that guy through some real shit I have to say. I'd forgotten half of it and Ritchie reminded me last night. "Don't you remember we did this and don't you remember we did that."

I think he was saying you heated the door knob?
Yeah that's right. It was about 200 degrees centigrade, so by the time he reached the door... aaagh, and as he pulled the door open there was a plank tied to it, and then he realised we had tried to brick him in! I think he realised that perhaps he wasn't the most popular man in the band at that point. That was just some of the stuff.

(Heide) Why wouldn't he be?
The problem is that if your dealing with guys with an English sense of humour, and I guess by that point Ritchie and I sense of humour was pretty warped, and your starting to come off a bit big time, which he certainly did. We'd say okay Tony , more or less on the second album, would you like to come and do a keyboard solo now, "Well man I might come down in a couple of hours if I feel like it." It's like...wrong! You don't do that. When Ritchie says "can you come and do a keyboard solo?" You go and do a keyboard solo. So he kind of made a rod for his own back in that respect. He asked for it. He really did. He was a very good player, but very cocky and a bit full of himself. So he had to go. There was no way he was going to last the pace. I don't really know what happened to Jimmy. Can't remember why Jimmy went. I think Ritchie felt his bass playing was okay but we needed to find somebody better. We went through a few other players. Should have got Neil in you see, he would have been good.

You had Mark Clarke.
Mark Clarke didn't last very long. 'Ding!' The tuning key. I remember every time we'd do a take. The red light used to go on and he'd go "stop... stop... stop." He's out of tune and I couldn't understand this and it went on and on. About thirty takes. "Stop I'm out of tune." He'd get this tuning key and go ding. So every time we mention Mark Clarke. It's ding-Mark Clarke. What he was doing was because he was getting a bit uptight he'd bend the neck before the start of the take. Just enough to put the bass out of tune. So we'd start the track and it would be all over the place. So he didn't last very long. In the end I think Ritchie did something terrible to him. I think I threw a tea cup at his son or something like that. I can't remember now. In the mist of time it's all gone a bit faded.

(Murray) He's in Colosseum now.
Mountain now isn't it?

Yeah. He's with Mountain.
And Colosseum as well?
(Murray) Yeah. How can you possibly be in two bands at once?
I don't know. It sounds a bit like two bands is not enough. Neil 'three bands' Murray.

The next question you probably won't be able to answer. You're probably not aware there's going to be a Rainbow anthology coming out.
I am now aware because I've read your article, and I hope I'm going to get some royalties out of it!

Well I can put you in touch with the chap you need to speak to if that's the case.
Either I will or I won't.

It's obviously the whole career of Rainbow. They're putting on 'Mistreated' from 'On Stage' but nobody seems to know exactly where it was recorded. I don't suppose you know?
I've got quite a lot of stuff. I've got tapes of virtually every live show we've done. When I hear it I could probably work out which one it was.

We think it's one of the Japanese shows but were not a hundred per cent sure.
Could be. We recorded several. We recorded several German shows. We recorded the Japanese dates. It wouldn't take long for me to work out which actual version it is. I've got most of them. I've actually got some outtakes of rehearsals which I might sell you at a vastly inflated price!

I might be interested at a vastly inflated price!
Funnily enough another friend of mine is a big Ronnie Dio fan and I said I'll try and make some copies. If I can dig them out, you can have them. They're quite interesting. Quite amusing I think there's one or two rows going on in the background and it's quite good.

Presumably the concerts are soundboard recordings?
A couple are off the mixing desk and a couple are from the actual recording truck. Some are actually quite good quality.

So we've established there are no outtakes from 'Rainbow Rising?'
I honestly can't remember if there were any outtakes.

What about the other albums you were involved in, because we heard at the time that you did a track called 'Night People' which you did on stage at times, as part of the medley for 'Man On The Silver Mountain.'
Could be.. yeah Night People... yeah what it was, all that was really was a kind of jam. Ritchie played a selection of chords, we all followed along and Ronnie came out with the words 'Night People'. He just sang whatever came into his head.

It didn't get laid down in the studio?
It never got finished, but yeah I do remember that now you say it. But I mean there were lots of bits that never actually became songs. We started off with a bit of an idea, then that would develop. It would either develop into a proper song or it would be binned you know. There's a few things like that lying around.

So again there are no unreleased songs as such?
I don't think so.

From 'Down To Earth' even?
I don't think so, like 'Weiss Heim' for example was an after thought that we did that eventually surfaced as a b-side. Most of the stuff we did, we did kind of...we'd have say three or four tracks that were really happening and the rest of them were fillers. What we call fillers really. We were always struggling to come up with enough for an album. We'd get most of it, but not quite, so that's probably why there's not like a vast amount of stuff recorded.

When 'Weiss Heim' was put out on a compilation you weren't credited as the drummer.
Yes, I know, yeah.

Bobby Rondinelli got the credit.
He needs that! No, it doesn't matter. I think most of the fans know it's me playing on that.

So it's obvious you still get on when you saw Ritchie last night?
Well perhaps we still get on, I'm not sure! Yeah I think so. He's okay.

Would you work with him again if he ever offered it to you?
I think if the situation was right that we got back together for the music side of it, and we were going to do something, I mean just getting involved to do... I've got mixed feelings. It's always nice, I mean whether I could ever work with Ronnie again it's like... I would have much more of a problem working with him as I find him. He's got very bitter over the last few years. I don't know. I would feel a bit uncomfortable in some respects, although I suppose some times professionally you've got to think about what a good thing would be. I mean if Rainbow got back together again as it was. Say we did a few dates just for the hell of it then I wouldn't say no. I'd be interested. I'd like to work with Ritchie again, because I've thought of a few other things I could do to him which I didn't do in the five years when I worked with him before!

And of course you've done some work with his current singer, Doogie.
Doogie yeah, well Doogie, Neil and myself. Some solo stuff I've done which has still not yet surfaced. Doogie came and did some tracks with us and...

He's got a good voice.
Yeah, he's got a great voice. Funnily enough he was actually going to do the album and then Ritchie stole him from right under my nose! That's another thing I've got to get him back for!

You've got lots of things to do tonight.
I'm going to be quite busy, aren't I? I probably won't have time to watch the show.

Are you going to clear his room out?
No, that's too obvious. No, I would do something much more subtle than that. But he's got his girlfriend with him which is a bit sort of... I wouldn't want to do anything. It would have to be just me and Ritchie and then we can get down to it. It's a bit unfair to involve young ladies.

An innocent party.
Yeah, though she probably chucked the glass of water over me.

Well, she had the video camera in her hand.
Aaah, that's what it was.

(Heide) Somebody else had chucked the water.
Actually that was very fortuitous because he didn't know I was going to sit out here and I didn't realise that was his room up there, but now I do know that's his room up there.

He's given the game away.
He's kind of blown it there, hasn't he.

I'm just thinking, maybe it was Rob's room. (Rob Fodder, Ritchie's PA)
(Heide) Yeah, he was there too.
He may have done that deliberately so Rob may get the wrap.
I don't think I'll be doing anything tonight. There will be another time, don't worry.

You also said the other day that you're very keen on his new album.
I think his new album is fantastic. We were in Greece about two weeks ago and the guy out there,

I think he's something to do with the Deep Purple fan club.

Stathis.
Yeah that's it. He did an interview with us and he just said here is Ritchie's new album. I hadn't heard it and when I got home I put it on, and kind of blimey. Ritchie's wanted to make an album like that for years and it's just a really good album, it's very well produced. I like Candice's singing on it. He's playing really well, it's just typical sort of... a really nice departure and it's very well played. I think it's really good. I hope he does well with it. Quite surprised, but very pleasantly surprised.

So going on to what you're doing at the moment with Peter Green.
Well the Peter Green situation is something that's been going on for the last year. Neil and I kind of got involved. Well I got involved first because I knew Mitch and Stuart, people that are managing Peter and they really wanted to get... I think Peter had seen some videos with me with Brian May or something like that and he said "Cozy would be good and I'd like to do some work with him" so I came along to do some recording and realised that he hadn't really got a band, so I thought he really needed some experienced musicians to kind of give him a bit of security. I phoned Neil and I phoned Spike (Edney) because obviously we'd just worked together on the Brian May tour and we were pretty tight. I mean Neil and I go back a long way as you know. So at least we kind of put the band around him and then let him develop from there. I mean it's probably gone as far as... So yeah it was a case of that. We've just been working for the last year.

You mentioned obviously there that you worked with Brian May.
Yeah.

Takes us back to something that may haunt you but you did 'Since You Been Gone' with Brian May.
Well that was my idea funnily enough.

It was your idea? Because we thought who else would have suggested it?
Brian wanted to do it. Brian said to me, "would you mind if we did 'Since You Been Gone?" I said "you better ring Ritchie 'cos he'll never believe it!" So after this track I refused to play, almost refused to play on, I've now had to play it for the last ten years. I'll probably have to play it in the next band I join as well, so it's kind of haunted me for that. Maybe that's Karma. Maybe that's Russ Ballard's way of getting me back. No he loves the song. It's a great song, no doubt about it. It's just... you can see why after having done stuff like 'Stargazer' and 'Gates Of Babylon', suddenly you do 'Since You Been Gone.' It's like Wha... are you sure. Obviously Roger's influence was much more commercial.

Sure.
And the band definitely took a left turn if you like.

I think Ritchie brought Roger in for that purpose.
Yeah maybe he did and I can't say it was a bad move because obviously they went on to have some success. I mean 'I Surrender' was another big hit, 'Stone Cold' which I thought was the best of the lot. I thought 'Stone Cold' was absolutely brilliant.

So you obviously listen to all the other stuff.
Yeah, I mean at the time I'd just spent five years with Ritchie, we worked together, we'd done a

lot, we've been through quite a lot together. Five years with Ritchie is a long time, believe me.

Probably the longest you've been with any band.
Yeah, Pretty much. I felt I needed a change. We left on relatively good terms. As you can still see, we're still chucking water over each other so it can't be all bad.

And of course working with Neil Murray, you say it goes back some time?
Yeah Neil was in my original band back in, when was it, blimey '75 I think, '74.

You obviously just feel that you click as a unit?
He knows what I'm going to play before I do.

Which band was that?
That was Hammer. My own band after the sort of singles. We worked together again with Whitesnake. Worked together again with Sabbath, then Brian. That's when we hooked up with Spike. We go back a fair way.

So Whitesnake. What was it like replacing Ian Paice? What did you think about stepping into those shoes?
Well, I mean Ian's a very good drummer. I didn't think about actually kind of replacing him. I'm there for what I do. I've had to replace quite a lot of famous drummers over the years. Carl Palmer's another one. You're hired for what you do. It's nice to be compared with these people that are very good and successful. I don't worry about that. I just do my thing.

Did you enjoy your time with Whitesnake?
Yeah, that's why it's quite amusing that 'Dolly' as we call him, dear David, and Ritchie of course don't get on too well. I had great delight in winding Ritchie up about that. In fact I've just put a photograph of David Coverdale on his dressing room door, which he'll see when he gets down there! It's all good fun.

Of course he'll know who did it.
Would he? Do you think so?

He would if it goes in print. If it's in the next issue and he reads it he'll soon know then.
I think he'll know who did it, yeah.

Maybe in another ten years when he meets up with you again...
Probably will be ten years before we see each other again.

(Heide) But obviously your style was different to Ian Paice's.
Yeah, I mean Paicey's much more of a kind of... what's the word; technical player than I am. A lot faster than me. Just a different style. He's a great player to watch. I've been lucky enough today, the last couple of days to watch some really good drummers here at the show. We've had Ian Mosley who's in Marillion who's a good player, Doanne Perry from Tull, he's brilliant. There's some good drummers on this bill and I'm looking forward to seeing my replacement many years on down the line tonight with Ritchie. I'm sure he'll be very good.

Who were your influences when you started?
When I started. Buddy Rich, Louis Bellson really more than anybody else because he used to use two bass drums. Cozy Cole, that's where the name came from. Then I used to listen to a guy from

the Hollies, Bobby Elliot and Brian Bennett from the Shadows.

It's funny you mentioned Bobby Elliot, because Ian Paice said he was one of his, said he had a very clean sharp sound.
Bobby's a really good guy, that's right a typically English player, he's also one of my good friends now and we kind of got to know each other over the years. He's great. John Bonham obviously.

(Heide) Didn't you work with Louis Bellson on 'Superdrumming'?
Yeah that's right. It was great. We actually played 'Skin Deep' and I think he's seventy something, forget how old he is, sixty nine or seventy and I mean he's fantastically fit and he still plays the same shit he did in when he played with Duke Ellington, Count Basie. Fantastic. Really fabulous drummer.

What about more modern drummers, not players that influenced you then but any new players you've heard recently?
Well obviously people like Simon Phillips. But I haven't really heard anybody lately that's particularly caught my eye. I think music's going through that kind of phase where there's been so many machines, there hasn't been many drummers come out of the last ten years which is a shame. Hopefully that will change soon and we'll get some younger kids that are coming up and playing really good. But I haven't heard anybody new that I've actually gone, cor blimey this is good. Most of the guys are in that sort of thirty five plus bracket. Maybe it takes a little while. I mean Simon was the last one I really heard that came from such a young age.

You've been on some same albums as him.
Simon, yeah I've done lots of sessions and different albums he's been on.

Jon Lord and Bernie Marsden.
Yeah, that's right. He was on Michael Schenker's first album. They were looking for another drummer and he was also talked about with ELP, I mean I kind of did that. Again he's a different style to me. Much more jazzy and possibly not so heavy. Different style.

So looking back on your career now, is there any particular era or particular band that you have fondest memories of: Happiest times?
There were a lot of good times with Rainbow certainly. It was also fraught with quite a lot of upheavals. Obviously the amount of personnel changes. We went through quite a lot of shit with that.

What was your favourite line up?
Well obviously the 'Rainbow Rising' album was good, although I thought the 'Down To Earth' album was good in some... I have mixed feelings about that. Some of the tracks I thought were great. I went on record in saying that I thought the last great guitar solo that Ritchie played in my era was 'Gates Of Babylon', and after that he hadn't really kind of... It was almost kind of like he got bored with it. Perhaps he had. Perhaps he needed to go in a different direction, whatever. Ritchie's the kind of guy that one night he'll play absolutely brilliant and the other night he won't be bothered, and if he's not in the mood he won't play particularly that great and he won't go on and do an encore. That's Ritchie and that's why Ritchie's Ritchie.

Would you say that's sort of similar to Jeff Beck in that respect?
Yeah Jeff's a lot more consistent now, but in the days I worked with him he was very unpredictable. He'd have out of five nights; he'd have one great night, two very sort of all right and two quite...

where he's all out of tune and all over the place. He's not like that now but going back twenty-five years: Unpredictable.

What was it like working with Graham Bonnet after working with Ronnie. Was that a breath of fresh air or was that just as fraught?
Great singer but Ritchie's kind of pretty much documented that. Graham is his own worse enemy. He can sing great, but how he gets through the day is quite beyond me. Very difficult. He's a nice guy. I've worked on a couple of things with him since. I did 'Line Up', 'Forcefield.' I don't know what he's doing now but I wish him luck, he's okay.

(Heide) Did you do some demos with Ian Gillan at one point?
No I've never worked with Ian. The only other thing you were going to ask, I think you mentioned about was this Malmsteen album which I thought was quite intriguing.

The tribute?
No the new album that I've just finished with him. It's quite interesting to watch. He's obviously a Ritchie Blackmore fan. Here he is suddenly, looking at him it's quite amusing. He's got every mannerism that Ritchie's ever done down, but he does it times ten! It's like quite weird really.

You mean personally or guitar wise?
Yeah I mean every thing about him. He's copied every thing Ritchie does. It's quite amazing. In fact I think Ritchie said last night that he'll probably come out with an acoustic album featuring some Renaissance material next year with a girl singer he's found in Yokohama or somewhere! Who knows.

Thanks for your time anyway.
Well it may have shed some light on some of the...

Well we'll put those points you made in.
Well just like to put them straight you know. I mean there's loads of others. I could go on all night but I'm not going to, there's a show we've got to go and see. There's some fireworks I've got to... oops let the cat out of the bag again. Oh shit, well never mind. So if that's it I'll see you all later. I've got to get ready to do some mischief. See you later.

Should be fun later.
Should be. Enjoy it!

Footnote: Regarding the points Cozy made concerning some of the comments in the Neil Jeffries interview. I'm sure that both his and Ritchie's memories were probably somewhat hazy. After all it was twenty odd years ago. The mischief and fireworks that Cozy talked of, never actually happened. The only fireworks to be seen were above the stage to celebrate the end of the festival, but they weren't of Cozy's doing! In fact it had been planned for Cozy to take the stage with Rainbow for an encore of 'Smoke On The Water' but the strict curfew ensured it didn't happen.

Later the same evening, after witnessing Rainbow's last gig, I spent several hours in both Cozy's and Ritchie's company. Cozy seemed to have a never ending supply of amusing stories to tell. The following day Ritchie and Cozy went their separate ways and less than a year later Cozy died in a car accident on the M4 close to his Wiltshire home. When I heard of his untimely death, I was deeply moved. I still find it hard to imagine that someone with so much boundless energy is no longer with us.

****

MARK CLARKE

Bassist Mark Clarke's professional career started when he teamed up with drum legend Jon Hiseman in Colosseum. He joined Uriah Heep, touring with them during a brief stint, that also saw him performing (and co-writing) on just one studio track, 'The Wizard' on their 1972 album 'Demons and Wizards.' He also continued his association with Hiseman in Tempest. When Tempest split he formed Natural Gas for one album before getting the call to join Ritchie Blackmore's Rainbow. Clarke's name is often omitted from the biographical details of Rainbow's career as his time in the band was very short lived. In the eighties and early nineties he replaced the late Felix Pappalardi in Mountain but as Clarke had cropped up in the interview with Cozy Powell it prompted *More Black than Purple* subscriber Helmut Gerlach to get Clarke's side of his brief tenure with Rainbow when he met him during Colosseum's 1997 Germany tour.

As Gerlach explained; "for a short time in 1977 Mark Clarke was the bass player with Rainbow. Even if you have all the Rainbow albums you might not be familiar with his name though. Mark only stayed with Rainbow for some of the 'Long Live Rock 'n' Roll' recording sessions. But Mark's name came up during the Cozy Powell interview. Cozy's comments about him weren't really all that favourable, so I thought it would be a nice idea to give the man a chance to tell us his side of the story. At the time this interview took place, Clarke was back playing in Colosseum, the band who reformed in 1994 after splitting up in 1971. "Together with fellow *More Black than Purple* subscriber Florian Gäke I approached Mark Clarke when he arrived for the soundcheck before the Colosseum show in Braunschweig. Mark suffered from jet lag after flying in from New York to Germany that day but although he was due to soundcheck he didn't hesitate to make himself immediately available for the interview. He turned out to be a very friendly guy and a very forthcoming interview partner, who also happened to be very intrigued with the photos of Candice in MBTP issue 5...

It was quite a short time you were in Rainbow, so from your point of view what went wrong?
Well, first of all I had known Ritchie for many years touring with Colosseum. Colosseum and Deep Purple used to do a lot of shows together. When I was in Uriah Heep we toured with Deep Purple extensively. And I had my own band called Natural Gas and we were living in Los Angeles. We were all rehearsing in this huge sound stage: Rainbow were on one side, Bad Company were there and we all took different times of the day. I wasn't happy with my band, so I went back to New York and I said to my wife that I was going to leave. We were going to fold up the band. That night, Ritchie called me and asked what I was doing. I said: "Well, as it happens I don't know 'cause I've just decided to leave (Natural Gas)." He said - and this is true: "Do you want to join Rainbow?" So I said, "Well, I'll go and see him." So, I went to see his manager and flew out back to Los Angeles. And what it was, Ritchie has this thing about bass players to use picks. He loves that. I use a pick, but I don't like using a pick. I'm

a lot faster without it, you know. That's basically all it was. And we were at a place outside Paris called the Chateau doing the 'Long Live rock 'n' roll' album and it just didn't work out. There were no real hostilities whatsoever. God, I just remember I was there for three months and it just wasn't working out, simple as that. We didn't speak for about four years after that... no, a lot longer after that actually. The next time we met was when Mountain were invited to tour Europe with Deep Purple (in 1985), *which surprised me. So I asked our manager why we were asked to. He said, because Ritchie requested his manager to ask us.*

He's a Mountain fan.

Yeah. So that was cool. We had done about three gigs together - this is a true story - and we were in the dressing room and Leslie West, (Mountain's guitar player) *said: "Don't you think it's about time you went and thanked Ritchie?" And I'd seen Jon Lord and I'd had drinks with Jon and Ian, but I hadn't seen Ritchie. So I said, "Yeah, I suppose I should really." And I opened the dressing room door and Ritchie was standing inside and he said, "I was coming to see you." So I said, "I was coming to see you." Anyway, it was fine. Then I've seen him many times in America. No, Ritchie is a real rock 'n' roll guy. He has very set ideas and that's fine, that's how he is. I have my own set ideas, you know.*

But he has got this reputation of being difficult to work with and not always treating people nicely.

Well, I don't know about that. You see, he paid very, very well. He paid people lots of money, so he could do that. He treated people around him, the musicians fine, you know. Yeah, he's awkward to work with, many gigs - I only did a few gigs - half the time he was just going to leave, he wouldn't do an encore, so he'd just leave. So he's awkward like that. And I think he thinks that's like a cool thing to do. I think so, you know, I don't think it is and most other people don't think it is, but everybody has their own ideas and Ritchie has his own. It's fine by me.

Did you get to play with Rainbow live then?

Yes, I did, in America. I can't remember where. One of them was Los Angeles, an off the cuff gig. We also did a gig in Paris one night. We just showed up at this club, and we actually played in Paris, and there was another one. We played two songs and Ritchie smashed the guitar and then just walked off and it wasn't even his own guitar. And the guy in this band went: "What?" I could see Ritchie's roadie paying the guy out. That's how it was with Ritchie.

Probably Ritchie had a big smile on his face or he was trying to hide it.

Yeah. Sure, he thought it was really funny. She's nice... (Mark takes another look at Candice on the cover of MBTP issue 5).

And she's very young...

Is she? What's her name?

Candice Night. *(The interview was eventually resumed when Mark took his eyes off Candice's photo)* Did you actually get to contribute anything to 'Long Live Rock 'n' Roll'?

Yeah, I actually did two tracks in the studio, 'Kill The King' and the other one, I don't know what it was. No, I did three tracks. I can't remember, 'Kill The King' is the only one I can remember 'cause Ritchie wanted the bass in quarter notes and I asked, "Why doesn't it go in sixteenth notes?" And he said, "can you do that?" and I said, "sure I can do that." But he wanted someone to do it like that with a pick. So, you know all about the picks. Yeah, I contributed something to the album.

On the finished album as well? When you listened to it...

I've never listened to it.

Really?

Never ever. I very rarely listen to stuff that I've done, very rarely. With Colosseum I always have to; Mountain - some of it. I've always listened to everything I've done with Billy Squier because it's very interesting, I thought. He's a very interesting kind of guy, great songwriter. But no, I've never listened to the 'Long Live Rock 'n' Roll' album.

Ritchie is also notorious for his practical jokes he likes to play on other people especially the members in his band.

He never did anything to me. We did something to him.

Right. Can you tell us?

Yeah, we were staying at the Chateau and the guest house is all suites and many, many famous people like Chopin stayed there, and he had the room that Chopin had stayed in. It had a huge armour, so one night we tied string to the door, we covered it with shoe polish and we took it through to the window, we took it outside the window and then, late one night, Cozy Powell and I put a ladder up and we pulled this string and you could hear (making eerie noise) *and all the lights were on and suddenly we could hear Ritchie going: "What the fuck...." And he was convinced of ghosts there, you see. He really was convinced of it. That was about it really. And then he came out and pushed Cozy off the ladder.... What else did we do? No, no, I think that was about it really, but he never did anything to me.*

Tony Carey wasn't in the band anymore at the time...

Yeah, he was actually.

There is this famous story about how he left in the middle of the night.

That was it at the Chateau. Well, I don't blame him really. We got as many candles as we could, hundreds of candles and filled his room with candles. And Tony is very frightened of ghosts. Tony went into his room to find all these hundreds and hundreds of candles and then Ritchie threw a grapefruit from outside through his window in the middle of the night when Tony was asleep, which really frightened him. That was the night he left actually. He got up in the middle of the night and just left. There were all kinds of things: Ritchie put food down on his seat and he'd sit in it and he put all kinds of cheese and stuff in his suitcase, you know. (Suddenly breaks out in laughter) *Very, very funny actually, you know. Tony - I found him to be a bit of a fucking idiot, weird, a bit strange. That's about all I can remember of that.*

So probably Tony being an American didn't have that sort of English humour.

No, he didn't. No, no, he didn't have that humour at all. He tried to be serious, but nobody took him seriously at all.

Of course, we don't only want to talk about Rainbow but about yourself as well. So could you give us a short overview of what you've done before Rainbow and after?

Before Rainbow... God... Colosseum, Tempest, I was actually going to join Manfred Mann at one point, I rehearsed with Manfred and I was asked to join. I did not want to join but I did rehearse with them. Then I went to America with Natural Gas, then Rainbow, then I worked with a keyboard player in America called Richard T, then I did a lot of sessions with Mink de Ville and Willie de Ville. Then I was asked to join a guy called Billy Squier and we had many, many very successful records in America for a long, long time. Then I actually started to produce people. I left Billy and I worked with Ian Hunter from Mott The Hoople and I co-wrote songs with Ian, I co-produced Ian. Then I did the same thing with a group called The Monkees, believe it or not. I actually co-produced a record, I co-wrote two songs with David Jones. Then I went back with Billy. ...Oh God, there's lots of other people: I wrote with Cher, I did something with Raquel Welch. God, I can't remember all that stuff.... Oh, Mountain, of course, Stephen Stills. One of my favourite nights was when I got a call from Mick Jagger the year of the Colosseum reunion and my wife said: "Jagger is on the phone." I said, "Hello, Mick." "Hello, Mark. How are you?" "What can I do for you?" "Well, you know, we're looking for a bass player." "I thought you had one." He said: "We have been everywhere. Are you interested in coming down?" I said, "Yeah, of course." So I went down and I spent a whole night with them. I played with them for four hours, which was, other than Darryl, I was playing bass, we were the only two that did. I mean, it was really fantastic: full equipment, I played all of the songs, it was really great. It was a big circle on the stage and we did 'Honky Tonk Woman' and all that. It was really fun. But I was never really a Stones fan, so I was interested purely because of the money, but then I went straight back with Colosseum and I've been really doing that ever since. I did another Mountain album since the last Colosseum tour. That really brings us up to date, that's the last twenty years.

That's quite an array of bands.
Yeah, I've covered a lot.

What was the most rewarding experience in a band or in a musical situation, also personally speaking?
One of them was actually spending the night playing with the Rolling Stones, definitely one of the highlights, and the other thing I really love is the Colosseum reunion. That was really astonishing. When we played together it was as if we had just played two gigs before. And I'm just about to start working with Billy Squier again in America, but if there's anybody listening to this tape, now I'd love to live in Germany. I would love for a German band to ask me to join them. I would love to live in Germany.

Really?
I love Germany, I really do. Over twenty years I've grown to love the place. The people are great, the place is great. People that work for us in Germany go: "Are you crazy?" Cause I live in New York, you see. They all go: "We want to live in New York." "So you go to New York and I'll come here."

Would you like to tell us something about the song you sing on the new Colosseum album?
Yeah, it was written by Dave Greenslade. It's a peculiar time signature. It's in seven four and Chris Farlowe had a lot of difficulty singing it. It's about the environment, it's a great song actually. It's not too clever either, it's just a really down the line song: "The playground is what we all live in." I just happened to say: "Let me try." And I went in and everyone said: "Yeah, great." And that's really how it came about. 'Cause I was actually going to sing it to Chris to show him how to sing it, but I just really got into singing it. It only took one hour.

The last question would be: what are your plans for the future - continuing with Colosseum?
We'd like to, yes. We're not sure about those plans at the moment. I mean, we will continue to do touring, you know, already next year we will be doing summer tours in Russia and other countries. I don't really know. I want to continue to play but it's getting more and more difficult to play because of economics. Like with Colosseum we can afford to swallow some of the cost, I mean, there are many, many gigs we did before the reunion that we didn't do any money during. Any money would just be poured back in and you can only do that for a certain time, cause you have families to support, you have to have a job, you have to work. Simple as that. So I'm not sure what I'm going to do, but I know I'll be doing some Billy Squier stuff and we will be doing more Colosseum next year after this tour. And again we'll have to see how this record does. The record has only been out a month, so we'll have to see. It's probably the best Colosseum record that we've made, without a doubt. So we'll just have to see.

Coincidentally at the time this interview was conducted, Colosseum also featured former Humble Pie guitarist Clem Clempson, who was auditioned by Deep Purple in 1975 as a potential replacement following Blackmore's departure.

****

RITCHIE BLACKMORE
& CANDICE NIGHT

In early 1997 Blackmore had released the first Blackmore's Night album 'Shadow Of The Moon', with a planned tour to follow, that was to commence in Madrid on 12th September. However Blackmore had been suffering with a recurring finger problem as a result of the break he suffered in 1987 whilst on stage with Deep Purple.

After Blackmore's Doctor stated, quite categorically, that he should not play the guitar for at least three weeks, a memo was sent to all the promoters along with a copy of the Doctor's report. As such the European dates were put back, some falling by the wayside in the process and Blackmore's Night was launched on stage in Tokyo on the 2nd November. Following eight gigs in Japan, four were booked for Spain, but the last one had to be cancelled when Candice Night was taken ill with food poisoning. After Spain, the inaugural tour concluded with five shows in Germany.

After the penultimate gig in a Berlin church (Passionskirche) on 18th December, Ritchie and Candice were interviewed by local journalist, Jörg Schulz, with co-ordination from *More Black than Purple* subscriber Christian Meyer zu Natrup, (who also chipped in with some comments). The interview naturally focused on Blackmore's Night but Blackmore also gave a good insight into his earlier life, as well as touching on other subjects. At one point he was asked about the subject of a Rainbow reunion with Ronnie Dio but Blackmore was quite coy with his answer. However, following his meeting with Cozy Powell earlier in the year at the Esbjerg Festival, there had been some serious discussions involving both Dio and Powell.

This interview was originally published in two parts in *More Black than Purple* issues 8 and 9.

You did your first show at Long Island in August.
(Blackmore) *That's right. It was in a small club and restaurant* (The Normandie Inn). *The club is very old and so it is perfect to play. We played there free and a lot of people came from miles around just to see us. That was a great feeling and we knew then that the tour would also bring a lot of fun for all of us - the band and the fans.*

Tonight you told the audience that the church is one of the nicest places you have played on this tour. Is that the reason for having planned playing this tour completely in castles and comparable places?
(Blackmore) *Yes, exactly. The story behind that was, we only wanted to play in castles and small halls, and the problem was, we had a promoter in America, a typical promoter. So we told him: "Blackmore's Night is specifically for five or six hundred people. We want to play in castles and have a great time with a particular atmosphere - a medieval atmosphere", and the unscrupulous promoter basically booked rock clubs. He booked us into rock clubs over here. "So we can make more money, 'cause more people come to the rock clubs," and we kept saying to him: "Are you advertising this as Blackmore's Night in Germany?" "Oh yes." "Are you sure they know that we will only be playing acoustically?" "Oh yes, of course." And then we found out a couple of months ago that there were clubs booked up, rock 'n' roll clubs and we said: "You're gone." So we got rid of them. Would you like to take it from there Candy?*
(Night) *No, you're doing a great job.*
(Blackmore) *But it was too late to change anything and we had to come here. The promoter here in Germany said: "You should be playing in castles and churches." This exactly was our intention, but we could not change anything for this tour, and last night in Cologne he put us into a rock club and that was tricky. It went okay, but I was nervous because we were playing very quietly and the people; "Rainbow rock 'n' roll, Rainbow rock 'n' roll."*

And the acoustics in this church tonight were good for such a show.
(Blackmore) *Exactly, and you have to play very quietly when you play to those acoustics.*

And the audience was brilliant too. It was very quiet during the quiet passages.
(Blackmore) *Exactly. That's what we look for when we are on tour.*
(Night) *We would have felt strange playing pure rock 'n' roll in such a perfect acoustic environment.*
(Blackmore) *That's why we didn't play the rock 'n' roll thing too long tonight. It was too loud. So I wanted to go back to the acoustic stuff. They didn't know what else we were going to do. So we played songs we've never done on stage. But I like to have a surprise. I like to surprise the band too. Not only the audience, I like to surprise the other musicians. It keeps the edge. I hate doing the same songs every night. That's what happened tonight. But again what we really want to do is play in castles and churches. Now we know the promoter in Germany knows about that. We asked him: "Were you told that we wanted to play in castles and churches?" And he said, "no." The guy in America did not tell him about that.*

Will you come back in spring '98?

(Blackmore) *Yeah, we would like to. Maybe in summer. Then we will change the set list a bit. When we started we were in a castle. Candy and I were just playing our songs and it was our road manager who said to us: "Do you play 'Sixteenth Century Greensleeves?' Or something like that. And we said: "No, we're doing our own stuff" but* (he speaks to Candice) *I was very surprised that you could sing 'Sixteenth Century Greensleeves' and 'Temple Of The King', 'Street Of Dreams', 'Perfect Strangers', I was very surprised, and* (in German) *das war ein überraschung für mich* (that was a surprise to me).

Before I saw Blackmore's Night on stage I wondered how it would sound when Candice Night sings 'Temple Of The King' and 'Man On The Silver Mountain', but it works very well.

(Blackmore) *It's my opinion too.*

(Night) *Thank you. Ritchie always writes very melodically. He doesn't write this typical kind of heavy metal. There is a lot of melody, and then it also depends on the band that is playing these songs, or the chemistry of the people. But then the songs always work because they are brilliant tunes.*

We have heard that Ian Anderson got a pistol from you as a payment...

(Blackmore) *... for helping us out. That's right. I didn't want to give him money or anything. We tried to find out what he would have liked. Then we were told he collects pistols and chilli peppers. So we said, okay let's send him chilli peppers or a pistol. Finally we decided to send him a pistol. A typical English customs pistol.*

Had it been planned to have Ian Anderson on the whole album?

(Blackmore) *No.*

But given a second Blackmore's Night album, will he be playing again?

(Blackmore) *We would like to use him again if he wanted to do that. I was very surprised that he wanted to play on our first album. I said to him; "Ian, you know I've been a fan of yours for twenty years. I'm going to send you a song and if you want to play on it, great, but if you don't play on it I won't be upset." I didn't want to put him in a position to say I have to play on this otherwise Ritchie is gonna be upset... but he liked the song and he did it.*

Candice, did Ian Anderson give you lessons in flute playing?

(Night) *No.*

Where did you learn?

(Night) *In California we went in a shop and Ritchie picked a penny whistle. It was a fifteen dollar one. A very, very cheap one and he brought it home, and he wanted to learn it. But he got so frustrated after the first day, that he was throwing the thing away. I also didn't want to get bothered with this anymore. But I picked it up and the first song 'Renaissance Faire' came out, and he got very annoyed that I could do it and he couldn't do it. He got very angry with me.*

(Blackmore) *I couldn't make noises with it.*

Ritchie, you described several minutes ago that you have been in the business for thirty-five years and nevertheless promoters still try to direct you to your past work.

(Blackmore) *Yeah.*

You will have to fight against this.

(Blackmore) *That's right.*

Isn't it a problem for you, having all these experiences and then another promoter comes along and tries to tell you what you will have to do. What kind of feeling is it?

(Blackmore) *Promoters and managers have very big egos. And so do record companies, and so do radio stations. The artist is the lowest. Then it's the promoter, then it's the agency, then it's the record company. That's the way music is. So the artist is down there. These things happen all the time.*

But you can deal with it.

(Blackmore) *I get angry- always. It's the same thing when trying to get radio stations in England to play our music. No one plays it.*

Why not, it's an excellent album. Here in Europe we have the middle aged, so why don't they play it?

(Night) *'Cause it doesn't sound like the Spice Girls.*

(Blackmore) *And I'm probably too old. If you are over twenty-nine you are old, and then you will have big problems to get played.*

Okay you are fifty-two, but you are looking quite good and even a bit younger.

(Blackmore) *But nevertheless the BBC doesn't want to have it.*

(Night) *But I am only twenty-six.*

(Blackmore) *It's the same problem in the USA. I saw a TV interview with Little Richard in America. At one point the journalist said: "you don't get played on the radio, do you?" He said: "No, no, they won't play my music. Know why not? I am too old." They play Paul McCartney and they play Elton John, and if anybody else is coming and asking, the answer is: "We just want young people." We tried to do television shows in America. We had an awful time getting the shows. Yes she's young but I'm the old man.*

(Night) *But there's no age on music.*
(Blackmore) *Yes, but I am sure if we didn't have you and Jessie, we wouldn't have done these shows.*
Jessie is obviously a very good guitar player. But I have in mind a passage of an interview I read where you said that you would not play with another guitar player on stage. But now you do. I only read this and so I don't know if you really told it to the guy.

She was not the first. Joe Lynn Turner played guitar (zu Natrup).

(Laughing) Okay, forget it.
(Blackmore) *I don't remember saying that. If I did say it, I did not say I would not play with another guitar player. It might have been I wouldn't play with another rock 'n' roll guitar player. But acoustic - it's a whole different thing. But in the rock 'n' roll setting I wouldn't play with another guitarist... I don't think.*

By the way a month ago I met Joe Lynn Turner in Hamburg when he was doing his acoustic tour. He sends you his regards.
(Blackmore) *Good, good. I didn't know he was doing acoustic. I should have known.*

He played guitar too.
(Blackmore) *He can play very well.*

You were born shortly after the Second World War, which may have been a difficult time for children. Can you tell me if you got any support from your parents when you started to play guitar, and when you decided to become a musician? I believe you were professionally on stage at the tender age of sixteen.
(Blackmore) *That's right.*

What about the people around you? Were they proud of you or did you have problems with them?
(Blackmore) *No, they were very proud. My parents bought me the guitar when I was eleven, and they encouraged me. My father just wanted me to do it properly, not picking things and doing things and then getting tired of them. His whole attitude was: "I want you to learn this instrument properly, and so I'm sending you to lessons. You're not just gonna fiddle and get tired of it and throw it away." That was his big deal and so he sent me to lessons.*

You had classical lessons?
(Blackmore) *Yes, I had classical lessons for a while. That put me on the right footing to play with all my fingers and to develop my certain style of playing. That helped. So my parents were very helpful. Then I wanted to become professional when I was sixteen and a half. My dad said - he was reluctant - but he said: "Okay" and that was it.*

It is wonderful for a musician who has no duties beside music. Were you able to make a living from your music from the age of 16?
(Blackmore) *Yes, I was. I was making a lot of money when I was 16 to the age of 18. A lot of money! From the age of about 19 to 22 - that was my rough period. I remember being in Berlin and starving. We had nowhere to stay and nothing to eat. We came here in 1964 to play in a club. It was a small one, a little tiny thing. And the manager didn't like the band. He said: "You don't play the right music." So the drummer went home and the three of us were starving. In Berlin with no drummer and nothing to eat. So I had bad memories of Berlin!*

Was it Screaming Lord Sutch at this time or the Three Musketeers?
(Blackmore) *In between.*

Okay, so you had a good start, then you had your starving period. But that was only for a very short time?
(Blackmore) *Yeah.*

And then you earned enough money to survive with Deep Purple?
(Blackmore) *Oh, yes.*

What has changed since you have reached that goal. Are there only advantages or also disadvantages? For example, being on tour permanently with Deep Purple, and then with Rainbow. I think Blackmore's Night seems to be a little more for your own private interest and for fun.
(Blackmore) *That's right, very true. The Deep Purple thing - we were very lucky that it became very famous - and with Rainbow it was very lucky too. But that constant touring makes you... not depressed, but it brings you down constantly, being on the road and being in hotels. I've done that for a very long time, but I really got tired of this business. But with this group we do short tours, very short tours, before we get crazy with each other. I don't want the same thing to happen, that's why with this band we do no more do than three to four weeks. That'll be the most and then we'll stop for one month. With Deep Purple we worked to death. The management came and said: "Play there, and play there..." all the time. Consequently a lot of us became sick because of working too much.*

So you would call your strategy of short tours a good way to overcome the problems on tour?
(Blackmore) *You are absolutely right.*

And is it better being on tour with your girlfriend now, being always together? Because I think that the main reason for the splits of relationships with partners is being on tour so often and not being together. (Looks at Candice) Okay, you can give the answer, Candice.
(Night) (laughing) *I've been with Ritchie for eight years already. When I first met him he was on tour with Joe Lynn Turner and Deep Purple for the 'Slaves and Masters' tour, and that was the only tour in our relationship that he was often away from me. But he would call me every day, and I got postcards from Holland and from the whole of Europe. With the 'Battle Rages On' tour I went on tour with him, and we had a good time. It was the only thing that saved him, because he was having so many problems with members of the band and having so many problems with the management. And he just needed somebody to come back to and be able to talk to, saying: "I'm going crazy" or "Wasn't he singing really bad tonight?" or "What's going on?" And I think that helped his sanity a little bit. Ritchie and I have a very strange, but actually very good relationship where we are constantly together, whether it's on tour or at home.*

And you are working together.
(Night) *Which is great, because when he gets a creative spurt, when he comes up with an incredible riff or song, I'm right in the next room and he can call me in and say, "sing something over this" or "write something for this." And I'm right there, and he does not to have to call me up and wait for me to arrive, and pay me some money and do the whole thing. And what else is great is that he'll go out and play soccer down the road for an hour, and he'll come back and say, "oh, I missed you," and he's only been away for an hour. So we're constantly together.*
(Blackmore) *We are used to each other's company.*
(Night) *We get along very well. It is strange 'cause although many parts of us are very different - age, blonde hair / black hair, happiness / sadness, whatever - people are constantly comparing us in a way that we are almost identical. We are really very well connected.*

Would you see each other a bit like the kind of the relationship experienced by John Lennon and Yoko Ono?

(Blackmore) *No. I have no talent compared to John Lennon, and Candy has a hundred times more talent than Yoko Ono!* (Candice laughs).

Is Ritchie a kind of dictator sometimes?

(Night) *Ritchie likes things to be right. He will know what you can do and he doesn't expect any less from you. If you're going to work with him you will have to give a hundred per cent of yourself. And he knows what you can do. So he doesn't let you relax in a corner and rest, slacking. If you're gonna come in and work with him, you'd better do the best you can do. And a lot of people see this as being very dictatorial, but I don't think it's a bad thing.*

(Blackmore) *I think some people call a person a dictator if they know that they have to follow his direction. I know what I want, and where I wanna go. So if that is a dictator then I am a dictator. A lot of people don't know what they want and they don't know where they are going.*

You are always trying to be perfect on stage. I think this is a very good aim.

(zu Natrup) I think Ritchie does not want to be perfect. Players like Satriani or Steve Morse are perfect, whereas Ritchie plays from the heart.

(Night) (clapping) *I like that.*

(zu Natrup) The new Deep Purple line up is very boring because every show is the same.

(Blackmore) *Yes, I know. They were always boring when I was with them because they always wanted to do the same show. I'm not joking!*

When I say "perfect", I mean that nobody in the band should be drunk on stage or full of drugs, or concentrating on other things. People should be on stage and think only of what they are doing at that time on stage.

(Blackmore) *Yeah, that's right. They have a responsibility. I feel that I have a responsibility to the fans. People have paid money, and every time I get a little bit tired or slack I tell myself: "These people have come here on a freezing cold tonight. You better play something properly." Sometimes I get nervous: I'll be nervous playing, and by being nervous I won't play as well as I would when relaxed. That is a dilemma sometimes. But there is a responsibility not only to the fans but to whoever is in the audience and has paid money to see something good. You just can't go and say: "Hey, who cares?" This was the problem with somebody in the last band who thought a tour would be a never-ending party, and people in the audience were just fools. Yeah, it's got to be right. That's why we are on stage.*

(Night) *I think he's (Ritchie) out there doing his part and doing it as well as he possibly can. And he just expects the same from anybody else.*

(Blackmore) *Sometimes I get annoyed on stage - many people ask me why I'm so often annoyed on stage - it is not because I'm an egotist. I get annoyed if my sound is bad, if I see someone playing something wrong, or if sometimes the audience is not very responsive. Sometimes you get people who really just seem to be there but not to enjoy themselves; it is kind of strange when sometimes people sit in the audience like a stone. I often wonder why those people come to shows. I've seen them in other people's shows too. Ian Anderson for instance, when he was in Hamburg. I went to see him play, and saw him jump off the stage and hit somebody then jump back on stage, and I thought: "What the hell did he just do?" I asked him later: "Why did you do that?" He said: "The guy was asleep. And I'm not gonna play to some guy who is asleep. If he comes to see me he's gonna stay awake." And so he smacked him! It was so funny. It is strange sometimes with some people in the audience who don't enjoy it. Luckily it doesn't happen very often.*

Would you say that your knowledge about the world is based only on your own experiences of life, or do you get advice from other people?

(Blackmore) *Mainly experiences. And my father told me a lot. School taught me next to nothing.*

So in the past you did not have any interest to take more lessons or to study?
(Blackmore) *No. I left school when I was fifteen and could not wait to leave! I just did not like school. I didn't like my teachers; many of them were very bizarre. I don't think they were normal. The subjects were really boring. I think it was also this way because times were very conservative when I went to school. And there I was, a bad little doggy!*
And then you went on stage and played. You began as a player and then you became a rock star. And then the sex and drugs and rock 'n' roll stereotype came straight to you.
(Blackmore) *Right.*

What kind of feeling was it for you suddenly being at the top. You were known as one of the best guitar players all over the world, and the fans loved you. Was it a bit strange or a bit of a crazy feeling, or what?
(Blackmore) *It's confusing, that side of it, because all the guitar players that I thought were very good were not known, and many people had never heard of. I was, and still am lucky to play my guitar well. But I find that a lot of people today choose players I don't feel are very good. I know really good players who people just ignore. So I've never quite understood that. Maybe I have two sides to me. One side is being the person at home where I don't want to do any more rock 'n' roll. And then I have a side where I go on stage and say, "Yeah, come on, let's play rock 'n' roll!" But that's me, and Candy probably sees both sides.*
(Night) (smiling) *Yes.*
(Blackmore) *But it's funny, when you're talking about the so-called drugs period, everyone says: "Oh, the Sixties." I still don't recall the Sixties as being any different to any other time. The drugs I never took. Until this day I've never taken cocaine. I want to be the only musician in the world who has not taken cocaine. That's my ambition. Okay, I drink. But LSD, cocaine, all that nonsense, I don't take, and I've never touched it - I was too nervous. I never needed LSD, it's not needed in the way that I think. I would have gone mad. I was lucky for that. I think I have had very stable parents. They did not even drink, and mainly my thoughts against drugs came from my parents.*

And you also don't smoke?
(Blackmore) *No.*
(Night) *He's not that party kind of a person. When he goes on tour he stays in his hotel room and I can't get him out of it. This is the first time out in the bar on this whole tour!*

But you're still playing football?
(Blackmore) *Yes, of course. But it's getting harder and harder.* (laughing)
(Night) *Only because we've been travelling so much.*
(Blackmore) *Because we travel so much I have to exercise my back, because I have a bad back. To me exercising can be very boring. I like to walk. To actually run I have to be running after a ball. If there's no ball I am not gonna run!*

(zu Natrup): I know that you are a fan of Bayern Munich.
(Blackmore) *Yes. The reason I like Bayern Munich is because of Franz Beckenbauer. He is one of my heroes. I have certain heroes of my life: Ian Anderson is one, Franz Beckenbauer another, John Cleese is another, Bob Dylan, Buddy Holly. But I don't have any heroes from today. I have heroes of comedians, even politicians.*

What about Aldous Huxley?
(Blackmore) *A little bit too deep for me. I haven't really followed his stuff. I don't know much about him.*

You mentioned other guitar players. What do you think about Randy Rhoads? He had his own style I believe.

(Blackmore) *The first thing I think about when I am asked, and I am talking about most guitar players, is how I find them as people. He was an amazing guy, a really nice guy. And so is Eric Clapton, a very nice guy. Okay, Randy: I've listened to a lot of his stuff and I liked it a lot. He was obviously a good player and he was very humble, and that to me is also a sign of a good player.*

Two of your solos tonight seemed to be inspired by George Harrison.

(Blackmore) *I doubt it!* (Candice laughs)

I think you should listen to his solo in a song by Belinda Carlisle.

(Blackmore) *Never heard it.*

Do you dislike George Harrison?

(Blackmore) *No. He's a nice guy. I don't really listen to him. When he was with the Beatles I took notice of him, because the Beatles were one of my favourite bands. But then I never took much notice of what he really did. Half the time on those records it wasn't him but session players.*

By the way, the basement tapes of Ozzy Osbourne were published a while ago. Christian told me that you played music in the Seventies together with Phil Lynott and Ian Paice?

(Blackmore) *Yeah. We made a couple of tapes.*

And you still have these tapes?

(Blackmore) *No, I don't have the tapes. The ex-management has them. They were not finished and there were only three songs, half-finished. But it hasn't got anything to do with Blackmore's Night* (laughing).

(zu Natrup) And these songs, what did they sound like? Was it more like Deep Purple or more Thin Lizzy or more blues?

(Blackmore) *No, more Hendrix stuff, because he* (Phil Lynott) *sang that way. We were going to form a band with the three of us. It was when I wanted to leave Deep Purple, and then Ian Paice asked why and I said: "I can't work with Ian Gillan." Then he said: "I've got a new singer". But it's not just Ian Gillan, there's somebody else." But I didn't want to even get in to that. I'd rather leave the band. And Ian Paice asked: "Who's the other person?", and he said: "Let's get Roger", and I said no. I said no, but on the other hand I couldn't tell anybody to leave the band. But in the end they went my way. That's what happened when Roger and Ian went. And Ian Paice, Phil and me had been working together cause I wanted to do a bit more bluesy music. But then we had new guys in the band and songs like "Mistreated." But I couldn't do something like "Mistreated" with Ian Gillan. He wouldn't have done it.*

'Mistreated' is a very good song, played also by Whitesnake and by Dio. But this is a very guitar-orientated song, and Dio's guitar player did not bring the right feeling into the song, although Dio sang like a god.

(Blackmore) *You have to open your soul for this. It's only three notes. But with them you can express yourself. And if you have nothing to say, you'll fall into a hole, 'cause there's no melody, nothing you can hang your head on. You have to improvise. It's true.*

There are rumours that Rainbow will also reform with Dio. Is it right?

(Blackmore) *No. This* (Blackmore's Night) *is far too important - what I'm doing now. I've taken like thirty years to do this. So I'm very happy doing this. I am very happy playing to people very quietly, even if it's fifty or one hundred people. I've done enough of this "shaking my fist."*

And so will you keep going on with Blackmore's Night and not have any other projects besides?

(Blackmore) *With the Ronnie Dio thing I might do a couple of weeks playing maybe, but way in the future. I haven't got the time right now.*

And if the management of Purple came to you and asked: "Would you play for the 30th anniversary tour?" Would you do it?
(Blackmore) *No! Especially if the management asked. If the band came to me as friends... maybe. If the management came, I would say, "fuck off!" I despise the management of Deep Purple.*

You very often played as headliners on stage, but you also played as support in the past. Are there only advantages being the headliner on stage, 'cause you have to say: "Okay, you will have to do this and you will have to do that," or did it have also disadvantages, being always the person people are concentrated on?
(Blackmore) *Yeah, that's true. There is more pressure on, but then you have more fans that are on your side. If you are supporting somebody, you are trying to win over their fans. That's the hard thing. I haven't opened for many people. I opened for Jethro Tull. And that was kind of difficult. Because you have to see all the people in the audience wanted to see Ian* (Anderson). *That was way back.*

(zu Natrup) Is it true that Keith Richards played bass on the Lancasters?
(Blackmore) *No, I never really met him.*

(zu Natrup) Do you remember where you played bass on the 'Long Live Rock 'n' Roll' album?
(Blackmore) *No, I really don't remember. But if the bass is very similar to the guitar, that will be me. I like to play the bass. I think it's a great instrument. Although it has only four strings, it's just as complicated as any other instrument. Our bass player in Blackmore's Night* (Mick Cervino) *is very clever, he plays very well, also very complicated things. It's amazing to see him play.*

(zu Natrup): What happened to the big rainbow you had with you for the 'On Stage' tour?
(Blackmore) *It still does exist! A short time ago it was used for a dolphin's show.*

Now you have almost reached everything a person in the business can reach. But nevertheless I'm sure that you still have some thoughts about the future, or a philosophy of life. Could you tell me a bit about this?
(Blackmore) *My philosophy of life basically is that I think we should just go out of it, get out of life.*
(Night) *That's not true.*
(Blackmore) *Okay. But we are gonna go through a bad time in the next few years. I think Nostradamus was correct. It's not looking too good with the Middle-East countries. I just see nothing but "doom." It's just a matter of time before someone blows up New York with atom bombs in a suitcase. Think of all these religious fanatics. We have to be really careful. And what we're trying to do with Blackmore's Night, is... we are trying to get away from computers, get away from stress, pressure, marketing, people like the Spice Girls. We're trying to just play music, even just to a few people. It's great, playing to a full place. And I am surprised that this is going down so well. It's amazing that people are so quiet. And they are listening. They are actually listening to what we are doing. 'Cause I thought... people used to say to me in the old days, "why don't you do an acoustic thing, why don't you play a quiet part?" Every time I used to play a quiet part if I was in Rainbow or Purple, people kept shouting and yelling. I'd be playing quietly and people shouted, "come on, get on with it!" This was the point, this kind of "negative" shouting. And I thought when we took Blackmore's Night on the road that we don't need people who are shouting out: "Get on with it... Dio..." But this way we are very lucky.*
(Night) *You know, it's great: making this album, whether it's writing it, recording it or playing it every night. It's like an escape for us. This is our own little fantasy world that we want to live in*

all the time. And we want to share it with people. And it's so great to see that people are really connecting with us; that they are listening. We are getting so many fan-letters where people are writing to us and telling us, "your album is like therapy" or "your album makes me cry" or "it really just helps me to get away from all the stress and pressures." And it is great to hear that people really understand what we are trying to do with that - it's amazing.

And what kind of dreams do you still have?

(Night) *What kind of dreams? I think I'm basically living out my dream right now doing this. Because doing this is more than I ever imagined. When I was younger, music was so important to me. But I never had confidence thinking that I could do it, that I could perform it. I wanted to listen to it all the time. But I didn't think that I would be able to create it or to help to create it or to perform it. But finally I met Ritchie, and hearing him play around the house and having him say to me, "hey, why don't you try singing this?" or "why don't you try singing that?", and bringing me into this whole process of creating it, I was saying, "maybe I can do it." And he really gave me the confidence by saying, "yes, you can do this." It's a wonderful feeling. So this really is the dream that I've had. I'm realising it now, looking back over all those years. This is the dream I've had and so it has happened.*

(Blackmore) *She picks up very quickly when we write a song. If I'm at home and just fiddling and I get an idea, and I think how it should sound with a vocal, she's just there and I ask: "Can you just sing these notes?" - that works! Immediately we have a song. Sometimes with the old bands I wouldn't see the singers, so I had to tape an idea and to send it somewhere else.*

(Night) *And you lose that spark and that energy.*

(Blackmore) *And it's very interesting because if I worked with Joe Lynn Turner he would always listen what notes I would sing and I said, "okay, listen to it" and he did change it slightly into his style. If I'd do it with Dio, he would say, "what do you hear in this riff?" And so he got an idea. So he would take the direction. But that was different than what I'd wanted them to sing, but I didn't bother. There was no point. They always sang what they wanted to sing. It is interesting. When I was in Rainbow, and obviously in Blackmore's Night, the melody usually comes from me. But the melodies in Deep Purple usually didn't come from me. I would come up with the riff and give it to Roger and Ian (Gillan), and much to Ian Paice's and Jon Lord's consternation, because the writing was done by Ian, Roger and myself. Ian Paice and Jon Lord always wanted to be in on the writing, but they couldn't write. It is interesting how in something like 'Smoke On The Water' or 'Black Night' my part would be (he sings). Then I would play a bit of a riff and just give it to Ian. I would never suggest to him what to sing. It was his job. And I've done my job. It's yours, I'm off. It was a completely different way of working.*

But it's maybe much easier working together with a person you love?

(Blackmore) *Of course.*

And when the both of you love each other, it is the best condition for writing a song.

(Blackmore) *That's right, very true. We write very many things very quickly. I wouldn't give a really big heavy riff to Candice.*

(Night) *I wouldn't be able to sing over it.*

(zu Natrup) The last song tonight, 'I Think It's Going To Rain Today' sounded very spontaneous, almost like a rehearsal.

(Blackmore) *We played that song together before, but the band hasn't.*

(Night) *And never in front of an audience.*

(Blackmore) *And the band tonight didn't quite know what else we were gonna do, because sometimes we go back and do 'Black Night' or 'Smoke On The Water' or 'Street Of Dreams.' Tonight I just did not feel that rock 'n' roll was the right thing for a church. I played the two songs ('Still I'm Sad' and 'Writing On The Wall') and I wasn't enjoying myself on the rock 'n' roll side.*

It didn't work. That's why I decided to play acoustically. I picked up the wrong guitar, and the rest of the band was thinking: "What is he doing? We should be playing rock 'n' roll." But I like to do that, be spontaneous. Every night doing the same show, it's boring.

(zu Natrup) And in my opinion the Blackmore's Night album reaches more people than 'Stranger In Us All' and it has sold more copies.
(Night) *Yes, 40,000 more copies.*

Let's talk about the album. You said that it is heading for a completely new market, which is so unusual for somebody who's been in the business so long and made his living in hard rock. Also

at the age of fifty-two to start reaching out to other people and succeeding in "their" market - it must be an amazing feeling.

(Blackmore) *I sometimes like to do things backwards. The acoustic thing - it's not really acoustic, it's renaissance music. I've always loved renaissance music, but I don't like acoustic music with that certain kind of playing, with these guys coming, strumming away on their guitars. That does nothing for me.*

(Night) *And actually we had a lot of people in the press area and also in the record company when we told them that this would be Ritchie Blackmore's new album. They said, "Ritchie Blackmore's stuff is too heavy for me." And they didn't want to listen to the album. But when they had actually played it, we suddenly noticed that they loved it. But his name sometimes tends to turn off certain people - maybe women or maybe old people - it turns them off, whatever the music could possibly be. But once they hear the songs, they love them.*

(Blackmore) *That's right.*

Are there any special funny stories from the tour or recording 'Shadow Of The Moon'?

(Night) *The possum story would be a good one.*

(Blackmore) *Okay, the possum story. In America they release the LP in January, so I gave them a new track, an instrumental called 'Possum's Last Dance.' We were recording, and the window was a bit open. And when recording I used to play in the dark. This little animal came up in the dark and looked through the window. It was so funny. It was watching us at work and then saying, "okay, I've heard enough," then going off. When the others came in, the animal had gone. So they thought it was like a joke. But it's a very rare animal and when you see it with its long nose - a very strange animal - you want to tell people that you saw it. Anyway, this animal became like a little mascot, and I had this instrumental that was kind of fast, and when Candy heard it she said, "it's like the possum's dance," because it reminded her of the little animal running around. That's why it is called 'Possum's Dance.' Then about a week later I was going to a restaurant, and I was driving along and a possum came running out in front of the car and I ran over it, and I thought, "hh no", because animals are my favourite things. I had killed a possum! That's why the song is called 'Possum's Last Dance.' But the rumour is that I did not kill him, because I could not face going back to the scene. I stopped the car , Mick (Cervino) was with me... a possum, my favourite of all animals! We went back a couple of hours later and I looked. But there was nothing there. And so we were hoping that he just went out of danger and I didn't kill him.*

(Night) *It's actually an instrumental that has been released only on the American version of the album. So it's gonna be a bonus track.*

And will you also go on tour in the USA?

(Blackmore) *If there were the right places, yes. But we'd like to concentrate more on Europe. To us we don't want to work too much. I'm not gonna work like Deep Purple. That's crazy.*

(zu Natrup) Are there any plans to release a live album? `Cause I think every show will be taped as a bootleg.

(Blackmore) *Of course, it's hopeless.*

(Night) *We did make a video last night* (Cologne), *we had some cameras.*

(Blackmore) *We wish we'd done it tonight in that church, it was perfect.*

The sound was better.
(Blackmore) *I think so, yeah. Last night was a weird sound.*
(Night) *That typical rock 'n' roll sound.*

I have a very short last question. Could you imagine another job, a second best job after being a musician?
(Blackmore) *Yes, I would be a psychic. So I could always tell people what to do. I can! And they* (pointing at the interviewers) *laugh.*
(Night) *And what about a doctor?*
(Blackmore) *Oh yeah I would like to be a doctor too. I love medicine. When something is wrong with a person, I love to find out what it is.*
(Night) *All the books we have in our library at home are about the paranormal and all this medical stuff, nearly all medical books ever written. If you came in and told him that you had a headache, Ritchie would ask: "Where is the headache, what kind, please describe what it feels like?" And then he would look it up in the book and tell you exactly what is wrong. It's great!*
(Blackmore) *Because health is so important. Some people just go, "hey, I'm sick and I go to the doctor's and get pills." I want to know, "what's wrong with me, what the pills are for, do they have side effects?"*

But music keeps you younger than other people of your age. Other people are just sitting down watching TV after having done their daily jobs. But you do other things.
(Night) (totally serious) *That's me keeping him younger.*
(Blackmore) *That's true. And all my friends are very young. I have one friend who's 54 and that's it. All my other friends are 25 to 30 years old. A lot of older people annoy me, especially English people. People who are always telling you that you are too old for this and too old for that. When I say, "come on, let's have a game of soccer." "No, I'm too old." "Do you want to play some music?" "I used to play the guitar, but I am too old for that now." But if you say, "let's go for a drink in the pub," they say, "okay." They are not too old for that. This is the English thing. The English are very creative people. But all that they want to do is whinge and whine. And I do it very well. Sometimes Candice goes, "I can't hear you complaining any more." Because I love to complain. National pastime - the English.*

(zu Natrup) I hope that you will be playing for the next twenty years.
(Blackmore) *Playing or complaining? Oh, it's healthy to complain. Rather than some people just holding it all in maybe.*

Okay, he may be complaining but he made you do this wonderful project.
(Night) *Oh, yes. And it's wonderful for me, indeed.*

I think that your voice is a bit similar to Sally Oldfield's.
(Night) *I like to hear that. I also get compared to Karen Carpenter. I hear a lot of comparisons.*

You should not compare yourself to Karen Carpenter because she has finished her life tragically.
(Night) *That's true. But her voice is so wonderful.*
(Blackmore) *Maggie Reilly is our favourite singer. We've played a lot of stuff by Mike Oldfield. He is also one of my favourites.*
(Night) *We had the idea for 'Shadow Of The Moon' from 'Moonlight Shadow.'*

(zu Natrup) That was what I thought when I first heard 'Shadow Of The Moon'. Mike Oldfield and Maggie Reilly came to my mind.
(Night) *That inspired us.*

****

RITCHIE BLACKMORE

When *More Black than Purple* was launched we were delighted that Blackmore freely acknowledged it, and through his management he happily answered some questions we had put forward (published in issue 2). Both Mark (Welch) and myself were also fortunate to have experienced Ritchie's company on several occasions, but pinning him down for a full scale interview always seemed elusive.

Then out of the blue, in early '98 one of our subscribers called to explain he had set up an interview with the man! Alan Whitman's name was familiar through his occasional letters to the magazine, but I knew nothing more about him. I was fascinated as to how he had managed to achieve what appeared to be a very difficult challenge. At the time, Alan's partner, Eileen worked for *Record Collector* magazine and they were very keen to get an interview with Blackmore. Knowing that Alan was a huge fan, and clearly had more knowledge of the subject matter than any of the *Record Collector* staff, he was put forward as the man to conduct it. Alan met Blackmore's manager Carole Stevens while she was in London for a business conference, and explained his intentions to talk about Blackmore's entire career, promising that the article would be the centre piece of the magazine, spreading over many pages. Because *Record Collector's* readership was at the time, one of the largest of the UK music magazines, at a time when the press was largely ignoring Blackmore, Stevens clearly saw it as potentially great exposure for Blackmore's Night. Gone were the days of magazines fighting over the rights to get an interview- the tables had turned and it was Stevens job to get the media interested in writing about Blackmore.

During her time in London I also met Stevens at her Hotel, and I could clearly see that she also wanted to get the lowdown on this guy who was going to be interviewing Ritchie. At that stage I had only chatted to Alan on the phone so I wasn't in a position to give a character analysis, but I could clearly tell he was a man of intelligence and was passionate about Blackmore's music. During our meeting, Stevens also invited me to join Alan on his journey to New York for the interview. Looking back at it now, he could clearly have conducted the interview over the telephone and saved himself a small fortune, but as Alan had never met Blackmore, the opportunity was too good to miss. By the time everything was in place, our entourage had increased to four. Alan had managed to get Stevens to agree that a friend of his, Neil Davies, another lifelong Blackmore fan and magazine subscriber, could also come along for the weekend trip to America. Finally, if one half of the *More Black than Purple* editorial team was going it seemed only fair the other half did as well, and again Stevens agreed to this.

Arriving at Heathrow very early on the Friday morning, was the first time that Mark and myself met Alan in person- the man who would interview Ritchie Blackmore the following day. We hit it off immediately. Given Blackmore's reputation with journalists, Alan was somewhat apprehensive and as both Mark and I knew the man, the moral support was going to help Alan no end. Furthermore, *Record Collector* wasn't planning on publishing the whole interview word for word, and it was agreed *More Black than Purple* could publish the full unexpurgated version after the article appeared in *Record Collector*. This indeed was a great coup for us, and the chance of getting some new stories was a fantastic opportunity. Alan had clearly put a lot of thought into the questions he was going to ask Blackmore, and had pages of them! The question was, would a man renowned for getting bored very quickly sit there long enough for Alan to get through them all, or would the whole thing come to an abrupt end within a few minutes?

Come Saturday, 2nd May, it had been arranged we would all convene at the Normandie Inn in Long Island; Blackmore's favourite restaurant, a few miles from his home. Stevens had suggested we dressed in mediaeval clothes, as she explained that Ritchie would appreciate that. We were taken to Medieval Mayhem, a shop in the vicinity of Lake Ronkonkoma, Long Island, where we were based for the weekend to hire some costumes. Once changed into our new outfits back at our Holiday Inn accommodation, we sat in the bar for a couple of drinks before wandering off round the corner to the Normandie Inn. We certainly felt like a bunch of 'Wallies' but had a laugh at the same time. Some of the other residents looked bemused and one asked us if we were part of a band! They were even more perplexed when we explained we were just off to a restaurant! Clearly mediaeval clothing is not customary in that part of New York.

Stevens met us at the restaurant, and shortly afterwards Ritchie and Candice rolled up in Blackmore's red Mercedes sports car. As he walked into the restaurant, there was no doubting who was the centre of attention. Dressed entirely in black, with a cape and familiar, Blackmore style hat, he took one quick glance at the four 'Wallies' in their mock mediaeval clothes and smiled. As we sat down to enjoy a meal before the interview was to get under way, we knew this wasn't going to be one of those clinical situations when journalists are wheeled in and out with a few minutes each to fire their questions. We were obviously here for the entire evening, and as it developed, a thoroughly enjoyable and humourous one. Blackmore's reputation for winding journalists up is legendary but fortunately on this occasion he was honest, forthright, and particularly funny through it's entirety.

Clocking in at nearly four hours, I've no doubt it's one of the longest, if indeed not the longest interview the man has ever done. It provided many new stories, particularly about his early career and remains one of the best interviews Blackmore has ever done.

How did you first get into playing guitar?
A friend of mine brought a guitar to school, when I was eleven, and the look of it was incredible - just the way it looked - the shape, strings, everything. It was so vibrant. That's how I got into it. I just wanted a guitar. Just like that! And it's interesting that people might say: "Is that because it's shaped like a woman?" Yeah, maybe - it's a good answer.

So was it more of an image thing rather than you actually liking the sound of the guitar?
Exactly - it was an image thing, yeah, because I just loved the way it looked.

So what were your influences at that time?
Tommy Steele, 'Six-Five Special' (UKTV show) - I don't know if you remember that - people like Johnnie Ray came out, then there was Bill Haley right in there. They were my influences.

So, in your early years did you manage to see any bands live, or was all your musical exposure on radio, TV… whatever?
It was on television, most of it. But I did get to see a band called Nero And The Gladiators when

I was fifteen - that was my favourite band - and they were big heroes for me. I will always remember - at Southall Community Centre - they were unbelievable. Just a three-piece band with a keyboard player / pianist, called Nero And The Gladiators, and they did 'In The Hall Of The Mountain King' and things like that. It was all classical stuff, but to rock 'n' roll, and that to me was... well, this is it! They dressed up as Romans.

Something that you had experience of later on.
Yeah. I tried to get into the band Nero And The Gladiators. I got close to an audition, but I didn't get an audition. I was fifteen at the time... fifteen or sixteen. I would have been very good for their band, 'cause I was really into that music. I think they got some other guitar player who I met later. They had Tony Harvey - have you ever heard of him? Great guitar player; he's since died - lived in Paris - brilliant guitar player. When I'm in a showmanship kind of mood, he's the one that's my mentor... that I used to really watch. He used to have some great effects on stage - the way he moved and the way he thought. But he's since died... After Nero And The Gladiators it would be Django Reindhardt, people like that - not so much because of his playing, but because of his name- Django! I just liked that name. And he lived in a caravan. (laughter) He actually had two fingers, so if you heard him play with two fingers.... this is true. And then I went from that to people like...

Wes Montgomery was an influence, wasn't he?
*Yeah, Wes Montgomery was in there for a while. Then the guy from the Edge... what's his name... The Edge... U2? He was playing violin back in those days. (*Blackmore pauses, waiting for our response and once it has sunk in what he has just said we all roar with laughter.) *That's a band I just can't comprehend. Thank goodness everybody else has now figured it out. It took them a while. But there are many guitar players - Scotty Moore, James Burton, Jimmy Bryant, Stevie West- very fast stuff. Country and Western I was impressed with...* (looks at the Irish coffee he's drinking) *as I'm not impressed with this drink - there's all lumps in here. Aren't there lumps in here? What the hell is that?*

So did you always want to play fast yourself?
I used to practice a lot, so speed to me was no problem. If I could play something I could play it really fast. It wasn't until the age of, I think, twenty, that I started trying to slow down. I always felt that I was playing too fast, everything that I did. It became like a nervous reaction - a bit like Mariah Carey. It's like (imitates MC's singing)... *this is meaningless crap. Slow down! So then once I started to slow down, that to me was very difficult. To play something and then hold a note for, say, a couple of beats. It's like: "My God, I can't do this, I'm too nervous" and I was back to that* (imitates fast playing). *It's a nervous habit.*

You moved from Weston-super-Mare when you were quite young. Do you think it was important that you were near to the music scene in London?
No! Absolutely not! It did nothing for me. The London scene to me was... I firmly believe that if you're in the country you practice more. If you're near the so-called "happening town" then all you're doing is out drinking with people when you should be practising. It's interesting, the first time I went to London - I was about seventeen - and I thought I could play the guitar okay. Until I saw this guitar player, playing in a small club. I didn't drink in those days, but they took me there. This was a club near the place where they had an office for Screaming Lord Sutch. And I was watching this guy who was unbelievable, and I thought: "Oh my God, that's it, every guitar player must be this good!" He had a Les Paul, a black Les Paul. That was Albert Lee. And he was just phenomenal. I was like: "I can't compete with this guy, he's just too good". Luckily, nobody else was that good. But I really thought that everybody in London was that good. He was really incredible.

You actually started by having classical guitar lessons. Is that where your love of classical music started?

Not really, no. I don't really love classical music. I think if anybody gets to the point where they can play a little bit... you want to make music that has some sort of integrity. Now with pop music or rock music, there's not a lot in it. You can just kind of go on stage and turn on the amp and blast out, shake your fist at the audience, and everybody's like: "This is alright"... and have a rainbow with different colours... (laughter) So they watch and are not really looking what you're doing. But it's the discipline and the challenge that I like. Obviously I could never be a classical player because I didn't start early enough, and it used to bore me too! I'd play Segovia stuff, not very well, and I used to go: "I don't want to play this Bach fugue", you know. Now I see the reason for it. When I first started playing, it was like: "This is too... involved". So I don't think it really did anything for me, classical... that came later.

So when you were having these classical lessons were you still focused on rock 'n' roll type stuff?

Yeah. I just wanted to jump up and down like Tommy Steele. I thought: "Why am I learning some sort of scale... what's the point? Tommy Steele just goes on stage and enjoys himself. I want to do that."

So at that stage were you thinking that you just wanted to play guitar as a hobby, or were you thinking that you'd like to do this professionally?

I think... it was interesting... because when I was going to school when I was about thirteen, I got the impression - and I think a lot of people may have got this impression when they were at school - that you're kind of picked on. Although I was a school bully - Gerald Flashman and I. But in school I kind of felt a little bit... I didn't really study, so I felt a little bit distanced from being accepted in school. This was great - the cause - because then I went: "I've got to apply myself to something to show these people I can do it". That's the motivation, to show people that you're worthy of something, you're not just an idiot. It would be: "Oh, Blackmore, he's an idiot". "I'll show them. I'll... take up guitar!" With a guitar. I'll need a guitar to do it. Small point, but...

So that was your way of expressing your inner emotion.

Yeah! That's my way of getting back at people - the teachers, and the way that I felt that the system was. You were either in or out, you know. In those days you were either brilliant at history, geography or maths, English - and if you didn't do that you were just a reject. I failed my 'Eleven Plus', so I was automatically a reject after that. You know, that hit me hard, 'cause my father and mother said: "Well, now you've failed that, that's terrible." I was eleven years old. Remember that test?

Yes.

So I didn't go to grammar school, so I'm going to be excommunicated. So I was like: "I don't want to die yet!" (laughter) Help! Give me a guitar. I can do this, I can do a bit of this... what about this? And I thought: "I'm gonna show people, I'm gonna play the guitar really well". So they would say: "He was a terrible pupil, but he could really play the guitar." That's exactly what they said! Later on. Isn't that weird? When you put your mind to it. But I couldn't follow anything they taught me at school. It's the way they would teach. We had very Puritanical teachers; my school was like a Victorian school - it was like, disgusting! If you missed something: "Please sir, I didn't understand"... "You didn't understand Blackmore? Go and stand in the corner". "Sorry sir!" It was just like Tom Brown's Schooldays; very similar.

So, what did your parents think of you actually taking up the guitar?

My father said, as I've always quoted: "If you don't master this, I'm gonna break it across your head". He actually said that! He said it in a jovial way, just walking out of the shop, 'cause it cost him eight guineas, you know?

A lot of money in those days...
In those days, eight guineas. This was before the war. (everyone smiling)

Which war? (laughter)
The French revolution (laughter). *It really was - eight guineas - was like a lot of money. Especially for someone who thought I was gonna just do my usual, and not practice. He was the one that took me to lessons, and said: "You're gonna learn this properly."*

So did you say to him at that point: "Hey, this is what I want to do for a living?"
No! Not then, no, 'cause it was like... this was my way of just playing. I could express myself more on that than I could in lessons at school. Quite a bizarre situation... when you go to school you're very impressionable between the ages of eleven and fifteen. And my father used to teach maths, and he taught me a certain way of doing maths which I would take to school, and they would turn round and go: "How did you come to this conclusion?" And I would go: "Well, I did this", and the guy would say: "Yes, I know what you did, but I didn't teach you that." I would go: "No, you didn't; my dad taught me that." I said: "It's a much simpler way of doing it." I remember him going through the whole book. They were all correct answers, and he would cross out all the answers... "No, that's not the way I taught you, so it's wrong!" Something hit me that day, like "this world is really messed up." That teacher - his ego's been hurt because I figured out a way of doing something - I didn't figure it out, I was taught another way which was much simpler. But he didn't teach me that way. So, that didn't help. But it did, in a way. It gave me that... "I'll show them..." Typical English school. Over here (USA) they baby them. They don't even hit them over here. If someone gets hit over here it's like... it's on the news! "He was thrashed!" We got that every day at school. Over here they go: "They hit you?" They can't understand it. "Yeah, they hit you..." Remember the fight with the grizzly bear, the compulsory fight with the grizzly bear?

(Bloom) In 'Ripping Yarns?' (a British TV comedy series starring Michael Palin, very Monty Python)
Yeah. Over here it's like: "The teacher looked at you badly? We're gonna sue." And they sue. It's unbelievable. So you've got all these little morons running round. When they're sixteen - look out! Sixteen-year-olds. We live right near a kind of little wood. We see these little gnomes going into the wood. It's the kids from the area, with their baseball caps. Okay... I go out, call my friends in the neighbourhood and we all go out dressed as spirits. That's another story. So they're very spoilt, to say the least, over here.

We have friends here in the States, and their kids are really screwed up.
You can't touch them over here. I used to get the cane across here (points to the palm of his hand). *That was a good one.*

(Davies) Our teacher used to do that to us, cane us when we were eleven or twelve.
Yeah. (straight faced) *Did you ever get nailed to the wall?* (laughter) (referring to another scene from 'Ripping Yarns')

(Davies) Yeah, usually at Easter...
What was your first guitar?
My first guitar was a thing called a Framus, a German guitar. Then it was a Hoffner, which was another German guitar. Then it was a Gibson.

So how much practice were you putting in in the early days?
In the early days, perhaps a couple of hours a day. I think it was when I was between fourteen and sixteen, I practiced quite a bit... as much as I could.

So did you feel you had a natural aptitude for the guitar, or was it something you had to work very hard on.

No, I fought with it. I did, at the beginning I fought with it. It didn't come easily. I'm not so much... I'm getting more musical as I get older, but in the beginning it was just feel - I could bluff my way around the strings, just from practice. But I didn't quite know what I was playing. If someone said, "hit a G", I wouldn't really know. Candy's like that, very musical. She hears notes, can copy something - especially in those days.

Were you just sort of playing on your own at that time, or were you messing around with friends or something?

I was with a band called The Dominators.

(Bloom) That was the first band you were in?

Yes, it was called The Dominators and that was cool. The very first band I was in was called the Two I's Junior Skiffle Group. Because there was a Two I's Coffee Bar Skiffle Group with Wally Whyton and people like that, and we were the junior band. That was my first band, and I played washboard in that! Then I went on to better things - I played the dog-box.

Can you recall the first time you played in public?

It was at a school show. It was quite funny - we did 'Rebel Rouser' by Duane Eddy. The audience started clapping, and it just drowned us out! You couldn't even hear what we were playing. It was great at the beginning (sings the tune), *like that, then* (mimics clapping) - *"where are we?"* (laughter) *Then the teacher comes on stage and says, "okay, that's enough - next!" And it was a ballet act or something. But that was my first. It was interesting that when we were rehearsing for that school thing, I couldn't get the amplifier to work - which was a little radio, 2 Watt radio - and I kept plugging it in, taking it out, fiddling with it, couldn't get it to work. And in the end, by mistake I had the guitar lead, and I plugged it straight into the mains - imagine coming out of a pick-up straight into the mains - and I blew the whole mains. I blew the whole mains in the school. All the lights went out in the whole school.*

Is it right that you electrified your own guitar and built your first speaker, at school?

I didn't build the first speaker. I built parts - I got the parts of the amplifier and put it all together, and then put it into a box and made it look...

You actually became an aircraft radio technician - did you have a natural aptitude for doing that sort of thing?

No. Again, I was like - this would have been London Airport - and I was....

(Ritchie breaks off to complain about the 'lumpy' cream in the Irish coffee - then we order port - Cockburn's) *...Co'burn's... we know that.*

(Davies) Even in Wales we know it (laughter).

Do you have the Spice Girls in Wales yet?

(Davies) No, we have the Spice Sheep (laughter). We marinate it in lemon and things like that and then eat it.

Yeah, I've heard about that.

So, at what point did you decide that it was guitars rather than radios for you?

I was in this band - they wanted to go on the road professionally - The Jaywalkers. That's when I was sixteen. So I went on the road with them. And that was when I started being professional. Travelling up and down the M1 (motorway) *with the door half open on a Bedford van. It gets really cold!*

Was it difficult adapting to your first proper electric guitar - was that a sort of big change?
No, because my first electric was the Hoffner - the Hoffner Club 50 it was, great guitar. It was much easier than my other Framus, which would always break down. I had this amplifier called a Watkins Dominator amp - and I was in The Dominators at the age of fifteen-and-a-half - and it would always break down every time we'd do a show. It would blow up. So I'd go and take it back to Selmer's which was in Charing Cross Road. To get there I'd have to go on the train from Hounslow West, with this amplifier. I'd take it back. "Oh, we'll give you another one." "Alright, great." So I took the other one back, and then the next weekend I'd be playing, and as soon as we opened up, sure enough... bong, bang... the usual. So the following Monday I'd be back to take it back to Selmer's. This happened five times! Every week I took it back, and they said: "What the hell are you doing, why do you keep blowing this amp up?" They said: "Next time you come in here, bring your guitar in, so we can see what you're doing." So I took the amplifier back. They said: "Right, got your guitar?" "Got it with me." The guy was really nice. He said: "Just plug your guitar in - what are you doing?" I said: "Well, I turn the amp up like this.." and they had a brand new one, in Selmer's, and I started playing until it blows up. It blew up, right in the shop. They couldn't believe it. They couldn't believe I blew it up in the shop. I said: "There you go, look." 'Cause it was getting like a Monty Python sketch - I was getting used to it by then. I said: "Take this amp. Can I try that amp?" "No, don't try that out. Get it out of here!" And that amp never let me down. Sixth amplifier.

When you were watching other guitarists of the period, how did you rate your own playing?
I never rated myself alongside of them. I just always thought... I just liked playing. If I saw someone that was really good, I'd look up to them. If I saw someone that wasn't as good, I would never go I'm better than he is.

So did you try to copy someone who you thought was good?
I had people like (Big) Jimmy Sullivan who was very good. There were so many guitarists around that were great. I was playing rhythm guitar in the band. Rodger Mingaye - brilliant guitarist - was the lead guitar player. We used to play places like Vicky Burke's in Twickenham, near Witton. I don't know if you know that area? A place called Vicky Burke's - a dance place - we used to play down there. That was my first introduction to playing live in front of people. And Rodger was the main guitar player; I just played rhythm. 'Cause he was just brilliant.

Was it difficult for you to get gigs in those days?
Yeah, we would play just small places, but it was fun.

In '61 you moved to play with Mike Dee And The Jaywalkers. What sort of music were you playing?
We'd play... first record that I ever recorded was with them. It was called 'My Blue Heaven'. Remember that old song? They wanted it rocked up. That was the very first thing I ever did - we did it with Decca Records. It got turned down, but that was what we recorded.

(Bloom) It never got released?
No, don't think so. 'My Blue Heaven', in 1961, my first ever record.

Was that your first time in the studio?
It was dreadful, awful.

What do you like about the Gibson sound?
The Gibson is just a very well-made guitar. The intonation is very good, very accurate. I like the shape of it... bright red...

So how do you rate Big Jim Sullivan, because I've read that he was a big influence on you. Is it true that he gave you some lessons?
Yeah, he gave me some lessons - I used to sit on his doorstep. I used to sit on his doorstep because he wouldn't answer the door, so I'd sit there. Then he'd answer the door: "What do you want?" "Jim, can you teach me that riff?" - because he was in Marty Wilde And The Wildcats. But he was phenomenal at the time. It was amazing to see somebody that good.

I don't know if you are interested but apparently Big Jim didn't pick up the guitar for years, but he's just taken it up again. And I noticed in *Record Collector* magazine that he's playing on Jackie Lynton's latest album.
Great!

Where does Jackie Lynton come into the picture, because you seem to be associated with him, but we're not sure where?
We were going to get a band together, when I was about nineteen. When I used to go to work, I used to work at this factory on the Great West Road - it was right next to Firestones - and in the workers' playtime they used to play Jackie Lynton And The Teenbees. This was about 1960. And he was great. Then I got to meet him in '61 or '62 - very nice guy. Then in '64 we tried to get a band together, I think. And we met Kim Fowley, who was doing P.J. Proby stuff, who gave us some demos to learn and to come back. Of course, Jack had the records and lost them and left them on the train! So we never did it. Typical! But Jackie Lynton - this guy can really make me crack up on stage. I love it when he'll start a number, and the band starts off, and he comes in and goes: "Hold it! What's the first word?" (laughter) They say it's so-and-so, and then: "Oh yeah, sorry, sorry!" Of course, the whole audience is crying with laughter, because they know that it's not worked out. That used to crack me up.

In the early sixties you started to play with Screaming Lord Sutch. Was that a big step up in your career?
Yes it was, because I went to rehearse for this guy who was offering a lot of money. I'd never heard of Screaming Lord Sutch, and I went to see him, and I passed the audition but turned it down. I just felt - I was fifteen-and-a-half, sixteen - they toured so much, I just didn't kind of want to leave home. That's basically what it was. But then I went back six months later and I went: "Okay, I'll try this." And the very first night with Screaming Lord Sutch , the guy enters - I didn't know, but the time that he enters the stage he's in a coffin. I was not amused by that. I thought: "This guy is nuts!" And I'm playing in his band. I didn't know what was going to happen. I just rehearsed with him, and we played 'Jack The Ripper.' We'd open with that, and I didn't know what the stage set-up was until I did it. We'd rehearse, then on stage he'd come out of the coffin. I'm like: "What's going on?" Of course he's got hair down to here. And I thought: "I've got to go home with this guy tonight - he's driving the van!" I wasn't too amused at that!

I actually know Dave Sutch, because the bank where I work - he used to have his mortgage with us. He used to come in, and he's such a quiet unassuming guy, you just cannot imagine…
That's right, until you see the other side.

He actually said to me how shy you were at the time.
That's right, and he used to grab my guitar neck and go: "Come on, move, move!"

Is it true that you'd be hiding behind your guitar amp.
Oh yes! Hiding behind the guitar amps and in the wing. They used to grab me - "Come on!" - and pull me out. It's very true. I learned a lot of showmanship from him.

That was going to be my next question. What did the experience teach you about stage-craft, and

how important was the experience for your own confidence?
He taught me that you can go out there and act like an imbecile, and people would think it's wonderful. But - it's very interesting, like a whole psychology kind of thing - if you get out on stage and you look self-conscious, people will watch you. But if you go out there, throw yourself around and act like a fool, they'll go: "Oh, yeah." It's like a show, a whole masquerade. But the moment you start taking yourself seriously and go into your shell, people see it immediately. But he taught me that. Just get out there and run around. I'd go: "Well, I feel an idiot." In the end I'm running around with a Tarzan outfit on, and I'm going: "These people are going for this; I can't believe it."

He commented that he thought your playing was brilliant at that time, but did you think otherwise?
I thought I was OK, I thought I was alright.

(Davies) Did you rate any other guitarists of your own age?
Yeah, I did. At that time there would have been a guy called Richard Hardin from Manchester - he was very good. Pagey was good. Albert Lee was the best. Jeff Beck came along when I was seventeen - he was brilliant.

Can you tell us about how your stint with The Outlaws and Joe Meek came about?
Yes, I used to do sessions with Joe Meek. With Sutch we went there, and Joe Meek liked my playing - he was a producer - so he used to have me on sessions, then I joined The Outlaws. And The Outlaws was the standard band that did all the session work for Joe Meek. There would be a point - unlike now - where I would listen to the radio and go: "I know that song, I played on it!" I'd hear so many songs on the radio, and I'd played on nearly all their records! It's a weird feeling. And now it's the opposite. (Laughter) Very strange.

So how did you adapt to playing in the studio? Was it a strange feeling?
Yeah, it's rigid. I was pretty good, until they'd say to me: "Play this melody." And as I didn't read music - we'd just read chord sheets - that threw me. I could not remember melodies to save my life. Except certain melodies. Chas, our bass player, used to play the guitar - I would leave it to him.

I understand that you had no idea who's record you were ultimately on?
That's true, some of the times.

Can you recall any of the artists you worked with, and who you were particularly impressed with at that time?
Mike Berry - we watch him over here now on 'Are You Being Served' (Seventies British TV comedy series). I did one record with him I think. Most of the records were with Rodger Mingaye playing - he was the guitarist. A lot of people credit that to me, but it wasn't.

Did you have any input into the material, or any freedom in the way you played the solos, for example?
No! It was always - we'd go in in the morning, and the producer would say: "This is the song that I want you to do today." And he would either play us a demo or he would sing it to us. And he couldn't really sing, so that became embarrassing. Chas was brilliant. Chas would make up his own melodies. Chas would go: "What do you want on this, Joe?" And Joe would go: (sings out of tune melody). "Do you want (plays in-tune melody)?" "Yeah, that's what I want." And of course you could see what was going down. Chas was writing it for him.

So you actually got to tour with Jerry Lee Lewis and Gene Vincent, with The Outlaws. What kind of experience was that?

That was interesting... (turns to Candice) wasn't it? (laughter) Jerry Lee Lewis was interesting, because we were supposed to have a week's rehearsal with him. Don Arden, Sharon Arden's dad (now Osbourne, Ozzy's wife), said we were supposed to rehearse for a week. Then it was five days, then three days, and then it was: "When are rehearsals going to start - we don't know what we're doing?" The tour was coming up, and I hadn't played one note with him. The day of the show we get to play with him - in the afternoon, he strolls in. And we're there, like, petrified, because I'd been told by Sounds Incorporated - another band - that if Jerry doesn't like you he'll give you a whack in the face. So I'm there, petrified, playing. Luckily he liked me! He wanted to bring me back to Memphis, where he lived. He'd come over to me and go: "Play, boy". I'd play, and I'd be looking up waiting for that whack. I'm like... (imitates scared look). This was before the show. Then when we'd finished he'd go (puts out his hand): "Put it there." To shake hands. A bit like Jon Lord. Jon Lord likes to shake hands.

So, you toured with him (Jerry Lee Lewis) in Germany. Was that your first time abroad, and is that where your love of Germany came about?

That's right. I saw a different country, and I immediately took to their... they seemed to work harder and enjoy life more than the English. In those days, back in '60 to '63, they were a bit class conscious in England - I don't know if it's still there, I think it's gone the other way now - but there was this class system thing which used to get on my nerves. You'd go into a shop and ask for a bar of chocolate or something and it's like - it'd give me the creeps - there'd be the upper class accent. And people judged you on your accent. The "stewed prunes." There were a lot of those people around in those days. You get that, or it's: "Oh-right mate, how ya doin'?" (imitating Cockney accent). Now it's gone the other way. Now it's not cool to be "stewed prunes", it's cool to be "oh-right mate." It drove me nuts, whereas in Germany I couldn't understand anybody, they couldn't understand me, and that was perfect! (laughter) A great arrangement. To me, the English language never meant much. I thought talking was people trying to cover up what they were up to. So going to Germany and hearing people speak a language that I couldn't understand - I couldn't understand what they were saying, it didn't matter what I was saying - let's just play music.

And now you have become a master of the English language.

No, not at all.

In 1965 you cut a solo single. What was the inspiration behind that, and how did it come about?

Derek Lawrence - (turns to Candice) we should get to Blackmore's Night in about three hours from now...

We can start skipping things. If you want to, we can go on to Blackmore's Night, then come back?

Okay. Well, in '65 I was thinking about forming this band called Blackmore's Night (laughter), and Derek Lawrence said: "Well, you have to make your solo effort first." So I said, "alright... but I'm in a hurry" and we did 'Getaway' - I think I actually wrote that. I think; I'm not sure. But then I think I wrote things like 'In The Mood' by Glen Miller, so I have to be careful. No, wait a minute, Jon Lord wrote that (laughter).

Then you rejoined Sutch yet again?

Yes, it was always when the bills started mounting up we went back to Sutch. You'd get to that point where everybody in the band would say: "I can't take this any longer, I can't back the Screaming Lord any more." And they would leave. And you knew they were gonna come back. It's like breaking out of a prisoner of war camp. A month later they come back in. They're back! They would hate it; it was like a penance. But he was the only guy that paid any money. Everybody else couldn't pay. You could go with all the fancy bands, but they didn't pay any money, so it was back to Sutch.

You actually got to record with him on your second stint with him, unlike the first one?
Yes. I can't remember what I recorded with him. As I said, a lot of stuff that he had really good guitar players on was not me, it was Rodger Mingaye.

The Three Musketeers got formed out of some of Sutch's band - is that right?
That's very true. Two players from Sutch: Jimmy Evans, who we're still trying to track down, and Silas Wegg - he loved Charles Dickens - his real name's Andy Anderson but he likes to be called Silas Wegg.

The band got a credit on 'Shadow Of The Moon', so presumably you must have some fond memories of that period?
Yeah, very fond memories, very fond memories. They were the days where - you left Sutch, and that was very intense - but it was the first band where I really enjoyed playing. We used to dress up as Musketeers, 'cause I always had to dress up as something, and we used to sword fence on stage. We were the first three-piece - this was in '64 - people had never heard of three-piece bands. So we'd be playing, and all the songs we had were very fast. The big thing in Germany was that you played music for people to dance to. And they could never dance to us, so we didn't really get much work. There was a guitar player called Joe Procter - we used to copy some of his stuff. We'd open up the show with a song called 'The Planesmen' (sings the tune), followed by 'Yackety Sax' (sings the tune), then we'd do 'Javes' (sings the tune), but in the middle of the act we'd do our speciality - a really fast number - 'Flight Of The Bumble Bee' (sings the tune). So you can imagine the audience watching us. And there was another song called 'Sabrosa' by Chet Atkins (sings the tune). Everything was like that (extremely fast!) which was great for me but was terrible for the audience. So they used to kind of disappear, and our work went down, and I was back with Sutch, I think. He'd be going (imitates out-of-tune singing): 'Johnny B. Goode...' It was brilliant that if you were in the key of 'A' - he's got these Chinese intervals in his voice (sings what sounds like Red Indian wailing, causing hilarious laughter). It was unbelievable. And people are going: "Well, why did you leave the band?" (laughter) It was difficult. That was difficult. I don't know how he did it. That's very difficult to sing in this totally unrelated key to what was being played. He could do it and stay on that note, and we'd be in this key and he'd be up here.

Presumably he wasn't aware...?
Oh, no! He was breaking things..., top hat..., yelling and screaming...

So didn't he join Deep Purple in 1984?
What, Sutch? Yeah! He did, yeah. It was like a bad nightmare coming back again. No, actually he was Okay then. Where it became a nightmare and reminded me of Sutch was in, like - where did he come back in again, was it '90, '89, when was it?

'92.
Was it '92? That's when it really got like Sutch. The whole thing - (grunts) - "What's this." And Roger and Jon are going: "It's great!" (laughter) And we (looks at Candice) just looked at each other and burst out laughing. 'Cause the management sent me a tape of what he had done, and I looked at her and we just started laughing. And I'm going: "What am I laughing about, this is serious business." It was a big political thing.

(Davies) Bring out your dead. (Laughter, Blackmore raises his eyebrows.) We were going to come in tonight doing the Monty Python sketch 'Bring out your dead', but singing: 'Bring out your Gillans.' (Laughter)
Oh yeah?

(Davies) The punch-line was…: "But I'm not dead!" And we said: "Yes you are, we've heard your new album!" (Laughter)
(Laughing) *Very true. It got to a point - that was very strange with Gillan - 'cause we'd be playing to a lot of people, places in Germany, ten thousand, packed. And everybody's going: "Yeah, great." And I'm going: "Why am I so unhappy with this song?" 'Cause the band can play. And Candy was saying: "What's wrong?" I'd go: "I don't know." I'd come off stage feeling like: "This is not right." I'd go to the lighting people, the roadies: "What did you think of the show tonight?" "Yeah, great! Yeah, we thought it was really good. I mean - Gillan - it was okay." "What about Gillan?" "Nothing about Gillan. Gillan was great… apart from… I didn't notice that he didn't sing for two songs. I really did not notice that." And I was: "What do you mean he didn't sing two songs?" It got that stupid, and everybody was petrified to say anything to Ritchie in case Ritchie goes: "I'm off!" Then everybody would be out of work. There'd be twenty roadies out of work.*

Was it frustrating in that you were enjoying playing with the rest of the guys?
Yeah, musically everything was great, but the singing thing was just a joke, just a pantomime. And he would take the piss out of the audience. He would just not sing, or he would forget the words. And he loved it. It was like a pig in shit! He can't do anything wrong. I'm like: "This is not fair to the audience", 'cause you could see the audience mouthing all the words to whatever it was that he would forget. And he would just look at me and laugh. I'm like: "It's not funny!" One night, maybe, it's funny, but not every night, the same crap. My favourite story though - he used to come across to me and go… 'cause when we first started again I said: "Look, are you going to start to sing 'Child In Time' every night or are you gonna say you can't sing it?" "No, Ritch, I've learned a whole different way to sing; I will never lose my voice again." Great. We're in the third night, he comes over to me: "Ritch, no "Child" tonight." "Why not?" "It's my voice." So, I let it go that night. The next night, he came across: "No "Child" tonight", and I knew he was getting into this routine. And the biggest number is 'Child In Time' to me. That's an amazing song, and he sings it amazingly well when he sings it. No-one can sing it like Ian. And I thought: "This is not right, he's getting out of it every night." So, of course, that night, after he'd told me we were not doing it, I went back on and went… (sings opening chords to Child In Time') *Jon's like* (imitates Jon, startled, joining in, laughter). *The audience went: "Yeah." And Gillan's like:* (sings the words). *Got him! Next night: "No "Child" tonight." "Right."* (then sings opening chords to 'Child In Time') *I got him every night. It's like saying: "No show tonight, I've been out drinking." That's how ridiculous it was. "I can't talk tonight." "Okay, so you're gonna go home, and go to bed and have some hot milk?" "No, I'm going out - all night - I'm drinking with the guys." Then tomorrow night be even worse. That really makes a lot of sense. And the places were packed; all these people: "It's brilliant." It's disgusting, you know. Nostalgia. So that's where I'd had enough. They needed that security, that safety net - the others need it - because they can't do anything on their own, so they're gonna all stay together. They need that Deep Purple security net. It's great. I mean, I would really love to get together once every seven or eight years and do a tour. Just go: "Hey lads", and play all the old songs - great! Then drop everything and all go our separate ways, and: "See you in seven years." We'd do 'Highway Star' again. But they take it so seriously. And I don't think they've got anything to offer musically. From a musical writing point of view, it's embarrassing, to quote Ian Paice. I mean, I was always put down: "We always used to have to do what Ritchie told us to do." I used to sit back and say: "Let's hear your ideas." They didn't have any ideas. Paicey put it into a nutshell. He came to me and said: "Come on, you didn't turn up for rehearsals today." I said: "Right, so big deal." He said: "It was embarrassing." I said: "What*

was embarrassing?" He said: "Jon Lord" "Why, what was wrong?" He said: "He couldn't write anything; we spent two or three hours at rehearsals, and because you weren't there, pushing, saying we were gonna do this and that, we ended up doing nothing." But that kind of brings it up to date, there, doesn't it? Rob (Fodder, Ritchie's PA) was there all the time, so they hated Rob, because they thought he was corrupting me. 'Cause Rob would go: "Yeah, it was awful tonight." And Candy was going: "I'll tell you all the reasons why you didn't enjoy the show tonight". I'd go: "Well, what were they?" She'd go to me: "Shall I write all the reasons down, why I think you get upset about the shows?" 'Cause I couldn't figure it out. I was coming off stage with "encore, encore, encore," right? And I'm going: "This was awful." But I couldn't remember all the reasons why I thought it was awful, until she started writing them down. She'd go: "Maybe this is why you didn't like tonight's show: Gillan forgot this, Gillan did this, Gillan sang out of tune here, the lights were abominable here, they showed Jon Lord under the lights here when it should have been you...." And I'm going: "That's all the reasons I'm so angry." I'd be so wound up after two hours of playing on stage. But it took her to write all those reasons down. 'Cause you can't stop playing and say: "Let me write this down for a minute." I would just come off remembering that I felt really angry. I could never figure out why. Then things started to be put into perspective. If I'm that angry, I'm just not enjoying this. Because I'd talk to the rest of the crew, and they'd be petrified that we weren't gonna tour any more if they said something to me like: "It's not working." If I complained about something, they agreed, but they were all told by the management: "Don't tell Ritchie if you don't like the show, just tell him it was great." And it was so weird, 'cause I could see this. "What did you think of the show tonight?" "Oh it was great!" There's something wrong here. I knew they'd been put up to something by the management. "Ritchie will leave if he's not told that it was great." A lot of that went down, believe it or not. Then I knew I wanted to get out. There was this pressure, too, just going round - like a security thing - travelling the world in a limousine, very safe and secure. And music shouldn't be like that. It should be on the edge. I've always thought it should be on the edge. That's part of the deal, the arrangement with the public. You don't go on stage going: "I feel totally confident tonight." You go on stage going: "I'm a mess." People relate to that, they don't relate to people going: "Well I don't need this audience, because I'm smug." As soon as they see that, you're in trouble. I'll tell you who did that: Judy Garland at the London Palladium. Her face was saying "I don't need you" to the audience, and they booed her. That was the end of her. After that she went downhill, remember that?

So, do you think you're one of the most misunderstood people in the music business?
Not really, I think they understand me, because I don't have much patience with people, and I'm a very moody person. Misunderstood, no. Because I want them to understand that I'm a moody person, and that life is not a bowl of cherries. In music you're always fighting. You can't go through life shaking peoples' hands and going: "Everything is wonderful." If you're a new born Christian, maybe. For me life is a struggle. There are icebergs everywhere, you've got to dodge them.

You have got an incredibly dry sense of humour. You're probably the funniest person that we know.
Really? (laughs) Dry? Non existent!

Dry, even by English standards.
What are you trying to say? You're a friend of Ian Gillan's, aren't you? I know your sort... But the one thing that perplexed me about that whole situation was the fact that I wanted to get out, off this ship which I felt was sinking, to make good music. That's all I wanted to do. I couldn't believe the finger pointing that went on. "He's a trouble maker" "Why?" "Because he's trying to make good music; we're trying to make money - he's spoiling it all!" That kind of bothered me. Even to

this day it really bothers me - what went down with the management, what went down with the band, the people that surround the band, the whole little clique. It reminded me of school. I'm a trouble-maker because I want to play some better music? They're still doing their thing. That's what I wanted them to do, they'd just get another guitar player. But it never came across that way. It was: "He's trying to ruin things for us.

Do you mind if we take a toilet break?
No! I want to complain more. Another thing I didn't like about Ian Gillan - I didn't like his shoes!

(interview continues after toilet break) *I'm exhausted now. Where are we, 1961?*

(Bloom) 1938. Hitler invaded Poland. What did you think about that?
It was not my fault. I said I didn't want to do it.

(Bloom) But Ian Gillan blamed you.
You see, that's typical, Gillan would blame me. He wanted to do it, I didn't want to do it. I like the Polish people. He wanted to go in there and get drunk and do his thing.

I forgot to ask you how much you weighed at birth?
I've no idea. It was probably at ten minutes past midnight, that would be the 13th, double summertime, two hours difference... Let's jump through to Blackmore's Night now. I think we've done enough drudgery.

(Bloom) We'd like to have talked to you about Rainbow for a little bit, but we can go back to that later.
Let's do some on Rainbow.

(Bloom) You were saying you don't want it too comfortable, and have always got to be on the edge. When things are going well, it often appears that you knock them on the head and do something different. Before Purple reformed (in 1984), Rainbow towards the end...
I shouldn't have done that, you know? I should have joined Purple for one LP and gone back to Rainbow. But I got lazy.

It seemed that the style of music you wanted to create with Rainbow at that time was more commercial and Abba-influenced.
That's right.

I felt that with the last album 'Bent Out Of Shape', you got the ideas almost the way you wanted it?
Very, very close.

Then you knocked it on the head.
That's right.

What drove you to do that?
I'll tell you what it was. It was money, purely money. The manager called me up and said that there was a lot of money in this. How much? OK, I'll do it. I shouldn't have done it. I shouldn't have done it, but I did. It's funny, but 'Perfect Strangers', the riff, I'd had in Rainbow about two years before. I didn't have a song for it.

So when you did those last dates with Rainbow in Japan, did the band know at the time?
No they didn't. It all happened very suddenly. It was Gillan trying to round up people doing the whole thing, resurrecting the Purple thing. But the money was so ridiculous, I went: "Yeah, I'll do that." Purely for money. 'Perfect Strangers' worked, but the one after that was probably one of the worst... I've done two really awful LPs: one is 'House Of Blue Light', the other 'The Battle

Rages On', although that was shaping up to being a good LP without the vocals - if you heard just the backing tracks they sounded really good. Then when the vocals got put on... (thumbs down)

Did you originally record the whole album with Joe (Lynn Turner)?
No. Two tracks. 'Stroke Of Midnight' - you should hear that - and 'Lonely For You', an excellent song. He did a song 'Lonely For You', it would have been a Number One had it been released; so catchy, Joe sang it, it was brilliant. I thought: "We've got to do this; if we take on Gillan we've got to do this song." Do it exactly the same. But I spoke to management: "Does Gillan realise that he has to sing that one song exactly like this?" Because I knew he was going to be a headache. "Oh yes, he knows all about it." I said: "Great, okay, that's one of the conditions of him joining Purple again". He didn't know anything about it when I spoke to him. I saw him in the studio: "Ian, do you know about doing this 'Lonely For You' song?" "No." "Bruce Payne didn't tell you that I wanted you to do that song with exactly the same melody?" He didn't know anything about it. That didn't help matters. That wasn't Gillan's fault, it was the management.

Obviously the first time you formed Rainbow was for different reasons - you wanted to start your own thing with Ronnie. Did you have a clear vision of the things you wanted to do then?
No. It started with the song 'Black Sheep Of The Family.. I put it to Purple: "Let's do this song." They said: "No, why should we?" I'm like: "Well, it's such a great song", and they went: "No, we didn't write it." "What's that got to do with it? Because you won't get any writing credits, you won't do this song?" "Yes." That was basically the bottom line. So I said: "Well I'm gonna do it with somebody else", and Ronnie was just around at the time. That threw me too. If somebody comes along and has a good song, you go: "Let's do that song"; you don't go: "It's not one of our songs". A lot of that went down with Purple, and I could never understand that. It was Paicey and Jon who were adamant about not doing anybody elses' songs. Roger would always listen to see if it was worth doing.

With the first Rainbow album came the first indications of your interest in mediaeval music, with the album cover etc. Ronnie was obviously into that music as well.
Yes he was, but he was more into the demonic kind of side, the nasty little gremlins. He was into hob-goblins and demons. I was into pixies in the wood. But I didn't know it at the time. He did a good job; came along, did very well, until... we started slowing down on the third LP ('Long Live Rock 'N' Roll') when we were in France. I remember being in the studio, and Ronnie came in with Cozy - I was kneeling down in front of my amplifier, trying to get the sound right - and he poked me in the back. I'll always remember it. "We're not standing for this!" "What?" "You're on the front cover of Circus magazine. We're not gonna be sidekicks!" And I then saw this guy in a whole different light. I went: "It's got nothing to do with me. I don't know if I'm on the front page of whatever you're talking about." "You're on the front page of Circus, and it was going (supposed) to be the three of us!" And I went: "So it's not?" "No, it's just you." "Who said this?" "Wendy just called me." "Oh, right; thank you Wendy!" That was it. I knew that we were finished then, because I couldn't talk to him (Ronnie) any more. I suddenly saw him in a different light. I saw him as this angry bitter little man. He got very bitter. And Cozy... Cozy's got another side to him.

When I spoke to Cozy last year, he was saying...
He was very nice then, he was great. That's the best I've seen him.

He said he would take your side more often than Ronnie's.
Cozy had some great stories. (Looks at Candice) Candy at this point is gonna get so bored with hearing stories.

Do you want to jump to Blackmore's Night?
Yes, and we'll come back to the stories later. Actually, there's a sketch I wanted to do by Monty Python. You know the "Cheese Shop" sketch? I want to change that into a "Beer" sketch, just for my home video. They'd use all the same words, but it would be just about beer - "Certainly uncontaminated by beer" - and all that stuff. Can you imagine? You could go through every beer name there is! "Do you have any Budweiser? "Not very popular around here sir." "Not very popular? It's the single most popular beer in the world." "Not around these parts sir." You could do the whole thing. I've been meaning to do it with some friends in my bar, but I never get around to it.

You have stated that you've wanted to do a mediaeval album for ages. Why 1996 / 97? Why was that the right time?
Actually, it was all to do with Frank Sinatra. Frank Sinatra once said to me… (looks at all) Why are you laughing?

We've heard this before.
He said: "Who are you?" So I thought, that's it, I'm gonna go with mediaeval. After that I felt devastated. It's very true. There's something about Frank that always brings out the best in me. "Who are you?" I just like that. I heard it on television once - it was brilliant.

Where did you get that from?
Someone said it on television. "Frank Sinatra said to me: who are you?" To me, that was my sense of humour.

(Davies) Didn't you say that to Jeff Beck in about 1966?
No. (laughter) I did say: who was he? My life gets very complicated like that.

This humour goes over a lot of peoples' heads.
Yeah, including my own!

When you did that Frank Sinatra quip on Japanese TV (promotional programme for 'Stranger In Us All' with Doogie White in 1995, called 'Bang Up Rock'), you were doing the interview with Doogie…
I don't remember that.

I was on the floor laughing.
(Suddenly remembering) Oh, yeah. I mean, it was ridiculous. You walk into the house. You go: "Right, what are we doing?" They go: "We're doing an interview. Right, go!" (Imitates a microphone pushed into his face) "Is someone gonna do an interview then?" "No, just talk. Just tell us about your life." "My life?? What am I supposed to say? Give me some clues here." Nothing. "The guitar - just talk about the guitar." Okay. (Turns to Candice) Remember that? I was like: "Quick, get me a Scotch! I won't talk about anything until I've had three Scotches." And this was early in the afternoon!

So, have you got rid of the smell yet? (referring to the odour left in Ritchie's home studio by his cats, as seen in the official 'Shadow Of The Moon' video)
No, you can't get rid of the smell.
(Night) *Now the producer has to deal with it; we don't.*
(Blackmore) *I go down there and his eyes are crying. He's like: "I can't breathe!" (laughter) And he doesn't even know why! "Are you okay?" "Yeah, I'm fine."*

Candice - you don't come from a musical background, do you?
No.

(Blackmore) *Yes you do; your mother's really good.*
Okay, I do.

So, when did you actually realise that you could sing?
My parents enrolled me in singing lessons when I was four years old; I was in singing and acting lessons. They had us doing little theatre productions out here in Long Island. It was all the Broadway stuff - "Give My Regards To Broadway" and "A Funny Thing Happened On The Way To The Farm", and all that stuff. I was just singing these show tunes. My parents: both of them play piano.
(Blackmore) *Can I interject for one second?*
Please.
(Blackmore) *Could you do* (impersonate) *Rob calling up Karon on the phone?*
(Ritchie then tells us about Candice's gift for imitating people, and moves from Rob (Fodder) to Joe Lynn Turner's girlfriend…)
Theresa from Kentucky. She talks in riddles and clichés - typical rock 'n' roll vibe, man. Everything is rock 'n' roll. She wrestles with pigs for a living. Typical Joe Lynn Turner, 'cause he's always… perfect for him because they both talk at the same time, and they won't stop to listen to each other, they just keep talking! And she just talks in all these clichés, in a southern accent. So… where were we? We called up the office… (looks at Candice) *You take it from there.*
We were at Roger's house looking at some of the mixes, and Joe was there, and he said that he had to take the 8-15 train back to Brooklyn or wherever he was going. Anyway, next day we woke up and said: "Let's play a joke on "the rockers." (Looks at Ritchie) *So, what did we do?*
(Blackmore) *Candice calls up the office as Theresa.*
She has a very bad temper, so just imagine. (Then does an impression of Theresa with a strong Southern American accent, to much laughter).
(Blackmore) *So they were convinced that it was Theresa on the phone! I think they eventually found out that it was us.*
(Blackmore) *When they* (the office) *found out that it was a joke, they didn't like it. They take themselves very seriously.* (Pauses, then turns to Candice) *You know who you remind me of? Freddie Starr!*

(Bloom) I can't see the similarity, but I'll go along with it. (Laughter)
Freddie Starr. That man, when I first met him… to go off at a tangent.
(Night) *What does this have to do with my mother's piano playing?*
Nothing. It's like everything's connected - but it isn't! (Looks at us) *Carry on. We'll come back to Freddie Starr later… much later.*
(Night) Let's do the Freddie Starr thing now, and get it out of the way.
Freddie Starr - it takes a lot to make me laugh - Freddie Starr had me crying. 'Cause I was backing the guy… I first met him in Joe Meek's studio. He came in - at the time he was just in a rock 'n' roll band - he came in; he was a singer. The Outlaws - Chas is sitting there half asleep - still got his pyjamas on. (laughter) *He actually had his pyjamas on underneath his trousers. You could see his pyjamas sticking out at the bottom. I'd go: "What's that?" "Oh! It's nothing." "It's pyjamas!"* (laughter) *And he was always late, 'cause he would get on the bus to come down to the studio and he would fall asleep. And then the bus would go back again to where he'd started! So he kept going back and forth to get to the studio. And when he got there, Joe Meek used to go: "Where've you been?" "Joe, you'll never believe this" - I remember this story once - "I was walking along, and this little bird was on the ground. It had fallen out of it's nest, so I had to take it to the vet's…" And Joe starts laughing. That was it, 'cause he had a soft spot for Chas. Of course, Joe was very gay, which I found out later. Anyway, Freddie Starr would come into the studio… we'd start playing…* (looks at Candice) *I think I've told you this story. In those days you'd put the solo on as you're playing rhythm - playing away - sometimes you'd have to the solo*

down as you're playing. Not like today, when you'd stop, do the rhythm four hundred times, then do the solo. In those days it was - right, now we're coming to the solo, and I'd start playing the solo. Freddie Starr dropped his trousers in the studio, and I'm playing, and he's now got his "thing" and he's trying to put it in my ear! (laughter) *I'm like: "What's going on? Get off! Get off!" And I'm trying to play the solo. Of course, Joe Meek heard the mistake - I made a mistake. In those days you didn't have a see-through thing, he'd have to come around the room to see what we were doing. He came storming round. "What the bloody hell's going on here... ooohhh!!"* (laughter) *I'm going: "This is getting to me. I'm seventeen years old and people are sticking things in my ear." That was my first introduction to Freddie Starr. He was Ian Broad's singer in the band - he was completely nuts! We used to be in Rhyl doing the summer season - we'd be playing with Arthur Askey, Jerry Diamond - and the bass player said: "The moon's bright tonight." And he'd just rush off down the road. "Got to look at the moon." "What do you mean, you've got to look at the moon?" "Oh, moon's bright tonight!"* (laughter) *So I was in this band with Freddie Starr's drummer, who was just like him - crazy - and his whole band must have been really weird. It was Freddie Starr and the Midnighters, and apparently when they played with the Beatles they blew them off stage. The Beatles could not follow them, in Liverpool, in '62!*

Was Freddie Starr a big Elvis fan?
Yeah. He used to make me cry!

(Davies) He once had Peter Stringfellow in the stocks.
(Welch) He also used to appear on TV on FA Cup Final Day, dressed as Adolf Hitler.
It's just him. I remember going to a party once somewhere - a debutante's party - and he just walks in. It was a very high society kind of place... "This is the Screaming Lord Sutch"... and we all walked in. Freddie would walk in, go straight up the stairs, and start washing his hair, dyeing his hair - in somebody else's house. He's dyeing his hair! So he comes down - we're all having tea - he pops his head in: "Have you got any more of that dye?" Who is this? It's Freddie Starr - he's just helped himself to the hair dye. Very odd!

Ritchie, would you mind telling the Tony Carey story - what happened when he left the Chateau?
It's a long story. He got excommunicated because he wouldn't play football. So we picked on him. I remember, Tony Carey once said to me: "Who are you?".... I used to throw the javelin all the time - I used to throw it at school - so I used to exercise by throwing the javelin. Just take it on the road, throw it around. And then we were in France, in the studio. I'd been throwing it in the garden, and I came back to my room. There was a corridor, and there was a wooden door at the end. So I thought, just for the hell of it: "I wonder if I could stick it (the javelin) in that door?" Nobody else was around. It went straight through the door! Of course, Tony Carey was on the other side of the door. I was trying to murder him... that's how it started. "He's trying to murder me, he's throwing javelins at me." So then he would stay in his room. He wouldn't come out. So Cozy and I just played jokes on him! There was one big incredible worked-out production that we did. What happened was... Tony was always taking drugs like cocaine and ridiculous stuff, so he was always hallucinating. And he always thought I was the devil! He was convinced I was the devil, 'cause I was the leader of the band. So I was the devil. (The lights suddenly dim, causing intense laughter.) *It took us a while to get into our first track at this place* (the Chateau), *which was haunted. I suppose the fact that we played football every day for ten days before we went into the studio didn't help to get things going... He'd keep coming down: "When am I going to put my part on?" "Oh, not yet, not yet." So when he eventually got into the studio, he walked in with a pint of Jack Daniels and a keyboard under his arm. The haunted studio! And he was already loaded - you could tell. Then he slipped, and all the Jack Daniels went down the control panel. So that was the end of him! He'd completely ruined the control panel. After waiting ten days, he came in, tripped, into the control panel... That was it! Back to his room. In those days you always*

needed a clown to pick on, and he was the one we picked on. Then he would start to... I don't know what drugs he was doing, but he was hallucinating... so he would stay in his room. Then he would come out at 8.00 in the morning until 3.00 in the afternoon. We got up at 3.00 in the afternoon, and worked all the way through to 6.00 or 7.00 in the morning. So we never saw him! He used to keep his door bolted. Then he started putting up crucifixes. Then he started obtaining all these flowers. We got into his room one day when he wasn't there, and there must have been a thousand flowers, and about twenty-five crosses up! Because he thought the devil was coming after him. So we thought, Cozy and I: "Right, let's really get him!" (laughter) *And Cozy and I together... that was really nasty! 'Cause we had a truce on each other, because that got out of control, too. We thought: "We'll scare the life out of him!" So, we were in this scary place to start with - nobody would actually go to the toilet alone, that's how scary it was. People would be like* (timid voice): *"Anybody feel like going to the toilet?"* (laughter) *"Yeah, I'll go with you." Two guys would go together... one would be looking around. It was so weird, because they were all so petrified of this place! Chopin's ghost was there. So, we used to do things to Tony's room.*

What did we do? We had it worked out that we'd play the tape across the studio to make out that we were actually recording. So Tony would think that we were recording, but in actual fact we were all hiding to get him! 'Cause we knew he would come out of his room. He would go: "Oh, I hear them playing... I'll go and help myself to a cup of tea." 'Cause we were across the courtyard. But it was the 24-track we started up, with us playing. Meanwhile, I was on top of the roof with Cozy, and we got this big 4 x 12 (plank of wood) *ready to smash through his bedroom window at the precise time that the lights were put out - it was synchronised. And we knew that he'd run for the door, and as he would open his door this other 4 x 12 would hit him in the head. Because it would have a piece of string tied to the door. He opened his door to run out, because he thought that the "Exorcist" was coming in through the window, and the wood hit him in the head! And we had it all synchronised. We were crazy! The music started up... Cozy and I were looking out of this other bedroom window, we'd got this big long battering ram so we could lean across the roof and go "smash"! Smashed his bedroom window. Now he would think the devil's coming to get him... because he could hear us playing... the lights went out, and of course he opens his door, and the string pulls and the thing hits him in the head. This is all in the darkness. But that was just one of the things we did to him. After that, he thought we were out to kill him. We used to heat up things. It was like he was in jail... and he'd be given his food - the cook would go up with his food, 'cause he wouldn't eat with us - the cook would go up and forget the utensils. And, of course, I'd go up with a pair of pliers and I'd heat up the knife until it was white hot, then slip it under the door... "Oh, thanks a lot." Then you'd hear: "Aaarghh!"* (laughter) *It was things like that that got me a bad name. It was funny, because Cozy was neutral at this point, before this... and then we went out playing football - because we were there to record so it's natural that we were playing football - and we came back and there were eggs all over my door. I was (staying) next to Cozy. And I went... aah, it was obviously Tony Carey, thrown eggs all over my door and ran away. So what did I do? I went downstairs, got my eggs, came back up, and threw them at Cozy's door. And you're thinking why did I do that? I went down to have dinner with Cozy. We were both eating away, and I'm going: "You know, that bastard threw eggs all over my door?" He's going: "Serves you right... for getting on the wrong side of Tony Carey... who's an idiot, and so are you!" I said: "Well, your door's got the same thing." And he went: "What? There's eggs on my door?" I said: "Yes. My door and your door! So he did both of us." "Carey! Carey!" And you could hear Tony in the distance: "It wasn't me!" And he* (Cozy) *went up and killed him, basically. But Cozy didn't find out that it was me. Tony Carey was saying: "Well, I did Ritchie's room, but I didn't do your room." "No, you did my room as well." I knew that the best thing for him was to get Cozy on his case. I wouldn't have to do anything. I just carried on eating. I could leave the whole thing to Cozy, and sure enough, Cozy just gave him hell! Cozy then, I think, threw everything he could find through his (Carey's) bedroom window. And, of course, Tony Carey couldn't say anything. "I didn't do it. I didn't do it."* But who else would do that to Cozy?

(Bloom) Did Cozy play tricks on you as well?
Yes, of course. I caught him coming up a ladder one day. (laughter) *I went into my bedroom and I heard this* (imitates tapping at the window). *"Wait a minute!" I crept to the window, pulled back the curtains, and there was Cozy creeping up the ladder. He was gonna destroy my room. I've forgotten what I did... I went: "Boo!" or something. "Aaagghh!" Crash! Bang! And he ran away. And next day he said: "That wasn't me." But there were a lot of stories like that. There were some great places that we played at. That one with Cozy in Don Airey's room... "There's the ghost!"*

Can you take the practical jokes as much as you can give them?
Oh yeah! It's just that Cozy would overdo it. It was like overkill. Have you ever heard this story about Cozy in Gelsenkirchen? He climbed to the thirteenth floor, went with the fire extinguisher into the wrong room, sprays this fire extinguisher, then sneaks back to his own room. (laughter) *The next day, this guy's in hospital... and it wasn't even one of our crew. He'd got the wrong room! He'd got this businessman. He was in hospital for two days... and nearly died!*

Cozy was a real daredevil...
Oh yeah! Unbelievable! We used to call him Spiderman. I've seen that guy on top of a roof, carting furniture out of peoples' bedrooms. I mean... this doesn't make sense... he's taken armchairs out of the window, climbed over the roof, with armchairs and things like that. I wouldn't have believed it if I hadn't seen it with my own eyes. And he did it to Colin Hart - the roadie with Deep Purple - have you met him? I remember this one night - we would take tablets to help us to sleep - and I remember saying to him: "I bet you couldn't finish that case of beer." And he actually went: "Okay!" It was like the Young Ones. And he had every beer in the whole crate! "I've done it." We carried him across the courtyard and put him to bed, and he stayed there for two days! (laughter) *That was Colin Hart. It was Colin Hart when we were in a little room where we used to congregate round the big fire, warming ourselves up. Cozy's taking the furniture out of Colin's room, 'cause - no one ever locked their rooms - but Colin had locked his room, thinking that nobody could get up to his window because it was thirty feet up. Cozy got over the roof, in through the window... was now taking all his furniture out via the window over the roof. But Colin was looking out of the window at him, watching him, and drinking! "What's that sod doing in my room?" And I'd been sent to get him to look the other way! But it was too late. Colin had seen Cozy. "The bastard. What's he doing with my furniture?" I went: "Oh shit! He's caught him." He said: "I know what I'm gonna do - I'm gonna let him do it." He just watched him. He was actually drinking away, watching Cozy take all his furniture out of the room over the rooftop. Then he'd appear at the rooftop again, go along the gutter, take some more furniture. And it was amazing! And Colin's just watching! Then two-and-a-half hours later, Cozy comes in: "Oh, it's a bit cold outside." Colin's like: "Now you can put it all back." Cozy's like: "What?" "All the furniture I've just seen you take out of my room, take over the roof... you can put it all back now." Cozy was like: "Oh shit!"* (laughter) *This guy had spent two-and-a-half hours scaling the roof. And he thought it would have a great effect, 'cause Colin wouldn't be able to figure out how the hell anybody got into his room.*

He was a character.
Yes - when you were on his good side. There were extremes. I think he had a sugar problem. When we were together in Switzerland or France (France but on the Swiss boarder. Ed) *in a castle, doing 'Down To Earth'... we had no singer. I said: "I wouldn't mind a bar of chocolate." He said: "What would you like?" "What do you have?" "Come into my room and I'll show you." I went into his room, and he had a big chest with three or four drawers. He pulled out the top drawer and there must have been two hundred Mars bars! Fry's Chocolate Cream... second drawer! Maltesers? I'm going: "My God!" I hadn't seen that many sweets in my mother's shop - she had*

a confectioners store - he had about one thousand pound's worth of chocolates! I'd never seen anything like it. And I think that was his downfall. That sugar thing....

Swindon was his team. I would be Bristol Rovers. 'Cause I was like the underdog. I didn't want to be with a fancy team that was just in the area. I was born in Weston, so Bristol was the nearest thing. Bristol Rovers. The only time I spoke to Cozy was when he'd give me the score of Bristol Rovers. Then we'd go back to hating each other. "Bristol Rovers lost today." I wasn't really interested, but he was very interested. He'd be picking it up on his long wave (radio). Don Airey was there. Don was always looking for Cozy! I wrote a whole sketch on this, which I still have. It's very boring to anybody who wasn't there. But we were in this incredible castle - again! To make a change we were in a castle. And we never got any work done. The first day, we found out that the singer we had recruited for the job couldn't sing above a top A. So that killed any song. So we sent him away. We then had to get other singers... so we were auditioning other singers. And it was costing two thousand dollars a day for the mobile (studio) that was already there. So we were in a castle spending a fortune, with the mobile there, and we didn't have a singer. So singers were flying into Geneva, coming to the castle - being driven to the castle by Colin - who would go through customs every day, going in and out. And the people were going: "What are you doing?" Eventually it was: "Hello, Mr. Hart, go on through." And he'd bring in another singer. And one singer once... we'd always come down for breakfast at one o'clock in the afternoon, and there'd always be a new guy sitting at the breakfast table. Once we had this Italian waiter who was a singer. He actually joined another band who became popular; I can't remember their name. But this one time I came down, and this singer was sitting at the end of the table. He looked like a wrestler! He was the new singer that we were gonna try out that day. And we'd always go through "Mistreated" - as a hard song to sing. Here we go again. "Ready, Cozy?" (Sings the riff). Points at the guy: "You're in." (Sings the first line in an extremely feeble voice, to much laughter) I just doubled up laughing! He was absolutely dreadful. But he looked like the Incredible Hulk. "How can we tell this guy he's awful?" I did the manly thing: "Oh, I've just got to go and do something. I'll be back." I ran away! Cozy's now playing on his own with Don. We had to tell him he was useless. I always remember running away, seeing Cozy holding his stomach and trying to play. It was so funny! That was in the good days. Then there were the bad days, when there was the ping pong tournament. The band, instead of recording, realised that ping pong was much more important. So, all the road crew and the band started playing ping pong. Everybody got into this ping pong tournament. Of course, I was out, because I hated ping pong straight away. But they became obsessed with it, to the point where: "Are we going to do any recording today?" Roger would always say that... Roger Glover. "I think we should record something today, lads." And everybody would be like: "Oh... but there's ping pong!" (laughter) Roger's going: "Oh yeah, right. We'll do that some other time." And the ping pong tournament became really intense.

Was Cozy into it as well?

Oh - Cozy was running the ping pong tournament! (laughter) That, and the Mars bars... Everybody used to get so brought down if you mentioned recording. Everybody was into their own thing. "We're going to record today." "Oh, but we don't have a singer. We'll do it tomorrow." Any excuse to get around it. And we stayed there for about two or three weeks. And Colin Hart used to come down every morning - every afternoon - and his hair would be wet. He was in a room - this was an authentic castle - there were something like two or three really good rooms, the other rooms were really bad. His room leaked, so as soon as it rained, the rain would come in on his head, and he'd come down in the morning: "I've had enough of this, this is too much... I can't take any more of this!" And I'd take one look at him, and he'd be like a drowned rat, soaked from the rain coming in through the roof. "It's not funny!" "It's incredibly funny!" "It's not funny! I'm not gonna stand for it any more!" It was so funny - like the Young Ones... just like the Young Ones. And he would look at me, and his hair was all over the place, soaked. Then he thought... some girl came from Norway - his girlfriend - came to stay with us for a weekend - Colin Hart - in his *room. So she came in, they went straight up to his bedroom... so we all took turns to hammer on his door for fifteen minutes! "Colin! Colin! Colin!"* (knocking) *We did this for the whole weekend. And the man was destroyed!* (all laughing) *Not only the water, but also this banging on the door. His girlfriend left! She came down, like a nervous wreck, and she ran out. Of course, to us it was incredibly funny, but it wasn't funny to him. Completely ruined the whole thing. I don't know if you've ever had someone knocking on your door every fifteen minutes! He was not a happy man. Then Raymond* (D'addario, crew member) *appeared. It was two weeks into staying, and Raymond appeared. I didn't even know he was in the castle. "What are you doing here?" "I'm staying here." "What? Where?" How strange. I didn't know Raymond was here... It's a long story... It gets more and more involved... Mrs. King! We didn't have a cook, so Cozy brings along Mrs. King, who's going to be the chef, 'cause we didn't have a chef to cook the food. So she came over, and her husband had died about six months previously. So when Cozy said: "This is Mrs. King, our new chef"... "Ah, hello Mrs. King." "Well, my husband always used to say that... before he passed away... and he used to say...". And we used to feel really sorry for her. Until you'd heard it ten times! After about three days, every singer who'd come in would get the Mrs. King treatment, which would be: "My husband has just died, and you know what, life is too short... so I take these tablets to help me to go to sleep...". And she favoured Cozy! Every time we'd go to the fridge, try to touch any milk, she'd go: "That's Cozy's milk; he's got to have fresh milk for his corn flakes." And we'd go: "Well, do you have any other milk?" "No, we don't. 'Cause Cozy's not up yet! Maybe Colin can go out and get some milk. But that's Cozy's. And you know what he's like if he doesn't have it fresh, and it's opened." We were like: "What the hell's this all about?" And the bass player we had - I've forgotten his name - I did a session with him...*

Jack Green?

Jack Green. Such a harmless guy. Every time he would go to the fridge - he's a part of the band - he'd open the fridge to look for maybe a piece of cheese, and Mrs. King would go: "What are you doing?" "I thought I'd have a piece of..." "No you don't touch that... that's Cozy's cheese!" "Sorry, sorry!" And she'd close the door again. Until I caught her... "Wait a minute... you can have whatever you want, you know?" She's going: "Well, that's Cozy's. Cozy will get upset!" "Well, sod Cozy!" And then Don (Airey) *would always enter the castle with: "Have you seen Cozy?" We're like: "No, I haven't seen him, no." And then about three hours later: "Has anybody seen Cozy?" "No, haven't seen him, Don." And this went on and on and on... after about the third or fourth day you'd be sitting there having breakfast, Don would come in: "Have you seen Cozy?"* (Speaking through clenched teeth): *"No, I haven't fucking seen Cozy. What is it with you and Cozy?" Have you seen Cozy? It was always that... he would open the door... "Have you seen Cozy?" "Get out!" Of course, we started to hate Don! Have you seen Cozy? He would do that five or six times every day! "Have you seen Cozy?" "What's the problem here?" It was really getting irritating after a while, you know. 'Cause Colin would be sitting there with his hair soaking wet, saying: "I can't take any more of this!" And there's Don coming in: "Have you seen Cozy?" And the local henchman at the end of the table was the new singer for the day. And Mrs. King going: "Well, my husband died, you know..." It was amazing! I've got it all written down. Every time I read it I cry with laughter! But nobody else would find it funny, because they don't know the people involved. I wrote it down as a diary... Day One: we arrive. Day Two: woke up, had breakfast, spoke to Mrs. King about her husband...* (laughter), *Don asked where Cozy was, saw our new singer and was told that he'd just scaled the walls... made a fire... And something like: Then it was time to eat... had dinner, became very tired, put the fire out, went to bed. Day Fourteen: met Mrs. King talking about her husband, Don was looking for Cozy... And it was like... the way it was done was very funny, to me.* (Candice whispers something about drugs) *Oh - that was Glenn Hughes. We were in Clearwell Castle, in 1974. We'd just got Glenn Hughes in the band, with David Coverdale. And he was always taking drugs... anything...*

Even at that time?

Oh yeah! Apparently his American girlfriend had just sent him something in the mail. And he didn't hesitate... he just popped it in his mouth straight away. Didn't know what it was! Just took it. And then I remember playing at rehearsals in this room, and then Glenn... We were going: "Well shall we play it in A or in B? Let's keep it in B... Jon, what do you think, B minor?" He's going: "Yeah." And I noticed Glenn was now going underneath the drum kit, and I'm looking at him like... oh, he's obviously lost something down there. I'm going: "Okay, Jon, so we'll keep it in B, and we'll not have that harmonic part... where are we going to put the bridge?" Now, Glenn has gone behind the drum kit, and he's making these wailing noises (demonstrates) *And every now and again I'd look over, then just play. And then he came up from behind the drum kit, and came up to me and went: "Ritch! Tell me! Tell me! Is my head getting bigger?"* (laughter) *"Be honest with me!" I'm going: "What?" "Be honest with me, Ritch. Tell me. My head's getting small." And then Jon comes along: "It's alright Glenn, it's okay... let's go for a walk." "Ritch! Ritch! Is my head getting bigger?" I don't know if his head's getting bigger. What the hell's going on here? I couldn't understand. I didn't know he'd taken these drugs. They told me afterwards. David Coverdale's like* (sings): *"Baby, baby, baby..." "My head's getting bigger!" I was like: "Christ, does he have to practice saying that word "baby"?" I don't know why he had to practice that word "baby". "Baby, baby..." "My head's getting bigger!" And then there's Jon Lord. "Hello, Jon." "Ritch - put it there!"* (imitates shaking hands) *"Okay, let's play something... so what did you think of that, Jon?" "Ritch - put it there!" "Baby, baby, baby..." "My head's getting bigger!" Paicey's going: "Why have we got so much melody in it?"* (laughter) *"Why do we have to keep changing chords?" "Ian, it's called melody." "Get rid of the melody - it's the drums that count. Without the drums it'd be nothing." It was very odd. It was!*

So, Jack Green was in Rainbow... playing bass?

Yeah, playing bass.

'Cause he sings as well, doesn't he?

Yeah, Jack's a really nice guy.

So Roger was there, just producing at the time?

Producing. Then Roger went on bass. But it was so funny to see everybody running through the castle. Roger would say: "Should we start recording, then?" "Aah... ping pong tournament!" And everybody went back to running through the castle, 'cause the ping pong tournament was on. Forget the recording. Roger was the new producer, and he would go: "Okay." It was so funny. It was excellent. We never got anything done. And then - we got Graham Bonnet in. This is where Graham Bonnet makes his entrance. We'd been told: "That guy in The Marbles... he's the best, he's fantastic!" We got hold of him, tracked him down... Roger's talking to the producer: "Do you know Graham Bonnet? What's he like in the studio?" "Brilliant!" "As a guy?" "Fantastic!" "So what's the catch? Can he sing above a top C?" "Oh yeah. He can sing an F sharp above a top C." So Roger's going: "Well, what's the catch here?" 'Cause he could sense that there was something missing. The producer at the other end in London's going: "He's great... great singer." But there was a "but", but you didn't hear it. So we had him up, flew out. Graham Bonnet comes in, starts singing... he was great! He did 'Mistreated', did it really well. I started talking to him. And then we started recording with him. And Graham's going: "I can't sing." I'm going: "Why not?" "I have to be in a studio." We're going: "But we're in a castle in the middle of France, it's fantastic! The ambience is unbelievable. You can't sing?" He's going: "No. I've got to be in the studio." It was supposed to be the other way round - I can't really sing in a studio but I could sing in a castle in France - a real castle. This guy couldn't sing in a castle in France. He had to be in a dirty little studio somewhere before he could sing! That was the first thing with him. Then that got out of control. "I'm not feeling too well today." We're going: "We'll do it tomorrow." Then the next day came, then the next and the next, and it went on and on and on... We used to ask Graham how he was: "Hey, Graham, how are you doing?" "Oh, I feel a bit strange." "Do you?" "Yeah, I feel really weird today." "Oh. Why's that?" "I don't know, I just feel weird." Colin would go: "Have you eaten?" And he'd go: "That's it! I'm hungry!" (laughter) *He actually said that in Denmark. Colin hit him across the head and went: "Come on, we're going to eat." I went: "What the hell was that?" And then he gets in the restaurant and apparently he sits there and... he's a vegetarian, but apparently he doesn't like vegetables!* (laughter) *He (Colin) goes: "What do you want?" "Ahem, I want a beer." They give him a beer. "Well... I want an omelette." And if they take more than two minutes to bring the omelette, he goes: "I'm not hungry any more... don't want it." "Okay." So he has more beers, and that's the end of his meal. That was Graham! So he fitted in really well with everybody else going: "Oh, my head's getting bigger" and everything else. And the haircut! "Graham - your hair's too short. The band... people that follow us like long hair." "I used to have long hair." "Okay, but you don't have long hair any more - it's very short and you look like a cabaret singer. Can you please grow your hair?" "I cut it off." "Right." At first it was like Mrs. King. So... by the time we were in Newcastle - that would be in 1980, 1979 - Newcastle City Hall - we had a watch on him. We actually had a guard on his door. Colin Hart was on his door, to make sure he didn't go out to get his hair cut. It was actually getting down to the back of his collar, and it was just beginning to be acceptable. Otherwise we'd go out on stage and be crucified because we'd gone out on stage with our new singer who had short hair. They're gonna hate that! You know what he did? He jumped out of the window, ran off and had a haircut!* (laughter) *So it came to showtime, we went on stage and the guy's hair was up here* (indicates with his hand). *And I'm looking at the back of his head - like a military-style haircut - and Colin was saying: "Can you believe it? He got out of the back window to have his hair cut!" He did. But I was so close to taking my guitar off and going "whack" across the back of his head. I was so angry! I'm so glad I didn't. But I was being pushed there... I was really being pushed.*

Is that where Roger's quote came from: "God gave you a great voice, but took away everything else"?
That's right. Oh yeah. Graham was always sick. So we'd send him down to Miami for a holiday to get over the cold. He came back and said that the air conditioning down there was so heavy that he's got an even worse cold in Miami! (laughter). *It went on and on and on. Can't sing this. Can't sing that. I said: "Graham, do you want to go out? Let's go to a pool hall and shoot some pool." "I don't play pool." "Okay, do you want to play some football?" "No, I don't like football." "Okay. What do you like? Swimming? What do you actually like?" He'd go: "I like my dog." "Great... you like your dog!" I said, "What do you actually like to do?" He said: "I like to run with my dog on the beach." Great! 'Cause we couldn't seem to get anything out of this guy. It was either "I've done that" or "I can't do this" or "I used to have long hair".... And what made me laugh was... the management called me up, and apparently when he went back to his dog - it was a big sheepdog, olde English sheepdog - he went back... His name was Barry, this dog. He went back to Barry, and Barry didn't recognise him... and bit him!* (All laughing) *I thought that was really funny! He went home to Barry, and Barry bit him...* (pauses) *The guy had a great voice... he could get up to F sharp.*

You liked his voice?
Well, no, not really. But it was better than the wrestler and the Italian waiter.

I thought he pushed his voice too far sometimes.
Yeah, he did. When we got Joe in, 'cause we wanted Joe, he (Bonnet) *said: "I'm not leaving." He wouldn't leave the band. I said: "Right. We're gonna have two singers on stage." And he went: "Well, I'm leaving then!"* (laughter) *He would not leave until we said he had to sing with Joe Lynn Turner. And Joe... Joe's a great guy. I like Joe. But Joe's very effeminate. Of course, we took him*

on stage in Europe, and I took him backstage, hauled him by the throat and said: "Stop that pansying! You're not Judy Garland!" He was doing this (imitates), *much like the guy with Van Halen.*

You were obviously aware that the fans weren't really warming to him?
Well, yes. I remember playing Leeds, and the place was jam-packed, and all the fans were going: "Ritchie... yeah!" And they were going: (imitates gestures being made to JLT). *And he's doing this across stage* (imitates JLT waving to fans). *I said: "Joe...", when I pulled him backstage, "You've got to stop that, or they're gonna kill us!"*

I think one of the best things you did to Joe was on the last night of the UK tour in about 1981, the 'Difficult To Cure' tour. You left Joe on stage to play the lead on his own.
I can't remember that. Really?

Yes. He was looking around with panic on his face.
The best thing we did to him was in France. We played France - this miserable... it was an outdoor gig. And, of course, France being so organised, as we know, there wasn't a roof. So it's now raining, and people are sitting in the rain watching us. There were only about 800 people in a 3000-seater arena. And it was such a miserable event. I didn't even bother changing. I remember thinking: "I'm gonna hate this... I hate France... I hate being here... just don't wanna play!" Playing away... Joe does his 'No Release' part, where he goes: 'No Release', and he usually gets the audience going, and we back off a little bit, then we come back. So what we did was... he's going: 'No Release', and starts hand-clapping, doing his improvisation bit. So I said to the drum and bass players: "Come on... we're going, we're leaving!" So we go off the stage, and Joe's on his own... doesn't know he's on his own... doing this (clapping) *to the audience, going: "Yeah, yeah, yeah." And they're sitting there in the rain, going* (glum faces with no expression)... *nothing! He's* (clapping and singing), *they're* (nothing) - *you know the French, all smelling of garlic. So we're now off stage, we're all off stage, right? Joe now goes... he looks around... then: 'No Release.' So we get down into the orchestra pit, and there's all these vegetables - perfect! I don't know why there were vegetables... it's France. We picked up all these tomatoes. We're now in the orchestra pit... now Joe is singing to the audience, but he can't really see because the lights are on him. We then started throwing the tomatoes at him. The audience meanwhile is still going* (arms folded, glum faces). *They didn't know what was happening. Joe didn't know it was us in the orchestra pit, throwing things. Now he starts swearing at the audience: "You bastards! You French bastards!" And he's now picking up tomatoes, and throwing tomatoes at the audience, who are going: "We're not gonna take this!" They now start to throw things at him! And it's still raining. Then Joe goes: "Oh!... it's the band!" It was too late then! He had the whole audience in uproar. So it was great! That was a funny event. To see his face! "No Release"... smack! I loved that! That was hilarious. He had no idea it was us in the orchestra pit.* (pauses) *I remember another time with Rainbow in Paris, or France somewhere, and the audience were so boring - it was about the third number - I got on drums, Cozy got on guitar, and we all started playing 'Peter Gunn'* (imitates) *The audience actually went crazy. They wouldn't clap because they thought we were awful. And then we did 'Peter Gunn' and they thought we were wonderful! Isn't that amazing? Only in France! And they're having the World Cup there! I read in an English newspaper yesterday which said that they can't get the tickets organised. Nobody knows what the hell is going on!*

They have sixty phone operators to sell a million tickets, and nobody can get through.
That's right! They won't answer the phone. Can you believe that? It's France. (pauses)

(More drinks are passed round, and Ritchie veers back on to the subject of Ian Gillan...)
Ian Gillan's always doing it backstage... He hires nannies and things to look after his kids, then

he comes down stark naked. I used to hear about it in rehearsals. "Another nanny left me today, she couldn't take it." And I'd be playing... "Couldn't take what?" "Oh, sitting there naked, she didn't like it... took offence to it and left." "What are you doing, naked?" That was his "thing", to be naked. He loves being naked!

Didn't you once hang someone up from the rainbow naked?
We did. Erik Thomsen (Danish tour promoter).
(Candice) *Didn't you do something to Roger?*
Roger we actually tied up in a Marshall amplifier case and left him on the Severn Bridge. (laughter) *He was the bass player - you had to do that to bass players. We went back for him later, and he was wriggling, trying to get out. We could see this wriggling Marshall thing! It's Roger Glover! We should have left him... But Gillan used to sit in the back seat and was always trying to play with him* (Glover). *It was unbelievable! Roger would be sitting there, and I'd be in the front - we'd all travel together in the same car - and I'd hear this: "Hey! Get off!" I'd look back, and Gillan's going: "Oh, just let me touch you, Roger." Roger's going: "Get off!" Jon would be reading a book. 'Cause Jon was there... the whole band... reading another book. Paicey would be counting the money.* (laughter) *"What's he doing?" And he was actually always trying to play with him! Very strange! Until this one day... we kept hearing: "Get off, Ian!". And I thought it was funny. But one day I looked round, and Roger's got his trousers half way down - Gillan's pulled his trousers down - and is now trying to perform oral sex... do the Bill Clinton on him, you know? I'm like: "What the hell is going on in here?" Of course, at this point Roger went berserk! "Stop the car! You pervert! Get off!" I'm going: "What the hell's going on here?"*

It must take quite a lot to make Roger angry.
Oh yeah. 'Cause at first Gillan would do that (does imitation of him doing kissing gestures). *Roger would go: "Don't start!" "Just a little cuddle, Rog." And then it would go worse. And now I'm thinking back... was that funny or was that a show or what the hell was that about?*

(Bloom) Roger got angry with me once.
Did he?

Birmingham - you know, the incident with the water? After the show I was talking to him. Some friends of Gillan were there: "What happened at the beginning of the show with the guitarist?" I just piped in: "I thought that was really funny." Roger said: "You thought that was funny?" He was getting really angry. I thought he was gonna hit me!
It was funny in a way. (Looks at Candice) *You know the real story.*

I'd never seen Roger so angry.
I always remember Roger, in this castle in France, the same place that Don was always looking for Cozy. So... now... I had to share a bathroom with Roger. And Roger would always go into the bathroom, and I'd hear him. This one night: "Let's play a trick on him... wait until he goes to the bathroom." And I had this big long pipe that I was going to wedge in-between the door and the wall, so that he couldn't get into his own room. But I had to wait until he went to the bathroom. It was about fifteen feet long, this pipe. I heard him go into the bathroom. "Right!" Ran out, picked up the pipe, ran down to his bedroom, burst open the door, walked in with the pipe... I was going to wedge it against the door, so he couldn't get in. "Right... right..." Going in with this pipe. And suddenly, I kind of looked over to the bed, and Roger's sitting on the bed. He's reading a book! And he looked up. (all laughing) *I went: "Oh! Right!" And I went back out of the room again with the pipe.* (laughing) *And... the way Roger tells it is very funny. He said: "I was just sitting there, and all of a sudden I saw the end of a pipe come into the room! Christ! I know this place is haunted, but a pipe!..." And then he saw me at the end of the pipe. Of course, I came in, then straight out again. "Oh! Wrong room!" I couldn't believe he was in bed. I thought he was in*

the toilet. I was gonna play this incredible trick on him. And he's sitting there, sitting up in bed, looking at me.

So who was in the bathroom? Was it Don Airey looking for Cozy?
What happened was... he'd come out of the bathroom, and I thought he was going in. I got it wrong. Of course, I tried to pretend... I was very cool. "Oh, Roger... I'm just..." ... whatever I'm doing. And Don was always looking for Cozy. "No! I have not seen Cozy." Slap! "I don't care about Cozy. Get out of my life!" (pauses) "Have you seen Cozy?" It was really corrupt. "Ping pong, anybody?" "Yeah!" "Recording?" "Nope!" Ping pong! Until Cozy started losing the tournament. And then it's: "Come on guys, this is silly, we've got to start recording."

It took a while to do that album? ('Down To Earth').
Yeah! But I have it all logged. I still find it funny, when I see that diary, 'cause it was definitely a Monty Python sketch. It was just unreal. With Mrs. King. She'd just sit there. "I'll tell you about my husband." "Yes, you've told me about your husband... tell him!" (pointing to someone else) "You know, my husband used to say..." It was like... (grits teeth) "What are you doing in that fridge?" "Just trying to find a piece of cheese." (wimpy voice)

We should run it as a serial in the mag.
Yeah! I must try and dig that out. (Looks at Candice) I think I've showed you that? It is funny, to me, if I see it. I thought it wouldn't be funny to anybody else, unless you knew the band, knew what was going on.

That's often the way with humour. You've just got to be there.
That's right. Like John Cleese with Fawlty Towers. He said that he actually stayed there - that's where he got the idea from.

Farty Owls. "Duck's off!"
That's the funniest programme I've ever seen in my life! I think my favourite sketch is when he's beating up the car.

"I'm gonna count to three..."
It's what everybody does, but we don't admit it. We talk to the car. "Now, you're gonna start... I'm gonna be nice to you, you're gonna start... 'cause if you don't start, I'm gonna beat the hell out of you... so you'd better start!"

I loved the way he was so sarcastic to people, and got away with it. What was the one when his wife was in hospital, and the nurse said: "Are you still here, Fawlty?" "Apparently, yes." "I'll go and fetch the doctor." "You don't need a doctor, you need a plastic surgeon."
"Doctor's coming." "My God, here in a hospital, a doctor?" (laughter) "Talking to me, or is there a dog in here somewhere?"

Apparently, they're (Monty Python) getting back together again.
Are they really?

There was a press conference. They had Graham Chapman's supposed ashes in a box, and they spilt them on the floor at the press conference! (Davies) He stopped it (Fawlty Towers) at the right time.
You could see at the end that he was starting to run out of ideas. And it was good that he stopped.

The characters made it. The two old ladies and the major.
His wife used to stick out like a sore thumb. Who else was there? Manuel! Apparently he really got hit on the head with a frying pan. Knocked him out! 'Cause he was explaining it on television over here, how he (John Cleese) hit Manuel, but he hit him too hard, and actually put him out.

(pauses) *That was Jon Lord's ambition... to be "the major." "I want to be the major." That's the way he is now. Major Lord. Shaking hands. "I hate you!" "Put it there."*

Have you seen ("Monty Python and) the Holy Grail"?
I don't like... the best one was in "The Life Of Brian" or "The Meaning Of Life", where he does the sketch where he's dead. The Grim Reaper comes to the American... they're having an American dinner. "Who is it dear?" "It's the Grim Reaper." Remember it? He walks in, and they're all eating. "Well, hello! Come in!" This skeleton's pointing at people...
The Americans are going: "Mr. Reaper, really glad to meet you!" And the English guy's: "Hello, awfully nice to meet you." And he's: "You English! You're so fucking pompous!" (laughter) I love that bit.
"Do invite him in dear. Does he want a drink? He doesn't look very well." He comes in... he's pointing this finger... That, to me, made the whole film. (pauses) I can't get into Blackadder. Maybe it's the medieval period. I don't like all that stuff. (Laughter).

That's why I thought it would appeal to you.
No. it didn't. You know who was very funny? Jasper Carrot. In the old days.

"Magic Roundabout" was a good Jasper Carrot sketch.
Oh yes, now you're talking... Magic Roundabout, Bill and Ben... I mean, it depends how far back you go...
(Ritchie leaves the table for a call of nature; interview continues with Mark Welch firing the questions to Candice...)

You've told us before about your musical background. So did it come easy when it came to making the record ('Shadow Of The Moon')?
It did, because even though I was singing from the ages of four to twelve, and then doing proper singing classes... I noticed that I would sing to my little sister, who is eight years younger than me; I'd sing her to sleep. She'd fall asleep in the first minute! So I knew I had that power to put people to sleep whenever I opened my mouth. And my friends would ask me to sing to them. But they were at the point where I'd be in my car and my friend would say: "I'm not looking at you, just sing." So I knew that some people in the close circle around me enjoyed my singing.

How was it- working with Ritchie, and then recording?
With Ritchie... when I met Ritchie I didn't meet him as a "singer". He slowly brought me out of my shell. He'd make me sing in front of his friends... But I loved to sing, whether it was to myself or to my friends. And then Ritchie made me sing in front of his friends. And at the Christmas parties and other parties we would have, he'd take out his acoustic guitar and get me to sing. And it was a fun thing, 'cause everybody would get involved. It wasn't just: "The spotlight's on you!" And we're all staring at you and judging you. It was: "Hey everybody, sing along." And it was great. And we'd be doing "It's a Long Way To Tipperary", and it was a lot of fun. So that was my real introduction to singing in front of a crowd - just singing at these parties in such a relaxed and friendly environment. And having Ritchie next to me, whether it's writing lyrics or performing on stage or in the studio, it keeps that kind of relaxed and fun environment.

The 'Shadow Of The Moon' songs began developing way before you actually recorded them. Was that during the Rainbow tour, or even earlier?
It was before the tour. It was before the writing of 'Stranger In Us All.' We wrote a couple of songs while he was in the studio waiting to do the vocal tracks. We did 'Be Mine Tonight.' Up on Long Reach Farm. And 'Ariel' was the first one, and that was supposed to be on our album originally. And then he gave it to Rainbow, and they recorded it on 'Stranger In Us All.' But we never thought that we would record an album like 'Shadow Of The Moon.' We just basically did it for our own

fun purposes. And when we realised that everyone around us really liked to hear these songs... Actually, Ritchie tells this one story where there's a neighbour of ours who's about fifty, and he came up to Ritchie at the end of the night one time, at about 5 o'clock in the morning, and said: "You know, I'm not a fan of yours, I don't really know the Rainbow and Deep Purple stuff, but if you put out an album like this I will buy it." And that's what made Ritchie say: "Okay, this might be a good idea. Because if somebody like that, who doesn't follow me, doesn't know what I'm all about, likes what we're doing together, then maybe there's an audience that will enjoy it too!" And that really clinched it.

The variation of moods in the songs reflects that.

Each one has its own separate identity, every one, even if you have the underlying Renaissance theme, they're also themselves, and to compare one to the other is very difficult. If somebody asks me my favourite track on the album, I can't choose it... depending on the mood... it's kind of like a story. Takes you through all these different emotions and all these different moods and all these different feelings. From the beginning of the day to the end of the day. I don't know how you could choose one particular part... "that's the one I want to play."

That's the strength of the album, because with a lot of albums you hone in on a certain one or two tracks, but on 'Shadow Of The Moon' there's no one track that stands out as being head and shoulders above the rest. Everyone has their own favourites.

Right.

When you wrote 'Shadow Of The Moon' you hadn't performed live on stage. Now that you have performed live, it must have given you a lot of confidence...

It was a scary thing at first...

Yes, but now you know that you can do it, you know that you can perform... So, how has this translated into the writing of new songs, 'cause you must be finding it a little easier?

Well, I think a lot of things have changed. We've changed producer, and even slightly the type of stuff we're doing; (looks at Ritchie) *don't you think?*

(Blackmore) *Yeah.*

'Cause a few tracks now are more like 'Under A Violet Moon', more up-tempo and kind of intense, without crossing the barrier to rock 'n' roll. I'm not a rock 'n' roll singer. That's not me. That's not my voice. That's not what I'm all about.

How easy is it making the new album now that you're more experienced?

Each day it's something new. Whether it's a new audience, or new ways to interpret the song. You're always dealing with something new! So I never feel it's like something I've done before. I feel strange about titles. But I'm having fun.

You must feel like the ideas are bursting out, 'cause you've gone straight back into the studio?

(Blackmore) *Yeah, we have a lot of ideas.*

(Night) *I was saying how many songs we've got already. Each day we sit down... and we decided to write all the titles down, see how far we've got, and how far we still have to go. We've still got like ten tracks to do.*

Obviously having a studio at home is not the same as being in "the studio."

(Blackmore) *That's right. It's taken me a while, but the more I record at home the less intimidated I get. The more I can get into the actual music without thinking that I'm being recorded... although I still go through that... it depends. If I go straight into the studio and I play something straight off, I'm okay. Second time... once I get into the third time around, I start to analyse what I'm doing too much. That's when I lose it. And I can't just keep playing one piece of music more than two times! I don't get bored, I become self-conscious. "I've got my finger there... what the* hell's this?" It all becomes... the first time you play something, it's like "music." "Do that again." "Okay." "And again." Third time! Someone will say: "The fifth bar in you're making a squeaky noise, a buzzing." "Oh!" So the entire performance you're thinking: "Oh, I'd better watch that buzzing." Then you start being very analytical. Analysis paralysis sets in. And it's not music any more!

If the producer said: "Just play it once and we'll record it", would you be happy with that?
Probably not! I did that last night. We were doing 'Katherine Howard's Fate' (new song) ...
(Night) *But you're good at knowing when you've got it right and when you don't. And I think that when you think you've got it right and the producer says: "Do it again", you start going: "Wait a second! What did I miss?"*
(Blackmore) *Last night with Joe* (James, BN's then keyboard player who was producing the second album at that point, but soon had a bust up with Blackmore and walked away from the project, allegedly with the master tapes)... *Joe's very good. He said: "Okay. Happy with that?" I went: "No, not really!" He knew what was wrong with it, but he didn't say "Do it again". He just said: "Are you happy with that?" I went: "Nope!" So it then became my responsibility.*

What about a song like "Possum's Last Dance"? It's only two minutes and forty seconds long, but there's so much work in there... it's so complicated!
Actually it was Rob... had Rob not told me about that song, I wouldn't have done it.

It must have taken a lot of work.
I just had it as an exercise. And he said: "What about "Possum's Last Dance"?" And I said: "What about it?" "It must mean something to someone." It was just an exercise.

Isn't there a story behind that song?
It's down to him (pointing at Rob).
(Night) *Tell the story.*

As printed in *Acoustic Guitar World*. Was he (Rob) the guy that ran over the possum?
Yeah. 'Cause you play certain things, and you need feedback from people around you. He said: "That was good, play that again. What was that?" I'm like: "What was that? Oh that's just a nothing." But I could tell that it must have come across as something worthwhile, or else he wouldn't have bothered saying: "What was that?"

It sounds like several exercises put together...
That's right. It's a very tricky piece to play. I play it differently now, but...

It will be difficult to play live...
No, not at all. We did that in about fifteen minutes. It was a second take. It's only difficult to play if you start to think about what you're playing, 'cause you can go: "Let's record", and you just play. It's when guys go: "Let's do that again." "Okay, we'll do it again." But it's that third time, you go: "I really don't want to play this again; I've played it twice!" But there's a follow-up to "Possum's Last Dance" on our new CD, which is very flash (sings the tune). *It's all orchestrated, too, so it's like overkill flash, you know. Joe Satriani should have a field day with this. The possum's making his return. I don't know what to call it yet.*

'Possum Comes Home'. Sounds like Latin, doesn't it (referring to the scene in Monty Python's 'Life Of Brian', 'Roman's Go Home.')
I'm thinking about "Possum's Peculiar Impromptu." Or something like "He Reaches The Other Side." 'Cause I don't know if I actually killed him that night or not. And that really bothers me. 'Cause I went back there later on, and he wasn't there. So I'm like: "Maybe he got away!" I'm

looking at Mick (Cervino) - *Mick's in the car with me - he's looking at me like: "But I don't eat meat!"* (laughter) *I went: "My God, I've just hit a possum! Aawww…" "But I don't eat meat!" I felt so guilty! I'd hit a possum, and he doesn't eat meat. Our bass player… who can play like you wouldn't believe. This guy is unbelievable! You know how he got the job?* (silence… then in a firmer voice) *You want to know how he got the job?*

Go on…
Right. You should have asked me that. (laughter) *He got the job…*
(Bloom, interrupting) But we don't want to know… but go on… (laughter)
He was a friend of Frank Sinatra's. That's how he got the job. And when Frank said to me: "Who the hell are you?", Mick was right there. "I know who he is." That's how he got the job… But Mick sent me a tape… (looks at Candice) *… how did it go? You tell the story…*
(Night) *Mick sent a tape to the fan club, and it was a videotape, and there was a résumé saying "Reasons why I should play with Ritchie Blackmore."*
(Blackmore) *He went through all this list of reasons, which I didn't listen to. And then: "Play the tape anyway." "I don't want to play the tape." Obviously a moron! "Play the tape anyway."*
(Night) *It sat on a table for five months.*
(Blackmore) *Eventually, cleaning the house: "What the hell is this?"*
(Night) *And he just throws things out, because he can't stand to see them sitting there any more. So we put it in, and it was Mick sitting there, and he played all these incredible things!*
(Blackmore) *He played the Bach "Invention" on the bass!*
(Night) *But played with his own backing track that he had made, and there were all these incredible Bach things. I went: "Oh, he's* (RB) *got to see this!" And his mouth just dropped open.*
(Blackmore) *I'm going: "I don't want to see it! I really don't want to see this guy. Sounds like a loony!" I sat there. "Okay!" It was great!*
(Night) *And it got to the end and he said: "Let's watch that again."*
(Blackmore) *Trouble is with Mick… he can't speak, can't talk! He has no voice.* (Imitates Mick's quiet voice): *"I want to sing on this next track." "No, I don't think we should get into this singing thing, Mick!"* (laughter) *Then* (whispering): *"But I'd like to try."* (Looks at Candice) *Remember? No, he can't sing!*

Was he a last minute addition, because wasn't Jessie going to play bass?
Yes, that's right. She was playing bass. But we're gonna incorporate his little showcase on stage, because he is one amazing bass player. I've never seen a bass player play like that - ever! He's a very nice guy, but he doesn't eat meat… doesn't eat possums! (Looks at Candice) *Remember when we played in Japan?*

Was it weird working with another guitarist?
No, 'cause you could never hear what she was playing! (laughter) *One of these days we'll hear what she's playing.*

You did give her two solos - a solo on two separate nights.
I tried to.

She coped relatively well.
That's right.

You must have been very pleased with the way the tour went.
I was! I was nervous in Spain, the first night, when they advertised it as "ex-Deep Purple", and all the people went: "Aaaarrgghh!" Before we came on stage… all the people shouting and screaming. We walked on with 'Be Mine Tonight', and they're (beating his chest and grunting).

I thought Cologne would be like that. 'Cause it was a rock venue. I could see a lot of the audience thinking: "What is this?"
Exactly! That's what we felt. That's why we won't do clubs again.

Stuttgart was good.
I loved the sound at Stuttgart, the PA... speakers this big (indicates small size with his hands), yet it was like: "What the hell is this PA?" Raymond said: "I've got the name of it." An incredible PA! Perfect! Whereas Cologne was big speakers... We have that all on video, which we will release. And it came out quite well, but... the sound wasn't too good. The video's an hour-and-a-half long. We might mix it with some new stuff.

I heard you were holding it back so people wouldn't have seen it before the next tour. But people will still come anyway!
Yeah. But I wanted it to be as good as possible, and the video... the sound in places is a bit strange.

Although the venue wasn't great, the music itself was good.
(Night) Yes. All the unplugged stuff came out great.
(Blackmore) (changing the subject) Want to hear a song? If you want to get the guitar and bring it in...

Candy - have you learned to play the hurdy-gurdy yet?
She's getting close; she's doing well.

It's about four months since I saw you...
No! I just got it! We got it two weeks ago from Germany, and we were playing it today - he was playing guitar and I was playing hurdy-gurdy.
(Blackmore) It was amazing!
(Night) It's as big as I am.

(Bloom) We were gonna try and get a crummhorn.
(Welch) I've got a shoe horn! (laughter)
(A discussion follows about the instruments played by Des Geyers Schwarzer Haufen, Blackmore's favourite band)
Some of the stuff (the Geyers music) is really peculiar. Really odd! Some of it moves me so much, other stuff is awful. They wrote some rubbish back in those days too. But David Munrow... committed suicide... the guy was just a professional. He gave it that spirit. He'd take an orchestra and go: "Come on, we're gonna do Renaissance music, but with spirit!" Some of those instruments - sackbutts, crummhorns, regals... There's a thing called a racquet. Amazing stuff! It takes you back to a nobler time.

When you started doing 'Shadow Of The Moon', did you want to do it like that initially? You said then that you weren't sure whether to make it authentic or not.
Well, yes, I still can't do it authentically completely. My thing is to take the emotion from that time, and the music, and play it today. I don't want to play it exactly as it was played then. Although I could sit here and get excited about crummhorns and racquets, but I don't think anybody else would.

So are you looking at it from a commercial point of view?
No. I just want it to be more palatable to the human ear. 'Cause I think that back in those days the tuning was so bad for a start. The tuning was really off the wall. They didn't really tune up. So if you hear a real Renaissance piece, it will be out of tune. I like things to be in tune. The Geyers - have you ever heard them play at all...? You should hear them live. They just play - they don't tune up, they just play... They're still in the 1600s. These men are fantastic. To witness one

of their concerts in a castle, you just never want to go back to reality ever again. That's it! "Let's stay here for the rest of our lives, listen to the Geyers playing... (hums 'The Clock Ticks On')*" Of course, this* (points to beer glass) *has a lot to do with it. They've had four hundred of them! Then you hear it on a record and you go: "Who the hell is that?"*

Was it you who said that they are trying to get a bit more contemporary, and you're trying to go the other way?
That's right. I'm trying to creep a little more in their direction, and they're going: "We're creeping in your direction; do you want to help us out?" And I'm like: "No!"... 'cause they're my heroes. When I first met them I asked: "Do you need a guitar player?" And they said: "No." They had no idea who I was or what I did. "We don't need a guitar player." "Well, I'm going to form my own band. I'll show you!" Now they're going: "Do you want to join the band?" (laughter)

Presumably in the past the medieval thing was a hobby. Now that you're into it professionally, is there a danger that your interest will diminish?
Not that my interest would diminish. But I don't want there to be any pressure. If you make a living by music, whatever that music might be, you're gonna be expected to tour... and the pressure's on!
(Night) *It's the business side of music that creates the pressure.*
(Blackmore) *Yeah!*
(Night) *When we just sit and play at home, then all that is fun and without pressure.*
(Blackmore) *Exactly! And I want to try and keep it that way. That's why as soon as we start touring, and I start seeing the capacities going up and the tour dates coming in, I'm like: "Oh no!"*

The kind of excitement you're feeling now - I think you must have had a similar kind of excitement when making the first Rainbow album (in 1975).
Yeah" That's right. (pauses) *I agree.* (laughter) (At this point, Ritchie gets his acoustic guitar out)

1974 - that's when it hit me with David Munrow. That's what set my mind thinking. But I used to love just listening to it - that was enough. Play rock 'n' roll. Listen to Renaissance music. To actually play it... "no, no, no, can't play it... too sacred!" It's only the last five years I've thought: "Maybe I should play it." Especially when Candice would sing it around the house. What was one of the first tunes that we did? "Renaissance Faire" wasn't it? (plays the tune) *We haven't done that one for a while, have we? That was the one I used to get Cozy, Tony Carey, and everybody to play. He'd go: "Ritchie's happy. We've played his little tune." Because when I saw Cozy in Esbjerg, he said: "I've got your CD... I really like that." And I said: "Do you remember that...?" "Yes, I remember!"* (laughter) *"I remember that!"*

You had the melody way back then?
Oh, yeah.

That's strange, because you say you can't remember tunes you write really quickly. But that obviously stuck in your head.
That's the first one that started it. And this one never had a home (plays 'No Second Chance' melody). *It's just a great little riff. Roger's going: "We should use that." I'm like: "Yeah." This was in '79. And we never did! It was a riff without a home. All these songs could have been anything.* (Plays 'Perfect Strangers' then adds 'No Second Chance' at the end) *I ended everything like that! Yeah! Everything we did would end with that.*

At this point the interview came to a close as Ritchie played songs both old and new (mainly Blackmore's Night) for the next ninety minutes, with accompaniment from Candice.

****

Above: Graham Bonnet, Cozy Powell & Ritchie Blackmore. Rainbow, Vorst National, Belgium 1st Feb 1980.
Below: Ian Paice and Ritchie Blackmore, Manchester, 5th November on Deep Purple's 1993 tour.

Above: Blackmore's Night performing at Burggarten, Rothenburg, Germany, 11th July 2003.
Below: Steve Morse and Don Airey. Deep Purple, Roeselare, Belgium, 7th August 2004.

DON AIREY

Hailing from Sunderland in the North East of England, Don Airey's interest in music, started in much the same way as most of the top rock keyboard players, namely by studying classical piano, which he did from the age of seven. In a professional career that stems back to his time in Cozy Powell's band Hammer in 1974, he has gone on to create one of the most impressive CV's of any keyboard player. Colosseum II, Black Sabbath, Gary Moore, Michael Schenker, Ozzy Osbourne, Thin Lizzy, Whitesnake, Jethro Tull, Judas Priest, UFO and Brian May are just some of the acts that Don has worked with throughout his career. Impressive by any standards, and amongst all that Airey also spent around three years in Rainbow, performing on two of Rainbow's most successful albums, 'Down To Earth' and 'Difficult To Cure.'

At the time this interview was conducted, Don had just done a few gigs with Deep Purple, stepping in for Jon Lord, who was unable to play after sustaining an injury. Don talked about the experience but that part of the interview remained unpublished until now. It makes for fascinating reading, bearing in mind what developed the following year when Airey became a full-time member of Deep Purple.

However, with Lord initially returning briefly to Purple, Don's career reverted to working alongside his former Rainbow colleague, vocalist Graham Bonnet. Bonnet had been touring for a while under the banner of Graham Bonnet's Rainbow, but by the time Don joined, a name change came in the shape of Rainbow Revisited. Or at least that was the way it was billed at Zaks in Wolverton, Milton Keynes on 17th November 2001. Completing the line-up were the the Thunder rhythm section of drummer Harry James and bassist Chris Childs, along with Italian guitarist Dario Mollo. Not only was the loveable James more than capable of Cozy Powell style drumming but Mollo, a huge Blackmore fan, who had also worked with Glenn Hughes, played the Rainbow songs with great style and passion. Thanks to Doogie White, it had been arranged for me to interview both Don and Graham Bonnet, after the gig. First up was Don...

For the uninitiated, could you give a brief overview of what you have been doing over the past few years prior to this band.
I left Rainbow to join Ozzy for four years, then I was in Jethro Tull, had a bit of a solo career, I had two years out of the business in the early nineties when my son was very ill then I came back in with ELO II, Uli Jon Roth, worked with a band called Ten, Colin Blunstone, I've just been working with Deep Purple. I'm always recording with people. I won the Eurovision song contest in 1997, so I'm pretty busy all the time.

Yeah I saw you on that conducting the orchestra. You did a solo project K2, what was the inspiration and thinking behind that?
I don't know I just thought... The inspiration was mountains. I used to do a lot of fell walking. It started being about Everest but ended up doing it about K2, which is a different kettle of fish all together. Quite a weird experience all in all.

Would I be right in saying that it was due to your involvement with Cozy Powell's Hammer that you got into Rainbow?
Well it was the third time they had asked me to come and try out for the band, and I thought this time I couldn't say know so I went over and I kind of hit it off with Ritchie. It was great to see Cozy again. It was just the three of us sat in a studio for three weeks just working out 'Down To Earth', that's where it all came from.

So you had auditioned for the band earlier?
No, no. I'd had the phone call "would you come and audition" but I never could. So that was the third time, so I thought I'd better go and see what was on.

This is also something that has perplexed me over the years, who was actually around then. It was obviously before Graham arrived but was Roger not there then?
No there was a bass player called Clive Chaman who was in the Jeff Beck Group and was in Cozy Powell's Hammer as well. So Clive was there and then Clive had something else on. I don't think they felt he was quite right for the band so it left just the three of us. Then you know singers would appear and come and go. There was a very nice guy called Ralph Thomson and he was quite good but he just wasn't up to it. Then we started recording the album without a singer. We had about seven or eight come over. Pete Goalby, Marc Storace, there was one terrifying man who was from the North East and he'd been in the SAS. A very nice man but he just assumed he'd got the gig, and he was walking around going "I'm really gonna enjoy this." and of course he never even got to sing because it was obvious he wasn't cut out for it.

It's interesting you say that because Ritchie said there were hordes of people coming over to audition as singers. He said one of them looked like a huge wrestler guy but he had a really weedy voice.
May have been the same guy.

He also claimed that Jack Green was around at the time.
Oh Jack Green, yeah. Well Jack Green didn't do much of anything I have to say. He was more of a guitarist than a bass player. He couldn't really play bass. It was a difficult situation. I think eventually when Graham came in he just said "what the hell's going on here, why don't we get Rog to do it, it would be much better." Ritch went "Oh all right then", that's how Roger got in thank God.

Roger was obviously just there to produce at the time.
Yeah that's why Roger came in. I knew when we had a rehearsal with Roger just after Christmas in England just the four of us playing it was the most incredible experience. What a band.

Ritchie has told some incredibly amusing stories about the period when you were recording the album in the Chateau. He reckons he kept a diary of the times. He said the band was more interested in playing Ping-Pong- that there was a Ping-Pong tournament going on and not much music was being written.
Nah.

I know he likes to embellish stories.
I read that and I thought no, that wasn't true. We used to work all day and he didn't play Ping-Pong and I think he felt left out because it got quite exciting! There was a big elimination. It was after dinner every night and I was the favourite to win but lost very surprisingly in the final to Amy, Ritchie's girlfriend. She was a very good player. I mean she was the ringleader of it.
The main problem with doing 'Down To Earth' was that we didn't have a singer. We just had a load of riffs and it wasn't until the fifth week that it suddenly all came together, very, very quickly. We did eight tracks in a week, or nine actually, very, very quickly.

Were you familiar with the previous incarnations of the band prior to joining?
Yeah, well I always kept in touch with Cozy you see. He always sent me the records when they came out.

So playing some of the older songs wasn't a problem?
No, no. I was a big fan of the band.

What are your recollections of Donington?
Well that was an amazing thing. I think the whole thing was the band's idea as far as I remember and Cozy wanted to do it at racing circuit so we picked Donington. We arrived on the Thursday and this deluge had opened and there was so much mud it was incredible. Then Cozy was trying out his explosives and he blew the PA out of the park really. So that was a bit of a disaster so anyway, come the day there was still plenty of mud but it didn't rain. There were some very memorable performances by different bands. April Wine were outstanding. Scorpions were good. Judas Priest were thrilling, and I think Rainbow that day were just extraordinary. It's funny Graham and I watched... a guy called Bob Richards, who's the drummer with Man sent me a video he'd got of Donington and when Graham first came over we watched it completely stunned at how good it was.

Was that just the half hour thing that was broadcast?
Yeah. It's a stunning piece of work.

What would be your view on somebody releasing the whole concert?
Well I don't think anybody's got it have they?

Haven't they?
No.

I'd imagine it's in the vaults somewhere.
It's long gone.

You reckon?
Yeah, it's lost. I was asking Roger about it actually recently, and it's lost. It's a great shame. The pity was the band went off stage and broke up. It was an amazing band and it was never even half as good again. I don't know why Cozy left. It just wasn't really any good with Bobby Rondinelli. and Graham couldn't sing... said I can't sing to that and he left, and I kind of felt all on my own then! The 'Difficult To Cure' year wasn't very enjoyable really. It was hard work.

Well I got the impression there was more of your involvement on 'Difficult To Cure' though.
Well, no, I mean I got more credit for my involvement. I had a lot of input into 'Down To Earth' but it wasn't credited. It's funny actually I've never thought about it much until Graham came back into my life and we thought about doing these songs again. I mean I've never dwelt on Rainbow, never talked about it much actually, not that it didn't mean anything to me.

Well you move on I suppose.
Never look back. I mean some guys spend all their time thinking about what they used to do. Bernie Marsden for example, he just longs to be back in the old Whitesnake, of course it will never happen. But I never felt that about Rainbow, never felt that about any band I've ever been in. I was always glad when it was over! Move onto the next thing.

Regarding the 'Difficult To Cure' tour there are some interesting stories Ritchie has relayed on that. Particularly one incident in France when apparently all the band left the stage and went round the front to the orchestra pit and started throwing tomatoes at Joe Lynn Turner.
Yeah I remember that! I remember the last gig I did with Rainbow. It was in Hawaii and Ritchie's

stack blew up and if that ever happened I used to take over and do a bit of a keyboard interlude. I did a keyboard solo lasting twenty-five minutes! Nearly half an hour, there was no sign of anybody and they'd all gone. Ritchie just went "ah I can't be bothered" and they all went back to the hotel and I was left on my own. Nobody came on to stop me. I was getting desperate I was playing 'Hawaii Five-O' and 'Hawaiian Love Chant' and eventually it just came to a stop. It wasn't very pleasant. When I got back to the... nobody seemed to care very much.

Probably a sign the band was disintegrating.
It was a bit. I mean it lasted another year or two until Ritchie got Purple together and produced that marvellous album.

You like that album then (Perfect Strangers)?
Oh yeah I thought it was brilliant because everybody I knew said, "oh Purple getting back together", I said, "Ritchie must have some great riffs up his sleeve that's all I can say", which of course he did.

He said he was working the title track out in Rainbow. In fact there are some rehearsal tapes of him doing it. I don't know if it was when you were still with the band or not.
I can remember the riff. I can remember that kind of Eastern thing. In fact that was a bit... I think 'Makin' Love.' I think that's how that started off.

It's interesting you mentioned that track because there were a couple of tracks you did tonight., that and 'Bad Girl', which if my memory serves me well, Rainbow never performed live.
No, I mean there are a few. We've also been doing 'Danger Zone.' You know we didn't know what to do really. We didn't want to make it too obvious so we've done three or four tracks that have never been played before.

It's nice to hear them. 'Makin' Love' was always one of my favourites on the album.
It was my father's favourite Rainbow track. He was quite a fan of the band. He used to ask why didn't you play that?

Probably Ritchie didn't want to.
Ritchie didn't want to, no. Well Ritchie never wanted to play 'Since You Been Gone' really. We only played that a handful of times as I remember, and Cozy as well- Cozy didn't like it.

I know Cozy didn't like it, he hated it.
Yeah he did, he hated it.

I think that was one of the reasons why he left the band actually.
I never understood why Cozy left the band. I don't think he did, and I think he scrabbled round for reasons afterwards. After he'd gone beyond the point of no return. I think he thought he would just swan off for a couple of weeks and come back but it was just too late.

I'm sure you must have some anecdotes about Cozy you can relay.
Well, when we were recording in the Chateau in France, I was in this bedroom that was called the Chapel and it was a very spooky room. There were all kinds of noises going on and I went in there one night and as I pulled the curtains there was a ghostly monk hooded figure behind the curtains, I just ran out thinking I'd seen something awful. In fact it was just Cozy! But he was dressed as a monk; it was pretty frightening. I wouldn't go back in there and I was hearing all kinds of things. It was just the band playing tricks on me and eventually Ritchie came over and said, "I've got a tape I want you to learn" and he played all these sound effects I'd been hearing. "Aaah you buggers!" I never felt such a fool in my life because they really had me going. I mean there was a great atmosphere in the band, it was like a kind of family. I was quite surprised I was expected

to be in with the Prince of Darkness and all that. Of course with the road crew everybody was so close, we used to play games and... how we found Graham was amazing. It was just Cozy playing his 'guess the single.' He had all these tapes and he just... "what's this?" You'd have a millisecond of it, get a bit more, but one night we heard (imitates tune) The Marbles 'Only One Woman.' What happened to that guy? Wonder where he is and that's how we found him. We sent out for him and of course Graham came, the eighth singer and he sang 'Mistreated' which he'd never heard before, and he didn't know who Ritchie was and he got the gig in three syllables. "I've been Mis..." Ritchie looked up and he had the gig. We'd found our singer.

Presumably the music had pretty much been written before Graham arrived.
Once he arrived it all suddenly fell into shape.

Are you saying he was the catalyst for getting it going?
Yeah, he's pretty much like that Graham, things start to happen when he arrives. It's been very strange working with him again. I didn't know what was going to happen whether it would work or not. We did a couple of gigs at Stourbridge last week we did two nights sold out and the second gig was great and we did a gig in South Shields last night which was wonderful, just wonderful.

That's near your home territory isn't it?
Yeah Sunderland. It was a bit hot in there and I took my shirt off and I had a Sunderland shirt on underneath and was roundly booed by the predominantly Newcastle audience!

I'm not surprised.
They relaxed... I don't think a lot of them knew I was from Sunderland.

Do you see this as a long-term thing or just a bit of fun?
I don't know what I see it as. I just see there's a kind of gap in the market. It's hard getting a good band together, if you want to get anywhere it's got to be really good. Doesn't matter who you are.

Well they're all good musicians. I was very impressed with Dario.
Yes he's marvellous and he's coming on leaps and bounds every gig. I mean Dario's a great writer, so we've got a live album deal with a studio deal in the offing so next year we hope to do a lot more. We've been offered so many gigs all the time.

Does that mean the Company Of Snakes thing is finished?
Well I left that in my head a year ago, but I was kind of coerced into doing the studio album with them, which I didn't want to do, and I went on that German tour, which was awful and that was the end for me then.

And as you said earlier you have been touring with Deep Purple recently.
Yeah.

Was it very short notice?
Yeah two days! They called me the week before saying Jon isn't very well would you be prepared, then I heard nothing, then on Monday Bruce Payne phoned me up and said, "we wanted you to do three gigs but we actually want you to do ten, be there on Wednesday!" And of course I was just about to do some stuff with Uli Roth and an orchestra. Two days of utter hell. I was writing arrangements with one hand and learning Purple numbers with the other. We had a brief run through the night before and I went into Steve Morse's room for a few hours and he coaxed me through a few things.

How easy or difficult is that when you are in that situation?
Very difficult. Just because of Jon being who he is, his part in the band you know. He's pretty unique and it wasn't like they said leave anything out. "We want you to do that solo intro there..."

And they would come up and say, "we think you should make the solo a bit longer." They were wonderful guys to work with. I was totally enchanted, being in the middle of them.

But obviously you are respected as being a good musician so presumably you could pick up the tunes relatively quickly.
There's one thing picking up the tunes but to go on stage in Purple in front of 22,000 people for the first gig- I defy anybody to be cool about it- nerve wracking, yeah! It was stressful but...

There have been rumours that Jon doesn't want to tour anymore.
I couldn't say what is going on there. It's not for me to comment, I really don't know I was just asked to be there and I had a wonderful time working with them. I had no thoughts that the gig was mine. I just said to them "I'll come in and do the tour", and it was great on those terms. I think coming in for him is one thing but replacing him... ooh come on! Big pair of shoes that one.

I think the band would loose a lot of credibility in a way if they just had affectively just one original member left with Ian Paice...
Well they've got three with Roger and Ian.

But obviously there was an original...
But the Purple that everyone thinks of is with Ian and Roger. And three out of five ain't bad. It's up to them. It will work; they're that kind of band. Steve is an incredible force in the band.

Another project you did was Quatermass.
Well I was a big fan when they were around. Pete Robinson was marvellous and Mick Underwood I thought the world of his drumming. A lovely guy. I said to them if you ever get back with John (Gustafson) and want a Hammond player I said I'll push my Hammond down the A1 to get to the rehearsals but he could never get John interested again. So I just went in for a day with them and very delightful it was too.

You weren't up for the gigs then?
No.

Well that's pretty much it unless there's anything else you want to say.
Well over the years I've seen Ritchie take a lot of stick from people and I don't know where I'd be today if I hadn't met him. He had a tremendous influence on me. I think he does with everyone who works with him.

That's what a lot of people I've interviewed over the years have said.
Yeah but he can be a bit hard to take sometimes, but he's a brilliant composer. The older I get the more respect I have for what he's done. Particularly a lot of the stuff he did with Purple. It's ground breaking stuff really.

Do you mean the early years?
Well 'In Rock' in particular, and 'Fireball.' I think 'Fireball' is extraordinary. It's funny actually I was in a record shop the day before Purple called me and I bought 'Fireball' and 'In Rock' and I just sat at home and played them all day, thinking how wonderful it was. Very odd!

Have you followed his career in recent years?
Yeah, I've got the 'Night' albums, I like them. I thought they were good. I got the Rainbow album with Doogie. I thought it was a bit on the dry side. I didn't like the drum sound very much but I thought the guitar... I thought the whole thing was... you know... master of his art, Ritchie.

****

GRAHAM BONNET

As mentioned in the pre-amble to the Don Airey interview, the Graham Bonnet interview was conducted after the same gig. Like Airey, Bonnet's career really took off when he was propelled into the spotlight, following his appointment as Ronnie James Dio's replacement in Rainbow. Prior to that he experienced a brief moment of fame a decade earlier with the top 5 UK single 'Only One Woman' under the name of The Marbles; a pop duo with his cousin Trevor Gordon. As the archetypal one-hit wonders, Bonnet spent the next few years in the wilderness, but kick-started a solo career in 1977, when he signed a solo deal with Ringo Starr's label, Ring O'Records. Produced by Pip Williams, the album also included former Juicy Lucy guitarist Micky Moody. The album included a powerful version of Carole King's 'Will You Love Me Tomorrow?'

A second solo album followed the next year, which was once again produced by Pip Williams, and interestingly included Ritchie Blackmore's former sixties bandmate Mick Underwood on drums. It was shortly after the release of this album that Bonnet was elevated to the ranks of Rainbow, who then under the joint guidance of Ritchie Blackmore and Roger Glover were masterminding a new approach for the band in the hope of opening the group up to a larger audience.

Although Bonnet was only in Rainbow for one album, it certainly gave him a springboard for the rest of his career. In fact, aside from Blackmore, Bonnet has sung alongside some of the world's top guitarists: Yngwie Malmsteen, Steve Vai and Michael Schenker amongst them. Although it was over an hour after the gig when I interviewed him, such is the way Bonnet performs that he still looked physically exhausted, prompting my opening question...

The astonishing thing watching you, and other people say it as well, is just how much physical effort you put into your performance. You're one of these singers that really goes for it.
Well tonight was a bit harder than normal. Because as I said we just had a bit of a problem in the middle, we had to change the battery in my thingy and I'm not used to using those damn in-ear monitors, they feel really weird for a start. I'm getting used to them when they work but if they don't work you are screwed and you get a sore throat obviously.

For the uninitiated, could you give a brief overview of what you have been doing since Rainbow.
Since then? Where do I start?

Well the things that stick in your mind the most. Things that gave you the most enjoyment.
Well I think probably one of the most important things that ever happened to me was joining Rainbow obviously. Because at that point in my career I had never done that kind of music, I'd never sung that kind of music, so it was something completely new to me. I'd been used to singing R 'n' B and pop tunes and stuff back in '68 when I was with my cousin from Australia... well he's not from Australia but he lived there for a long time and worked with the Bee Gees. ... do you want me to go that far back?

Yeah it would be interesting.
Well '68 was when I really kind of went into the studio for the first time and Barry Gibb wrote a tune for us called 'Only One Woman.' My cousin and I recorded this thing and it did really well. It got to number three I believe in Britain and Joe Cocker got to number one which we were kind of pissed off about but never mind. From there I got offered... we were called The Marbles and that thing only happened, only lasted for about three years. It was like I guess a British, what can I say, Hall and Oates or Righteous Brothers, white blue eyed soul kind of thing. From that happening I got offered jobs by different bands and tried to do things on my own which sometimes worked and sometimes didn't. Really when I came back and people started listening again; in England at least, was when I joined Rainbow. Before that I had stuff that I'd recorded which did okay overseas but never here or never in America. Just like in Australia or Germany and France. I did some solo albums and stuff. But Rainbow was when it brought me into the whole picture.

How did you first get to hear of the gig, and get invited to the auditions?
It was Cozy, they were playing a game in the house where they were all staying, spot the tune or whatever and they played my old record and said, "who's this?" and Cozy said... "and oh yeah I heard he gave up the business" or something and Ritchie heard it and I think Roger Glover at that time was working with Micky Moody who is a friend of mine and who was in a band called Snafu I think at that time. He called him up and through him he got to my manager and said "bring him over and audition" so I had to go out and listen to Rainbow albums and learn my party piece which was 'Mistreated.' That was my audition song. So I went over there and did that thing and they offered me the job. I wasn't sure about doing it to be honest with you. I thought I'm not sure if I like this music because I was into a completely different thing. Not that it wasn't great but it wasn't really what I had done. I felt a bit nervous about it. So I went back to London and I spoke to my manager. I said, "I'm not sure about this I don't think I fit." He said, "yes you will" (because I can make money out of you!) So he took all my money! Yes, anyway that's another story! So anyway I basically got the job and it was probably one of the best moves I've ever made I think.

So I'd be right in saying you weren't familiar with the Rainbow material before?
No, not at all because it wasn't what I listened to. My music, things I listened to back then were The Beatles, The Beach Boys, Stevie Wonder, anything but that kind of music, a completely different thing because that was what I was doing. The kind of songs I would make up would be

in that kind of area, r 'n' b or even blues stuff. Real blues kind of thing. I was never really into whatever that was called back then, it wasn't called Heavy Metal, what was it called?

Hard rock, heavy rock.

Underground even. Led Zeppelin I was never into either. All the guys that played drums and guitars were into Zeppelin but I was more into singers and being a singer I always listened to people who did harmony and had great melodies for vocals obviously. That was The Beatles or The Beach Boys or whatever you like.

So your recollections of that audition, just doing 'Mistreated'- that was all you had to do?

Yeah that was it. I remember Don said, "now can you do it on the microphone" because I did it without a microphone. It was in the Chateau and it had nice acoustics so I just stood back and didn't use the mic you know.

Believing in fair play Ritchie relayed a number of stories involving you during your time in the band, so I thought it was only fair to get your side of the events.

What did he say?

Firstly he basically said you felt uncomfortable tying to record at the Chateau and wanted to do the vocals in a proper studio.

Yeah absolutely.

He was saying "it's great we're in a castle in the middle of France."

I hate being stuck in the middle of nowhere with nothing to do when, if it's not a good day in a real studio you can at least go out into the street and you see other people instead of just the people you are working with. But there that was it, however many were staying there, guys and their wives and that was it. Where do you escape to just relax, and there was nowhere just a little village. I remember Roger Glover put me in the Chateau, in the dining room or whatever it was and we tried to do vocals in this room, which was... I don't know it just didn't work. It wasn't right and we didn't know what we were doing. We had no songs as such, just grasping at straws and it really needed to be done in 'the office' so to speak instead of the middle of the countryside with... I don't know... I can't explain it, I just love to be in a proper work area and this just didn't feel right to me, so it didn't work. But as soon as we went into a studio then it started to happen.

Were you just rehearsing in the Chateau then?

No we tried to record there with a mobile. It was great for drums and all the rest of it but for vocals it wasn't right, the place was so damn echoey. It was an old building.

I wasn't aware of that. So you actually went into a studio to lay the vocals down then.

Yeah, yeah, I went into a place in Syosset, which is a studio in Long Island (Kingdom Sound), *fairly small place. That was when it kind of came together.*

I got the impression that some of the songs had already been written and you came in at the last moment.

They had vague ideas of things but it was never really actually a song as such. That kind of came later. When we did get into a studio we did each song probably four or five different ways. Not the whole song but a verse, a middle bit and a chorus or something. Try it this way, try it that way and then kind of pick which was the best. It seemed to take forever but I don't think we actually recorded for that long but it seemed like it was taking too long because it was really hard work. and I wasn't used to it, working that way I mean.

I was completely thrown into the arena there (The Chateau). *These guys knew what they were doing and there I was standing there going I don't think this is right for me. Thinking that in my head, going they're not going to like it, I've got short hair, I'm not right, no, I like 1950s music!*

How long did you have those thoughts for?
All the time! No not really, after a while they got used to me. But it was always a thing that I wasn't wearing the uniform of the so-called heavy rock thing or whatever it is you know.

It's interesting you say that because that was going to be my next question. Another thing that Ritchie claims is that he wanted you to grow your hair and he claims he had Colin Hart guard your door, but you sneaked out of the window just before a gig in Newcastle to get your hair cut and he went nuts!
Guard my door? I don't think he guarded my door but I...

Ritchie likes to embellish stories.
Yeah I think he's added a bit there. I remember that day; my hair to me was like a bloody mess; it was all over the place. If you've got short hair you have short hair. Now people shave their heads and that's kind of cool now, but back then to have short hair wasn't the thing, it wasn't the uniform as I said of a so-called rock singer but yeah before a gig I went and got my haircut, didn't say anything to anyone and I came on stage that night. I remember the look of shock on his face, jaw dropping to the floor.

He said he wanted to whack you over the head with his guitar.
(Laughing) *I don't think he would do that. I think he actually quite liked what I did in a weird way.*

The other strange thing he said is that he claims he wanted you to leave the band but you didn't want to go. As such he reckons Joe Lynn Turner had already been lined up and said, "if you don't want to leave we'll have two singers on then," at which point you turned around and said, "well I'm leaving then." Is that true?
It's sort of, something like that. But what it was, it was very unproductive rehearsals for the next album and nothing was happening in rehearsals. Everybody was bored with each other, Cozy had left the band, Bobby Rondinelli came in playing drums and rehearsals were basically, well I don't think I want to be here, shall we go to the pub or something? Not quite like that but basically that yes. And there was one song that was written for us by Russ Ballard, 'I Surrender' and that was the only song there was, a whole song as such. So Ritchie would come to rehearsals and play his bass pedals stand there and go (imitates sound) do his thing and look around and say, "have you got any ideas?" Don and I played something to him one day. He said, "no I don't like that." "Oh all right then. Okay so what shall we do, is the pub open? Go for a walk. I'm hungry; anything but..." it was very unproductive. So it was an unhappy time too because Cozy wasn't there we were all kind of friends and it seemed to break up the family a little bit. I started to record 'I Surrender' and put down some backing vocals and then I thought, I'm not enjoying this anymore, this is not fun and I went back to Los Angeles and they called me up and said, "why have you gone back home?" I said, "I don't want to do it anymore." That's when they said, "how about if you sing the songs that you like on this album, the tracks you like to sing, we'll get another guy to sing the other ones" whatever they maybe, in the future, once they are made up, written or whatever. I said, "well that's not really going to work, you don't have two singers in a band. It's like having two guitar players. Can you imagine what that would be like? I don't think that will work, I don't want to do that." Because I had in my mind that maybe I could do something by myself at this point. So that was it. I left. I wasn't fired: I left.

It's interesting you saying you were working with Bobby Rondinelli because I was always under the impression you left the same time as Cozy after the Donington gig.
Well it was really in the end.

But you'd obviously gone back in the studio after that for a brief time.
Yeah so we went into Copenhagen I think it was. When we were rehearsing to do the new album but as I said I put some backing vocals down and that was basically it obviously they were changed later on by the new singer and that was it.

It was a relatively short time thereafter that you did your solo album 'Line-Up'. It came out pretty soon after.
Yes it did, riding on the...

Very much in the same mould obviously.
Yeah, using the same musicians.

Cozy was on it.
Yeah and Jon Lord.

Obviously you played 'Night Games' tonight but I was surprised that maybe you didn't do one or two others from that.
Well, you know what we are doing now is just kind of at the beginning of stuff. We are testing the water seeing what we should do and what we shouldn't do. How we should play it, if we should play it, when we should play it, where it goes. Kind of working out things. Kind of some rough edges to smooth out a bit.

You had some big hits. 'Night Games' was quite a big hit. Was 'Liar' the follow up?
It might have been, yes.

Two or three singles from that album were released.
'Liar' was another Russ Ballard tune. It didn't do well I remember that. I remember my parents saying to me, "I hate that song, what a horrible title, 'Liar'!" They didn't like it at all. You know I'm not sure what they released here. Because I didn't live here I didn't know what was happening sometimes.

From my recollections I think 'Liar' got in the top twenty. Donington was your last gig with the band, a massive gig.
And something I will never forget. I've said this over and over again, it was the first time I think about it that my whole family was in the audience for one thing, but it was the most magical day. It was horrible because Cozy was leaving. I remember after the gig we sat up until... I don't know we didn't go to bed that night. We stayed in a hotel in Leicester and said goodbye to Cozy and everybody cried and it was like the best day ever. It's something I'm really proud of, what a band. What a fucking band! I think that was the best line up with Cozy playing drums and everything. You might have your own opinion, I'm sure you do but to me it was like something about it, those guys because we were all so different as well.

I mentioned this to Don as well. Obviously that show was filmed and recorded and some tracks have been released on record. The BBC did a half hour broadcast. Don seemed to think the full footage is long gone, been lost.
I think it has, yeah. I've got a copy at home, but the copy I've got it's all over the place.

The whole show?
No its like bits, it's all cut up.

Yeah the BBC did it, very poorly edited.
The only time I did see it actually was when I left the band I went home to LA and they did the whole damn show one night on... I can't remember the name of the show but since then... nah.

It's a shame because I think a lot of Rainbow fans would love to see that released. What's your view of old live recordings being released?
I hate them, because they always sound a bit iffy.

The band was recorded a few times when you were in it. I don't know if you know. US radio broadcasts and things like that.
There's got to be some really bad ones. I remember... because you know what it's like when you record something live the show might be great but when you hear what the sound is it can be really, really bad. I remember Don and I, one night we did a show in the States, it was a fucking great show, all patting each other on the back and we got the tape from the board out front and it was awful, absolutely bloody awful. But the actual show and the audience, the thing between them and us, little guys on stage playing guitars and singing and stuff, and the crowd was absolutely amazing, but the actual thing was crap. It was absolute crap. Out of tune all over the place. It's weird. I remember listening to a concert once by the Pretenders. Chrissie (Hynde), *she was singing in a completely different key all the way through the show, but perfectly in another key, and that's what this show we did, that day was like. So I'm always a bit scared of live recordings.*

I've got quite a few of these things and I actually think they are very good.
Oh they are? I guess sometimes there can be one.

I know Ritchie's not keen on having these things released.
No, I can't listen to it.

Obviously someone who keeps cropping up in your conversations is Cozy Powell. One of the stories that fascinates me is about the time he scaled up the wall of the hotel in Gelsenkirchen and got into the wrong room with the fire extinguisher.
That's absolutely true.

Have you got any other interesting stories you can tell about "Spiderman?"
He always wanted to do everything, to quote an album, "over the top." He liked to drive fast and the rest of it, but he said, "It must be great to drive a jet plane." He always wanted to fly a plane, be in a fighter plane. Get even more of a buzz. He was always flying not falling. I did a track on the album that's just come out here; 'The Day I Went Mad' it's called. There's a song on there called 'Flying Not Falling' and it's all about him, because he would ride the roller-coaster but stand up. He was never falling, always flying, you know, nothings going to happen to me. He was always immortal, infallible. Nothing would hurt him so he was always on the side of danger. Don and I used to travel with him a lot, say where you can drive fast. Let's say Germany. The guys would take the plane and we would take the car with Cozy and we would get there ten years before everybody else, always early.

It must have been very upsetting when you heard of his death.
Of course, I remember the next day. I won't get into weird things but the next day I looked outside my door... and Don had called me the day before and told me about it... and I looked outside my door and there was a rainbow and it came right down. It looked like you could touch it in my back yard so to speak. Not literally but near enough to touch. So I got my video camera. How stupid. So I went out there and I filmed it and said, "is that you?"

Unfortunately the interview came to an abrupt end as Don Airey and the others were all sitting in the vehicles downstairs, waiting for Graham, and waiting to drive off into the night!

****

JOHN McCOY

John McCoy is best known as the bald, colossus of a bassist, who was in Ian Gillan's band Gillan for four years. His earlier career included the jazz-rock outfit Zzebra and outside of his time with Gillan he has has had something of a checkered career. On 18th June 2001 I had a lengthy phone conversation with John. It was primarily to talk about his time in Gillan, and to garner some new stories for the sleeve notes I was to write for the live Gillan release 'On The Rocks' that McCoy was producing. During the chat Ritchie Blackmore also cropped up and John had some pleasant things to say about the enigmatic guitarist. Those comments were published in issue 17 of *More Black than Purple*. The rest of the interview has remained unpublished until now.

How was the Gillan band started? I think I'm right in saying Liam (Genockey) was the first one to be approached?
Well Liam and I along with Steve Byrd were involved in a lot of sessions at that time as a rhythm section, particularly Liam and I. And Liam did a session with Colin (Towns) and I believe that Colin was, I won't say a fan but I believed that he liked Zzebra, which was the band that Liam and I had a couple of years earlier. To cut the story short they just asked me and Liam and Steve Byrd "would you like to cut an album with Ian?" That's how it started really.

So you were actually working with Liam at the time then?
I was working with Liam, and since the Zzebra days we continued to sort of pay our rent by doing sessions. We were really busy with session work, mostly anonymous film music and fairly crappy TV jingles and stuff but it pays the rent. At the time I had my own band running, doing gigs all over the place but the session work I had with Liam did keep me busy all the time. I wouldn't say it was just another session but it was a session more interesting than most.

I heard somewhere that there was a chap before Steve Byrd called Richard Brampton.
Yeah Richard, he was in the same clique of session people at that time but his name was mentioned and it was a thought but he wasn't really the right sort of player. He was a fairly laid back, jazzy sort of player.

He didn't get to play with the band then?
No.

So then you suggested Steve?
Yeah, he was working at the time with Sonja Kristina. The whole thing is very incestuous anyway. I worked with Sonja with Curved Air and later in the event when Liam decided not to continue, Pete Barnacle was also working with Sonja Kristina. But I think in actual fact Steve and I were recording an album... and it eventually came out under the name of Neo, an American guy called... The American! I can't remember the bloke's name. But we were working on an album and I was producing and paying bass and we were working at Kingsway so obviously Ian and Colin were having a listen to what we were up to. I had done quite a few production sessions at Kingsway on various projects so it just fell into place from there.

So at that stage had Colin already written the songs, and you just did it like a session?
Yeah the bones of the songs were written some of them were finished. The best song on the album in my mind was 'Fighting Man.' That was a song that Colin wrote and that just blew me away. But some were in rough form and we sort of threw in our little bits to help the thing a long as you do.

So was it implied that a heavy album was required or was it just assumed given that Gillan had been doing his jazzy phase?
Not really. We did have deep and meaningful conversations about Ian's career. I think Ian was the last person to realise that basically everybody thought he was pratting about and it was about time he got back to some good songs and a bit of balls. I mean I have every respect for IGB and the players in the band. Johnny Gustafson- one of the top three bass players in the world, he's fantastic and I was quite honoured to replace him as Ian's bass player but what they were playing just didn't do it for me at all, it just left me cold. And having been through that band Zzebra, which was jazz overkill! I was jazzed out! To me the jazz-rock thing had disappeared up its own arse and when I listen to an IGB album, I just think Ian sounds like a fish out of water. It's a shame because it should have been a great band with the calibre of the players. But there wasn't really a

conscious effort at the time to say let's do a heavier album. If I play a ballad it comes out heavy. Everything I do tends to be on the heavier side, it's just the way that it worked. It wasn't until after that when Ian suggested, "this is a great band and lets keep it together and continue," that we had serious talks about the direction. It had to be pointed out that the reason that first album was only released in Japan was that Ian couldn't get arrested. People were totally disillusioned with him and what happened with IGB and to the labels that put money into it, and to the people that put money into it, it was a disappointment. And to most of the fans I think it was a disappointment. Don't get me wrong; I was a big fan anyway. He's still the best singer in the world, not mentioning his performance with Pavarotti, embarrassing or what: Really embarrassing, very sad. But we had serious talk about the direction, and my own band at the time, McCoy was definitely a heavy band. At that time, and in between the Japanese album, and deciding we were going to continue fully, I was recording an album with Paul Samson- the first Samson album and so consequently Ian and Colin heard what was happening because I recorded it at Kingsway. So the whole thing just grew really. When Ian said let's continue, I said, "yeah brilliant let's continue but let's make it successful, commercially successful," because to me it was like a wasted talent. Because everybody I knew and everybody I talked to me said "oh fucking great, Ian Gillan what a fantastic singer, Deep Purple", and obviously everybody wanted him to get back into that kind of area. And I was one of those people. I think we were fairly successful.

So it was as much the band pushing him in that direction?
Yeah, like I said I think he was the last to realise he had been barking up the wrong tree. But it was a strange period the mid seventies; I'm not surprised there was a Punk explosion. And obviously that had a bearing on getting a record deal as well.

Were there any other tracks recorded for that first album that never made it?
I was looking at a rehearsal tape the other day actually. There were a couple of songs, which never really got finished. I can't remember the titles. There wasn't a lot from the first album.

I suppose it was pretty much done and dusted by Colin I suppose?
Well I think we had a few days rehearsal spread out over the course of the album. We would rehearse one day and record the track later that same day. Then if it wasn't right we would go back to it the next day. But we recorded it fairly quickly; some of it went down in the first few takes.

Although Pete Barnacle is given a name check on the album I assume I am right that he doesn't actually appear on it?
No, that's right. That was just a gesture because by that time we knew Liam wasn't going to be in the band, and we also knew we were going to Japan and that the album was getting released in Japan and he would be with us, so it was like this is an introduction to Pete really to let people know who he was, but he's not actually on the album.

Did the band have much time to rehearse before that first gig at Reading festival?
No not at all, we just jumped in and did it. It was a pretty daunting thing to do but we coped all right.

Do you have any recollections of it?
I think we went down pretty well but I don't remember too much about it. I may have been slightly drunk! I can just remember it being a great event and thinking yeah this could go a long way, this band could really happen. I was really upset that Liam didn't want to stay because I had worked with the guy for about eight or nine years and we were a good rhythm section. But I think I've

mentioned to you before he just said, "I don't trust Ian or this situation at all." He thought Ian was taking the piss and the sort of money that was available so he declined it. But I don't remember the gig very much.

I presume the set list was pretty much Ian's choice?
Well it was just a matter of what we actually knew, and a couple of old Purple numbers thrown in for good measure.

If I'm right 'Not Weird Enough' was the only track not played live?
Probably because it was not weird enough!

Good answer!
I really don't know. We all had our favourite songs that we wanted to do but it was ultimately Ian's decision because sometimes he couldn't handle certain songs. I think that's the beauty of this album because he's singing so great. His voice is excellent. It's very sad, because like 'Child In Time,' it wasn't our song, to me it's always been Ian's song and as the years progressed we went through all sorts of tricks. You know, tuning down the instruments and changing keys so that he could manage to sing it. But back then in '78 he was singing like an angel.

Were there any other songs considered for inclusion in the set at that time, or was it just basically do the album plus a couple of Purple songs?
Well we were out there to promote that album, so as much of the album as we could possibly do.

Initially after Reading there were a few dates in England and Germany in small clubs. Did you sense from the fans that there was any confusion, with them expecting the jazz-rock stuff still?
It was a strange time. As I said about the punk explosion that had just happened. People were really expecting the jazz-rock fusion band but they didn't get that. But it seemed to go down pretty good; I think they were quite pleased, well ninety-nine percent of them. A lot of people really liked IGB and preferred it to Gillan but I think the majority of people were really pleased that we were getting back into something a little simpler and heavier.

So what was your first impression of that first trip to Japan?
It was a long time ago but I remember it fairly well.

Were you playing larger venues than the few dates you had done in UK and Germany?
Yeah they were sort of medium size clubs when they still existed, when there was somewhere to play. Yeah the gigs in Japan were sort of large concert halls and full to the brim. And early evening shows, which is a weird thing in Japan. You sort of play about 6 o'clock show time, so it feels a bit strange but then the whole thing was very alien. It's a fascinating country but the first time is a real culture shock. But I just loved it and the people. I just thought the whole thing was tremendous but the gig that the album is from in Tokyo, I think at the time became known as the night of the broken strings. I think Steve and I both broke a couple of strings that night, which is really bad luck. If you pay attention you can actually hear things going out of tune and popping but overall I think it was a pretty good gig.

Do you recall the two TV shows you did over there as well?
Yes I do recall them.

There was the 25 minute five songs live in the studio that we talked about the other day, then a miming to Message In A Bottle on a show over there. Do you recall that one as well?
Vaguely. I remember being in a TV studio but the thing with Japan is that it's like being in a

production line. When you arrive you are handed a schedule. It's not just a sound check at this time, and a gig at this time. It's like the whole day is mapped out for you. Sort of hourly and half hourly events that you get driven to and taken to this place and that place and meet this guy and it all becomes a bit of a blur. Well it did to me, but then a lot of things do.

Have you any amusing stories from that tour that you can recall or are they all a bit of a blur?
I remember Steve and I got very, very drunk on Saki the first time we had it, which is a wonderful drink. But a lot of things that happened will have to remain unsaid. A lot of very interesting things happened but...

Not family entertainment then?
Not really prime time, no! But then that's Japan.

The words Geisha girls probably spring to mind, but we'll leave it at that then!
Mmmm yeah very accommodating.

Basically after that tour there were a few dates elsewhere then a couple of changes in the band.
Yeah, Pete was a great drummer but he lacked subtlety in his playing, and in his attitude generally. He was a real live wire of a guy and it just didn't gel somehow with him as a band. You've really got to get on with everybody to a certain extent. At least you've got to tolerate people's differences but it just didn't work with him.

So he pushed himself out in a way?
Yeah, in a way: It just wasn't gelling how it should do, socially and musically

And Steve Byrd was that a question of him wanting to move on or Ian wanted a change?
Well Steve was and is an amazing player. I first met Steve when he auditioned for Zzebra and he was only seventeen years old and his playing just really impressed. I think really his playing was second to none but as we got more and more of the older Purple type fans, as we got more of them coming to gigs I don't think they really took to Steve. Gillan was a band that really listened to what fans said and took on board the feedback that we got from... you know some fans they are just idiots but some fans you could have a conversation with that's serious and they've obviously got an opinion because they are watching it. I just don't think they took to Steve. He looked like... well he looked like a fucking skeleton on stage!

There were times I think when it looked as if he was almost sending the music up a bit, his mannerisms.
Yeah, well it's the same thing that dreaded word; he was a little bit punky. And I don't think people took to him really.

I think visually the band was a mixture of the old and the new wave. Ian and Colin with the hair and you, and Steve, who looked like Wilko Johnson. Both of you leaping about and Pete looked quite punky, an unusual blend.
It certainly got us a lot of press. At that time I had just kind of reinvented myself image wise. I'd got a thing called Alopecia and I used to have masses of hair and a great big beard. I woke up one day and half of it had gone and within the space of a week I'd lost all my hair. Little bits came back including the beard and I found it really worked for me and the things I was doing at the time. People- it wasn't just "oh that fat bass player guy, blah blah blah let's get him," it was like "fuck have you seen that bass player" because back then nobody had a shaved head, especially in a rock band. I found it really worked for me in terms of recognition, which meant more work.

So I just sort of got that image as I started working with Ian and Colin. And I guess it did look unusual because I was about three times the size of Steve Byrd! I guess it was a strange looking band.

I think that was part of its appeal. Not only was the music powerful but also there was a visual impact, which can be crucial for a band, and a lot of bands don't have it.
Yeah, I think we got it right visually when Bernie (Tormé) joined.

Yeah, I remember the first time I saw you with Bernie, it was like who is this guy?
When Ian said to me he had reservations about Steve Byrd, whether he could continue, he said, "do you know anybody?" I knew that this was the gig that Bernie had been waiting for and vice versa. He was the guitarist the band had been waiting for because I had worked previously with Bernie in a band called Scrapyard. And we sort of stayed in touch, and he had his own band at the time, the Bernie Tormé band. So I set up some support gigs for Bernie to play as support to Gillan and just said to Ian, "the guy I'm talking about, he's the guitarist in the support band check him out." I think in actual fact we didn't even get the gig over before he asked him. I think... oh yeah, Bernie was sound checking and I said to Ian, "come out and check this guy out." Bernie was doing one of Bernie's solos as only he can do, even at a sound check and Ian just said, "fuck where's he come from?" And I introduced them and that's it and off we went.

And the rest was history as they say and the band took a leap forward from there with Mick Underwood joining on drums as well.
Yeah, in terms of material it started to head in the right direction with the 'Mr. Universe' album. Mick came in, really at Ian's suggestion. It was like we know who we are going to have as guitarist. I mean Ian and Colin and I were tight from the outset but the drummer it was like who do we get? We tried a few things with a few different drummers, Mr Paice being one of them!

Really?
Yeah, that was interesting. He came down for a play. How serious it was I don't know but the opportunity was there. He probably wanted paying! And there were other sorts of people in the frame but Ian suggested Mick and Mick is such a lovely bloke. He's just like real old school, and he'd been in Episode Six with Ian and they went to school together in fact. And Mick came down and he's so experienced that it all just fell into place. We built up a good relationship as a bass and drum rhythm section. We played good together, it seemed to work. He had a good, not old fashioned, but old rock school sort of attitude to his playing. There are certain things that he did that just fitted naturally. I think in actual fact he really shone on 'Mr Universe', on that track 'Mr Universe.' He's quite an exceptional guy.

But I don't think he's doing much these days. There doesn't seem to be the places to play anymore.
Life goes on, nothing stays the same does it? Everything changes.

Which is why it's fortunate we have these recordings.
You can look at as many photos as you like but there's nothing like hearing the sound of the gig. It's a real document to what was going on then. It was a struggle, there's no doubt about it. Over there because of Purple and IGB, who had great success in Japan, we were going to a ready-made audience. It was a bit different in other areas in the world but the audiences were gagging for it.

So you basically found the Japanese dates a bit easier, less daunting?
I don't know, it just made it a bit more of a worry! I think in some respects we were probably trying a little bit too hard.

Will Smoke On The Water be included on this new release for the umpteenth time?
Yeah, "fuck Smoke On The Water" as Steve Morse says.

I must admit it wouldn't bother me if I never heard it again.
You say that now but you get yourself drunk and in the right mood you want to hear it.

It's good rock 'n' roll but I always refer to it as the fuck off song. At the end of the night, "that's it, that's all you're going to get now fuck off!"
That's true... thank you Ritchie, it's worked well for a lot of people. It's one of the classics of all time.

I don't know if you are aware but this gig was released on a bootleg in Japan a few years ago but it didn't include 'Fighting Man.' There has never been a live version of that released to date.
I think people will want to have this album.

Well it's the first document of this line-up.
And as you said about 'Fighting Man' I'm so pleased that is there because Ian sings that great. I don't know what the band is like on it really but Ian is great.

It was dropped after that tour though wasn't it?
That is a very high range song and in the set at the time I think we were doing 'Child In Time' most nights and that's a very high range song and I think it started to get hard work. But Ian was weird about that song anyway. I always thought it was the best song on the album. It's a Colin Towns song; it's not an Ian Gillan song.

But I always thought it had the potential to become an Ian Gillan signature tune like 'Child In Time' had.
Absolutely. I think it did in fact.

But he decided to knock it on the head after that tour.
Well make your own judgement but he didn't write it so maybe there is something in that.

Colin was responsible for coming up with a lot of good stuff.
Yeah - excellent writer.

And you got more involved in the writing as the band progressed.
Yeah it was all part of the loose sort of plan to get success. I had the arrangements for 'New Orleans' and 'Trouble' floating around for a long, long time. I think that's what helped us to cross over. It became a chart band, a singles band. And then when you have that kind of success I think it spills over onto the albums that you try and retain some sort of commerciality. Plus the fact of trying to make things a little heavier and a little more rocky.

There was quite a variety to the band; it wasn't just an out and out heavy band.
Oh no. I thought we did some good songs. The ones that stick in my mind from the later albums are 'No Easy Way', 'Are You Sure?'

Thunderous bass on that track. There always seemed to be one big epic number on each album, normally one of Colin's.
That is Colin's forte. He is a real sort of epic writer and scores really well on that kind of material. I'm probably a lot more basic myself. The thing is, I have worked with a lot of singers and you try and write to suit the singer and what you imagine they are capable of. Obviously Colin had

worked with Ian a long time and they worked well together.
I thought it was worth mentioning, it's not a rumour it's a fact. There's an album coming out of live Purple stuff from 1971, the European Tour. That's when I first met Ian because I was on that tour.

Was that with Maldoon?
That was Curtiss Maldoon, yeah. We were signed to Purple Records and we did the Deep Purple European tour. Now that was a band! That was absolutely... I was there every single night I was just like- ga-ga. It was so good and there were no sort of huge egos between themselves they were really a band then.

I think they were at their musical peak in '71. I think the commercial peak probably came a year or two after.
Yeah they were so hot.

Of course these days there is so much politics.
Particularly in the Purple end of the business it's all so fucking petty, It's unbelievable, I mean come on, grow up.

You would have thought that over the years people would just bury the hatchet.
I can't talk, but the shit that happened with Ian, I'm surprised he's still alive. The people I know who would gladly just kill him. Johnny Gus is one of those- he hates Ian. What a shame.

It's a shame the way the band fizzled out.
It was such a mess. You say about Mick, Mick was heartbroken. I mean I went into a total fucking depression for about a year, I couldn't believe it but Mick; he went to school with Ian. Ian is his daughter's Godfather- they were close. Even when it was written down in black and white and we saw all the figures for ourselves, Mick could not believe it. It took him a long time to except it. Horrible, terrible stuff.

Well hopefully these albums are a way of addressing the balance?
Maybe but it's too little too late really. The sales the band generated at the time were phenomenal, compared to what these albums are doing.

What were the biggest markets for the band, I know it was essentially Europe and Japan, you never really cracked the States did you?
The States was a difficult one. Once again it was the legacy of IGB because they totally bombed out there. Ian couldn't really get a good tour so we ended up doing a stupid tour in some awful places in the middle of nowhere. Plus the fact at the time we were on Virgin and in America I think it was distributed by RSO Records at the time, and that agreement came to an end the week we arrived in America so there was nobody there to represent us and help the tour along. There was no publicity of the tour. Never really did crack America but I think we could have done if we had been back again and kept working but you've got to tour America for a year to start breaking through.

I always imagine it's a tougher place and also brand names seem to be a bit more important. It's not the fact that it was Ian Gillan from Deep Purple. If it had been Deep Purple, yeah but the fact that he was on his own, whereas in Europe, particularly places like Germany they just like what they like and if you do good quality music they will go for it.
The whole of Europe right down to Spain and Portugal; the whole of Europe, right up into

Northern Europe and the old Yugoslavia, just absolutely everywhere. We worked it absolutely everywhere and did really well in the Far East as well. Even Thailand and Malaya.

Australia, I have some footage from a show there. From a programme called Countdown. Not the one with Richard Whiteley!
Oh what a shame! (Laughs)

I think it was Australian, doing a couple of tracks on TV.
All I can remember about Australia was that we had to get somewhere for a gig quickly and we got in a helicopter and it was the first time I had ever been in one and it frightened the life out of me! I can remember the Australian Tour manager was called 'Ghost train head' and he did actually look like one of those heads that popped out of the dark at you in the ghost train! (Laughs) Really frightening when you woke up in the morning and you see this head. So 'Ghost train head' was on that tour yeah, good chap. We stayed in Bondi Beach, very disappointing.

It would be nice at some point if you could get a video compilation out but I guess it's problems with copyright and tracking all the stuff down.
Well let us talk to Peter (Purnell, head of Angel Air Records) *about it. As I said to you, the record companies seem to be happy as long as you give them a royalty. When you look at seventies and eighties bands, Gillan is really under promoted. First of all the shit that went on and is still going on: Ian and his 'damager', they have kind of closed the door on Gillan as much as possible. The title of Ian's compilation album 'What I Did On My Vacation' says it all. He never talks about it, he never gives it any space at all and fuck we were successful. We had a lot of success and a lot of hit records. The fact that it broke up the way it did, they are really missing the point because Gillan tracks should be on compilation albums that get TV advertising and you never see them. And the reason is, it's buried in legal shit.*

Didn't his publishing companies go bust?
Yeah but at very convenient times when people started asking to be paid they suddenly go bankrupt but it's such a shame. Even with all that shit that has gone before there is nothing that can't be repaired its just peoples attitude to it. Really we should be doing an album and a tour, it would be great. If we got the Bernie and Mick line-up it would be fantastic, there's no reason at all why we couldn't do a reunion album. I think it would do really well and it would do us a hell of a lot of good, but there doesn't seem any chance of that.

I don't think the singer is going to be interested.
What a silly prat!

Well hopefully you can keep bashing out one or two interesting concerts.
Yeah.

I listened to Brainstorm (McCoy's solo album) last night, which was enjoyable. Some of it, the last couple of tracks were a bit off the wall and reminded me a bit of Frank Zappa.
Well I take that as a compliment.

Well I'm a big Zappa fan.
Good man! I'm always very scared of saying that because a lot of people don't understand.

I thought Zappa was a brilliant musician.
I love Frank and he's my favourite guitarist. I just love his guitar playing. Actually he was one of

the few people I would get up off my arse to go and see.

I saw him on the last tour he did in '88.
Did you get that epic album 'Shut Up An' Play Yer Guitar?'

Yes. I've got everything he did. Some of it's a bit hit and miss.
I think a lot of that's because of contractual obligations and he just churned albums out. A lot of the orchestral stuff didn't do much for me. I saw him at Hammersmith Odeon and the band was just absolutely unbelievable. He's always had great bands. Sadly missed, he's one of my all time greats. He always cheers me up. So come on, what's your favourite track?

If I had to pick one I'd probably say one of the more accessible, 'Peaches En Regalia.'
Oh yeah what a track. Mind you there are a couple of dodgy versions of that.

The one on 'Hot Rats' is the best.
The original version.

I tend to go more for his instrumental albums. I know a lot of people go on about his lyrics...
But that's fair enough because he set out to shock. I think my favourite track is probably 'Watermelon In Easter Hay.'

Probably one of his more emotive solos.
But I also appreciate his work from a production point of view. Because I'm into production I can't listen to albums objectively I can't help but think that's a so and so reverb, or that sounds like this kind of amp or that sample sound is wrong. I'm always analysing what things sound like and Zappa's production was second to none. He had the talent to have millions of things going on in the track but you could hear everything. He was absolutely a master at it.

They reckon he had the magic ears.
Yeah he really was a special person.

I'm also partial to one of the lesser-known albums 'Sleep Dirt.'
Yeah there's an acoustic guitar track, that's a brilliant track.

And the last track on it ('The Ocean Is The Ultimate Solution') has another great guitar solo that is one of my favourite solos.
There's a great one on 'Ship Arriving Too Late To Save A Drowning Witch', there's a good solo on that album. I keep saying I must go through the albums and make up a couple of compilation CDs. Because it's the same old thing, you buy an album and there are two good tracks. He's definitely one of the all-time greats.

Absolutely.
What a connection!

Frank Zappa yeah, what a star.
How did we get onto him... talking about Ritchie.

I think they are similar guitarists because they improvise and take chances. A lot of players do it the same every night.
It just came out. You must chase Peter up to get a copy of that Zzebra album because you will

appreciate Steve Byrd's playing because he's a big Zappa fan as well. I just thought about Ritchie actually. When we did that 1971 European tour with Curtiss Maldoon he was the only one in the band who was nice to us! The rest of them just treated us like "oh you are the support band" even though we were on the same Record Company and same management, but Ritchie was really nice to us. Strange how I remember these things. I think he got a lot of bad press.

Yeah, but he can be difficult at times.
I don't think it's difficult; he just blows hot and cold like the rest of us.

He's always taken an interest in support bands anyway. I've noticed that. He quite often watches support bands from the wings. Even now I think he will do that.
I just wished that he and Ian hadn't been you know… all that shit hadn't gone down.

But they are like chalk and cheese.
Did you see Gillan at the Marquee when Ritchie came down and played?

No but I was at the one at the Rainbow Theatre.
It was really odd because they still hated each other. I couldn't work out what Ritchie was doing there.

You may not know this then, but at that time he'd asked Ian to join Rainbow. Did you know that?
No I didn't. I think there were some whispers about it.

It was in December '78.
I think there were whispers about it.

And he turned up at Gillan's house out of the blue one night when Ronnie Dio had left Rainbow and asked if he wanted to join his band. Ian said know but asked him to join his band.
Yeah, I remember that now.

And then they went their separate ways again.
Which I think is just as well, I don't think either of those plans would have worked.

Ian obviously sensed his band was going places and starting to re-establish it again, it was just a question of time and pursuing it.
In Britain we really took off like a rocket.

There was plenty of stuff on TV: OTT, Tiswas etc.
It was non-stop.

Some of those videos were hilarious; Living For The City was so funny. I don't know who the janitor guy was though!
A good-looking guy I thought. Obviously very hard working!

I suppose in that day and age the rock bands generally just went in for performance videos, just playing on a stage, so for your band to come out with things like that…
It was a bit different.

And No Laughing In Heaven was as quite an interesting video.
It didn't really work as well as it could have done but the ideas were there. It's just that some of

the shots in the video didn't actually come out as well as they could have done but it was like the theatrical side of everyone coming out. It was a band full of ideas. So have we finished now?

Yeah we're just rambling.
I do a lot of rambling. Think I might get another glass of wine and listen to some Ritchie. I haven't listened to Ritchie for a long time. So if you speak to him at all say hello from me.

I will be seeing him next month.
Brilliant. Is he still away with the fairies?

Yeah did you see that programme, 'Top Ten Guitarists' show on Channel Four?
Yeah.

I think people miss his sense of humour at times; it goes over most people's heads.
Yeah I thought it was funny.

I think he seems happy doing that.
Yeah, but fuck what anybody says, he is stretching out. He's trying some unusual things. Okay, it might not work for everybody but as a musician he's growing. And I think he will turn around one day and just blow the balls off everybody with something. I think it's just a matter of time but I think it's interesting what he's doing.

Within the magazine I think some fans are disillusioned now because they are out and out heavy rock fans and they can't take this music, they don't know how to react to it, but it's healthy. If he just did a rock album for the sake of it he would be going through the motions.
But I think he'll do another rock album when he wants to do a rock album. When he's actually got the feeling to do it and it will benefit because of that. Right well I will go and play something.

Footnote: During the interview John mentioned a Deep Purple album from a live 1971 recording that was to be released, but to this day it has not emerged. With regard to the other Gillan members mentioned, Liam Genockey joined folk-rock legends Steeleye Span in 1989, departed in 1998 but returned in 2002, and has been a member of the band ever since. Steve Byrd spent 17 years working with Kim Wilde as both guitarist and composer. Pete Barnacle joined Girl, and later Spear Of Destiny, followed by Girl spin-off band Sheer Greed. He was also part of the touring band for Yngwie Malmsteen's Eclipse tour. His latest project has been with a Japanese band called Soldier Of Fortune.

In 2006, John McCoy reunited with his former Gillan band colleague, Bernie Tormé and created the critically acclaimed trio GMT with drummer Robin Guy.

****

STEVE MORSE

Although I wasn't aware of it at the time, I suspect like many others I was first introduced to the guitar playing of Steve Morse through the Dixie Dregs track, 'Take It off The Top'; an instrumental used for many years as the theme tune to Tommy Vance's Friday Rock Show on BBC Radio 1. Morse is one of those players who is extensively revered by readers of guitar magazines, and for year on year regularly a firm favourite in readers polls. Aside from his work with Dixie Dregs, Morse recorded two albums with Kansas, and has also pursued a healthy solo career with his own band. His choice as permanent replacement for Ritchie Blackmore in Deep Purple, was a surprise choice for many but since joining the band in 1994, he time with Purple has been almost as enduring as the two stints Blackmore had with the band he co-created.

I first met Steve Morse during his first UK tour with Deep Purple in 1996, and was instantly impressed by his intelligence and politeness. But I have to admit that I have always struggled to accept his playing style within the confines of Purple. Sadly the lack of improvisations on that 'Purpendicular' tour was one of the main things that distinguished the new line-up from the Blackmore led versions, but Purple has re-established its image with a mixture of long term fans who have stayed loyal and a growing legion of younger fans who were too young to even remember when 'Perfect Strangers' was released, let alone the classic days of the seventies.

It's disappointing that Deep Purple has only produced four studio albums in the thirteen years that Morse has been a part of the band, but their appetite for touring ensures that Purple is still one of the hardest working bands on the circuit. In addition to being kept busy with Deep Purple, Morse has managed to find time for outside projects, the most notable being Living Loud, the brainchild of Bob Daisley. Having contributed heavily to the early songs from Ozzy Osbourne's solo career, the former Rainbow and Uriah Heep bassist, along with fellow ex-Ozzy Osbourne drummer Lee Kerslake created Living Loud to re-record some of those classic Ozzy tracks, plus a smattering of new songs.

Jimmy Barnes was brought in on vocals, Deep Purple's Don Airey on keyboards and of course, Steve Morse on guitar. The 'Living Loud' album impressed me greatly, and particularly Morse's playing. It has a grittier and more aggressive feel than the majority of stuff he has done with Purple. It was in conjunction with the launch of the Living Loud project that this interview was carried out; conducted via telephone on 9th December 2004 from Steve's home in Florida. The majority of it was published in *More Black than Purple* issue 28, but some parts appear in print for the very first time.

Who initially approached you about being involved in the project?
It was Drew Thompson, the executive producer guy. He's just a guy who likes to make musical projects and he did the legwork of drawing everybody together and the attraction for me, having worked with most of the guys before in some capacity or being aware of their ability... I love to work with seasoned pros who are really good. You know that no matter what happens it's going to be enjoyable.

That's kind of answered my second question as well because I was going to ask what was it about the project that appealed to you and made you decide to commit to it?
And also the idea... first of all the idea of recreating the Ozzy stuff without anything different wouldn't have been for me and when I first heard that I thought, "there are a lot of guitarists who can do that, great Drew I'll talk to you later." And he said, "wait they'd like to do some material that's original." And that's more like me, and when I was working with Bob and Lee, Bob was "yeah let's try some different things." That's more my style because I can't help but change arrangements so that worked out very well, the fact that there was room for creativity in every tune. Especially for half of them, a clean sheet of paper.

If I could use an analogy, football clubs don't normally allow their players to play with other teams in case they end up preferring the style of play or the team spirit and as such they would invariably end up wanting a transfer. Is that something that you are conscious of or is it ever a concern for your fellow players or manager?
There's a little bit of a weird thing. Say for instance if Living Loud was playing a gig just before, opening for Deep Purple, I don't think the guys would like that at all. However the fact that it's something occasional fits right in with Deep Purple very well because every one in the band does that, and it's encouraged and every one says it makes a stronger band because the musicians are stronger. They come in with more perspectives and better able to judge the ideas they are putting into the band. We all believe it makes the gene pool stronger that we draw from.

Again you have pre-empted my next question as I was going to ask if you feel it's important to have side-projects and if so why?
Extremely important- in fact I do more than this. I think it's absolutely a necessity. With the band, out of necessity you end up with a repetition when you are doing a tour and musicians can only stand so much repetition, especially musicians used to improvising and needs to do that, so there's got to be a creative outlet: For me it's a necessity.

The album was recorded quickly by today's standards. Is this your preferred way to work in the studio or are you the type of musician who is happy to spend a lengthy time crafting the songs?
That doesn't really count the time we spent working on the songs, which is probably another ten or fifteen days and I wouldn't have minded if it had taken sixty days to record because I got a little bit rushed through the guitar parts. That's just schedules and the way it worked out but it was very close to ideal to me and I think Purple is leaning the same way; that have really good musicians and work out songs beforehand; go in, be able to play them as a group before you get into the studio then play the songs. I think everybody likes that better.

My favourite track on the album is 'In The Name Of God', and in particular its the style of your guitar work that I believe helps to make it stand out. Did you use any special effects or equipment to get that 'Sitar' type sound?
All the sounds were straight from the Variax Line 6, sampling guitar. They sent me one to evaluate and I just used that for the 12 string sound and the sitar.

In my review of the album I have said that I feel the quality of the new songs are so good that you should all consider abandoning your current groups and projects and make Living Loud a full time band. What do you feel about that?
I'm firmly entrenched with Deep Purple and I think everybody in the band is very loyal to the band. However the ease of writing with everyone and just the rock solid professional playing was so rewarding for me. I'm used to that with Purple but to walk in with guys I hardly knew and instantly make music like that was very gratifying to me. The best thing about my job is being able to work with really good people and I can't say enough about them. All the people I've worked with in the last decade have blown me away. And each of them I could write a little book about the points I like about them. When you're dealing with guys that are literally on the other side of the world it's really hard to think about a full-time gig there. Everything you do involves travelling 12,000 miles!

The new songs are all credited as joint compositions. Was there a specific approach to the writing or did the songs come together randomly?
Bob, Lee and I basically started on tunes and Jimmy came in some days later and we'd already changed the arrangements of the Ozzy stuff and done the majority of the music for the new songs but Jimmy just sat with a sketchpad cross-legged on the floor and came up with line after line right there on the spot that sounded great. 'In The Name Of God' we were looking for another track to do and Bob is a great producer and he does that in the writing sessions, he naturally steers things. So I was throwing ideas and he was saying "that's interesting." And that's just like in Purple. Purple would grab an idea that sounds like something they like. Bob was eclectic enough, with his ears, to grab something and say "let's go, let's take that out." He's great to bounce stuff off. My forte is I can spew like a machine gun, lots of different ideas and it works best with someone who knows when they like something and when they don't. And Bob immediately knows. He's very quick to work with.

When working on a project such as this, do you approach it differently than you would with Deep Purple, and is the method in which the album is put together different?
I'd say it's very similar but the difference is because there are fewer players ... bass, guitar and drums at first with an added vocalist and then when the album was recorded Bob put keyboards on. But basically it was a trio working together. Now that is easy for me to work with. My own band was a trio for fifteen, twenty years and it's easy to have your own ideas translated quickly. With Purple we have to grab a consensus of more people with five people in the room. That's the only difference though. But my approach is the same. Throw out lots if ideas I think are good and

let the band that are there choose it. The filtering process just takes a bit longer with Purple because there are more people, that's all.

More arguments!
The arguments are not very heated like people would imagine. There's a quick disagreement and if someone's unhappy its easy to just abandon something. If someone isn't feeling it's the best, the best approach is to abandon it unless someone really, really, really fells strongly about it then they can wage a long term campaign to talk everybody else into it. That's usually not a good idea but when someone has a vision that no one else can see sometimes that's the only way to do it.

Does that normally come from the producer?
With Michael Bradford with Purple we had that, where Michael said "no I want to do a more commercial tune and I'm going to bring it in and you guys are going to make it sound like you" and change the guitar riffs or whatever.

Do you think that is the benefit of an outside producer. Someone who is independent of the band and not involved with it emotionally?
Yeah, I think the real benefit is steadying things quickly. Not that we have really heated arguments with vitriolic things, it's just great to quickly decide if something is working or not. And with Living Loud, Bob is the guy and he does it instantly. With Michael he'll go ahead, listen to the versions and be polite but he'll eventually say no this is the way it should go and everybody wants that after so many albums of committee.

Given that you are constantly revered in guitar magazines and have built a reputation as a guitar virtuoso, do you ever feel it's expected of you to be flashy or show off your technique, particularly as I imagine quite a high percentage of your audience are aspiring guitarists that have been inspired to learn the instrument from listening to you?
I'm not so sure about flashy because I sort of agree with the way Bob was putting it. Like when we were doing a Randy Rhoads part it would be good to do something that sounds good. Something that's in the same level of technique he was doing, which was some of the Ozzy Osbourne stuff. But the way Bob usually says it, it doesn't have to be technical it just has to sound good, feel good, period. And I've always believed that. I believe good technique is a powerful tool and of course like all things if its over used it becomes an unwelcome tool. But I believe it's very important to have some musical technique to be able to play some difficult things and especially where I can put them in to landscapes where there are features jutting out from landscapes as opposed to an endless sea of skyscraper type licks. But that's the challenge, to make music out of it one way or another. For me personally I think to have some technique in the toolbox is really important.

I understand Living Loud will be playing live next year. Do you know yet the sort of venues you will be playing, size of places?
No because like for instance there's a tour laid out in Australia but one thing; we don't know the promoter, my manager doesn't know the promoter so we don't know if that's really happening or not. But Jimmy's quite big there and it's very possible we could be doing a few thousand seats.

Will you be playing in Europe as well?
Yeah, there's already been some offers of show dates in those big festivals but it's hard to do being in Deep Purple. It's really hard to just say okay I can take this gig and take that gig because Deep Purple is chronically always waiting to see if something is panning out or not. The booking agent and the manager are always checking into things around the world and that means usually having

to check out people and go through this whole negotiating process as well as long... well we need a deposit, waiting period!

You seem to be touring pretty constantly with Deep Purple so I guess logistically it must be pretty difficult to fit it in. Not just for yourself but with the other guys in Living Loud to fit it together at the same time.
It's very difficult and it's a shame because these guys are great to play with.

So who had you worked with before, did you say you had worked with Jimmy?
Not really worked with him but knew him and been to his house and he sat in with Deep Purple when we played in Australia. And I knew Bob Daisley because he worked with Jeff Watson-guitarist from Nightranger. We got to be good friends when I was touring in Kansas and Nightranger was doing that tour with us. So we were like best friends. We're like extremely American, like dry sense of humour for Americans and we share a lot in common with our sense of humour and stuff. Anyway Bob worked with Jeff making an album Mother's Army so I hung out with him, hearing this stuff and I knew Bob was a very musical guy. And Lee, we (Deep Purple) did a tour with Uriah Heep in South Africa many years ago and Lee is just one of those guys who is super nice. You can see why he's in a group and people love to have him in a group. he's just a wonderful guy and extremely tasteful drummer.

It's interesting you mention South Africa there because again that leads me onto my next question as astonishingly it's ten years now since you joined Deep Purple...
Actually eleven...

According to the bios the only question you asked them was is there a dress code? Had you followed their career before joining? How familiar were you with the music, did you ask questions about the music?
I was familiar with the music but what I wasn't familiar with... I'd never seen them live so my question wasn't so much about dressing but the point was do they know what I do, do they have any idea that I'm different than what some audience members might expect of a Ritchie Blackmore replacement. Basically do they know what they are getting into. So neither they nor I wanted to commit until we worked together so we agreed to do four shows. I was quite pleased that they knew the Dregs stuff and especially Roger, and Roger had seen me play live I know that. He was really ready for something different and they wanted me to... well I came to the gig as a fan, and it's easy to be a fan of Deep Purple for me because one of the things I love most about the band is they are very musical and intense interplay between the organ and the guitar that they did. That was groundbreaking for me and it led to me liking groups like Soft Machine and ELP, also for the intense keyboard stuff. I easily came in as a fan and as a fan I said, "you know what; I wish we could do this and we could do that and I really missed that when I heard your live tape" and it took them a while- to talk them into some of the things, but eventually they did sort of cave in to my constant requests to make the band more like I remember in some ways.

Again that ties into what I was going to ask next. You seem to be able to read my mind! Given that the band had a reputation of being quite free-form and improvisational on stage was this aspect of the band emphasised to you before joining, did they sort of say what was expected or was it a case of them just wanting to start from a fresh canvas?
No one told me anything actually, they just said, "here's a tape." I had a tape of Ritchie playing and I had a tape of Joe Satriani playing and I didn't know which parts were improvised and which bits were for sure, cues to learn! So I thought I'd just absorb it the best I could and we had just one days' rehearsal before we played to 13,000 people in a sold out colosseum and that's kind of

intense for a guy just flying in from Florida!

It must have been a bit scary.
It worked out fine. The fact that they like to improvise and had open sections, I love. That was one of the deciding factors for me. I'm totally into that. I love bands that do that and especially rock bands are so rare to do that.

A lot of them just play by numbers.
Oh yeah. So I really appreciate that about the group. That was one of the things that sold it to me. I was improvising and I heard Jon immediately pick up on it and Don has got the same ears. It's uncanny. I love working with super, super pros like that. It's people with above and beyond talent and it's been two in a row, Jon Lord and Don Airey.

I guess it makes the job a bit easier when you've got guys who know where you are going musically and can follow what each other are doing without really having to work at it.
Yes the job is easier but it sort of... I guess it's like looking at a fine diamond or something too. it's something I stop just to admire. A lot of times on stage I will be playing along and that is just amazing, what a great keyboard solo, that just kills me. To me Ian Gillan has showed me how great it can be to work with a singer. He just loves singing in the band and he loves being part of the band and he always... from the very first day, and I mean literally from the very first day he would just drag me into the centre of it and he's been one of my biggest cheerleaders too, about coming up with ideas and stuff. It's amazing to have that. Roger was the guy with the all-around producer ears in the band. He just loves any style of music almost. But Ian Paice he's able to swing while he rocks and that is so rare. That is the stuff that made rock 'n' roll originally so appealing.

I think Paicey came from a swing background, big band kind of thing.
He does, definitely- but he doesn't throw it in your face. He realises the band is a different vehicle so he plays with that sense of swing but with rock 'n' roll sensibility. It's a wonderful mix.

As you said it's eleven years now since you joined the band but was there any trepidation from

your point of view to start with, given Blackmore's reputation and iconic status in the band?

No I think he did fine by the band he left without starting a whole war with them or stopping them from continuing and he basically left me alone. He could have easily murdered me in the press! But I'm really happy none of that came about. He left the band willingly so it wasn't like I was stepping on anybody's toes. There was a vacancy and they had to fill it. In fact they did fill it with Joe Satriani before. Any time I go in front of an audience, ever since I've been playing I feel there is a big responsibility to show the people I've got a lot of respect for them, that I want to entertain them in the best possible way by getting into the music completely and letting my years of practice and everything hopefully allow me to select notes randomly as I feel them, and that will move the audience too. I'm kind of corny with that expression but it's heartfelt emotion.

Going back to what you were saying about not getting any negative stuff from Blackmore, on the contrary I think he was keen to see the band carry on anyway, and he quite admires your playing and thinks you are a good choice for the band.

That's a great example of really the way it's been and that I was able to hear some of the stuff he's been doing and what a cool career he's had. Playing for so many decades in one of the biggest bands in the world and then going on and doing a different style of music but doing it very well and again keeping it very musical.

It's quite a radical change what he's done.

Yeah, but at the same time it's really cool because he's a very creative guy. I sort of imagine him like Jimmy Page. A lot of different ideas and heavy riffs but some of those heavy riffs work quite well with the acoustic thing.

Is he a player you admire then?

Definitely. I've had to sort of know his music very intimately really, it's part of my job. When I was a kid the very first song I heard with Deep Purple was 'Hush' back in the sixties, we played that, my brother and I in our little band because we just loved it. We loved Deep Purple especially in that 'Machine Head' era when they really hit their stride.

In the eleven years you have been in Deep Purple you have only recorded three studio albums so how much importance is placed on new recordings by the band these days? I guess not a lot!

Well surprisingly we're getting ready to do another one. And all indications for anybody who isn't doing Rap music, why bother recording? Why bother making free downloads? The band really feels strongly that it's something that needs to be done to keep the band viable and renewed, so that's the reason. Really for the fans, and interestingly enough we're still touring the world- to new places. But a lot of the places we are returning to things are getting better audience wise so it's awe inspiring that there are people who still seek out what we are doing.

When you say getting better you mean drawing bigger crowds?

Yeah. All indications are that the mass media is all about Rap. It's just weird there is not a wider opportunity for rock musicians but that's the way it is on the media but in the world stage where people vote with their tickets it's still happening very well.

I certainly sense a lot of younger kids are getting into rock music. In the UK sales of guitars are better with the youngsters than they have been for years.

That's neat. My own kid is doing that, he listens to Motley Crue and he's learned to play the guitar.

You mean you're not teaching him?

I'm teaching him a little bit but I want him to learn something on his own too. You've got to have some instruction at first.

Do you have any particular ambitions or aspirations for either Deep Purple or any of your other projects such as Living Loud?
I would love to be able to tour with Living Loud and I'd really love to continue to tour with Deep Purple. My wish is always that we'll do shorter tours in Deep Purple so that I can spend more time with my family but if you are going to go on tour it's a great band to do it with. We just finished a very long tour and we were all sad to say goodbye. It was strange we really gotten close. It's neat the way that's happened. The band really gets along very well. I'm saying this because it's amazing to me that a band that's been around that long- everybody's just happy to play.

It's had a lot of ups and downs in its history.
Like everybody in the band was all kicked out at some point except for Paicey, no not Jon Lord. I've learned the history!

Are there plans for another album with Living Loud?
Yes there is. That's something we can do. The recording computer or machine or whatever can wait while somebody just goes and does some gigs. With a tour the overhead monster is so big that there's this mythical belief and I say mythical because I'm against this concept but the mythical belief is that you've got to play a certain number of gigs just to break even, you can't do it with just a short tour. One of my crusades with any band I'm in is to do a lot of short tours and pack them together and manage the business end of it very carefully so it can be done. I think bands are fresh and really explode on short tours. Unfortunately I don't seem to be able to draw any quoin with a crusade, the exception being the Dregs and my own group. We all love it. We don't sing though. So when we do ten shows we do ten shows in ten days. One tour we did 24 shows in 12 days!

So with Living Loud if you did a new album would it be all new songs?
I'd imagine so. But you never know what Bob's thinking. But he's a very natural producer. In fact it might be a very difficult and uncomfortable thing to pull him out of that spot. But as it is he's really really good at it. I'm surprised at what a natural he is. I'm very impressed. And he really whips Lee into shape. It's funny watching them. They sort of interact like the Odd Couple.

They've obviously worked together quite a lot in the past so they know each other quite well.
They're very comfortable, nothing is toned down. Coming back and fourth, it's hilarious watching them but they communicate sometimes in monosyllabic gestures and things like that and instantly come up with parts that are great. Like I said, just suddenly making music with somebody in a few days that's just an amazement. It still amazes me.

I think the initial idea was to have different musicians on the album. Bob wanted to get different guitarists etc for different songs but it ended up as a band when you started working together.
I didn't really know too much about what they had planned before. By the time I had heard about it. When Drew was talking about just doing Randy Rhoads stuff I was becoming less and less interested. Not because I don't love Randy Rhoads but there are guys that know it inside out who really live for that day of being able to do his stuff, who could do a better job. And some fans just don't want to hear someone interpret something. They want to hear the thing. So I wasn't too sure at first until they started talking about changing things around and letting it breathe and doing new stuff. I wasn't really privy to what had gone on before I got involved.

But clearly from what you are saying it feels more like a band than a project?
Oh yeah, that's the weird thing. I think just the collective... you know the four of us sitting in my practice room here in Florida and we were working on the tunes so quickly. Like you could throw into the middle of this circle of people a 120 years or so or maybe 150 years of experience. And that collective body of experience was awesome. I had the same feeling, the first experience I did with Purple and the first time I went on stage with Lynard Skynard it was just like sitting in a big easy chair, it's like, "wow that ain't working!"

Obviously if you tour you only have about an hours worth of material from the album. Has there been any talk of what other songs you would do?
We already did a couple of gigs when we were in Australia and we did some covers. One of my favourites is 'Gimme Some Lovin'' and luckily I talked them into that since Don was doing the live gig with us it was a cinch to do. And also there's another tune that Jimmy had a hit with that he recorded with INXS. I think he cut a song with them, a live track (sings); *"Gonna have a good time tonight, rock 'n' roll music gonna play all right." That was a hit here in America. So I was really keen to play that so between that and the album tracks we had enough to play the gig. We could always add some more to it.*

So you don't know what time of year you will be touring?
I wish I could just suddenly convey how big the schedule always is. More than a month ahead. Oh man! Sometimes with the UK tour we knew about that in advance. Because UK tours with Deep Purple are somewhat sacred events. They really push the management to get it down and get it done. But the rest of the stuff, there's a lot of things up in the air constantly. And when you are dealing with home turf you can say this will work and this will work. These worldwide gigs are difficult to pull together. I'm a broken record, with everybody I know, I say the same thing: I don't know.

Despite Morse's desire to tour with Living Loud, since this interview was conducted there has been no further activity from the band. He continues to be busy with Deep Purple

****

BOB DAISLEY

Being labelled as merely one of many of Rainbow's bassists would do little justice to Bob Daisley's career. But like so many who were in Rainbow the stint he enjoyed was the springboard for a successful career that has more than its fair share of ups and downs.

An Australian, Daisley moved to the UK in the early seventies and soon established himself as a member of Stan Webb's blues based Chicken Shack before going on to play with Mungo Jerry on their 1974 album 'Long Legged Woman Dressed in Black'. Following his stint with Mungo Jerry he joined the Black Sabbath-inspired Widowmaker. After appearing on the band's 1975's self-titled debut and 'Too Late To Cry' in 1977, his grounding was sufficient to get the call to join Rainbow. After Mark Clarke's brief three months during the making of 'Long Live Rock 'n' Roll' Blackmore tackled some of the bass himself but with gigs looming Daisley got the call to step in and complete the touring line-up. Although Bob Daisley was in the band for barely a year, it was a pivotal time in Rainbow's career when the relationship between Blackmore and Dio started to sour.

I interviewed Bob Daisley on 9th November 2005 in conjunction with the research for 'Black Knight', the Ritchie Blackmore biography. Although Daisley had been based in the UK for much of his career, he now resides back in his native Australia, and the interview was conducted via telephone. Prior to the first question we talked about the well documented story of how Daisley was approached for the band via a mutual friend Dick Middelton.

What was the audition like?
Really the first part of the audition was actually meeting Ritchie and socialising a little bit, because as Dick had mentioned to me, Ritchie doesn't really want to audition people unless he meets them first and finds out if they are probably compatible as a personality because it's kind of pointless, either finding out they are a great player or might be right, but he doesn't

get on with them. So I suppose that was the first thing. The first thing Ritchie wanted to do, and Dick told me this, was to have a few beers and a sit and a chat. So Dick organised that with Ritchie and we just went out... we may have gone out for a meal or we may have just gone out and sat at the Rainbow (Bar and Grill) *for a little while. I think we just went there and see if we had compatible personalities. We got on okay so Ritchie said, "come down and have a play."*

When you first joined then, did you have to audition with the whole band?
I went down to where they had been auditioning and rehearsing other bass players, down at a film studio in Hollywood: Met Ronnie James Dio and Cozy Powell and they had a new keyboard player, David Stone from Toronto. Immediately I got on okay with Cozy, we had things in common and we knew some of the same people. Ritchie put me through the paces playing wise. First of all he wanted someone who used a plectrum, and I did, so that was a natural thing. He just put me through a few different things, "play this and play that. Keep on playing this." Like hard, fast right hand stuff with the pick hand to be sure I could keep up and we played for quite some time, like jamming and playing definite songs, and pieces and at the end of it... It's not that clear, but I think we downed tools and had a tea break or something and then they came back and said to me "you are what we've been looking for and the gig is yours if you want it." The funny thing is, and I even have to laugh about this myself now, is that I said, "I'll think about it!" Don't get me wrong I loved the idea of playing with Ritchie and Cozy, and Ronnie and the name Rainbow and all that but people... when I mentioned I was going for an audition with Rainbow some people tried to warn me off by saying "be careful. You are in a band that is a democracy, and it's your own band." That was Widowmaker, and "you will be a hired gun and a sideman and quite often people will get chewed up and spat out and three months down the track you could be without a job." So I had to think about that. I didn't say it in a big-headed way or anything like that, I just said "I'll think about it" and I phoned my wife in England and she said "what" Are you out of your fucking mind! Take it!" And I was still umming and aaahing and didn't know what to do.

Do you think he was a bit taken aback when you said that?
I don't know, possibly, I suppose your average... I was twenty something at the time, they were older, more experienced and been in huge main bands, and there was me coming along and saying "I'll think about it" but I did mean it. I really did want to think about it because of the situation but really the decision was made for me anyway because with Widowmaker we had a couple of... this was at the end of an American tour, we had done. They quite often squabbled and fought and punch-ups and arguments and all that. We had a gig to do at the Whisky A Go-Go. We played there, in fact I think Ritchie actually came to that gig and watched us. At the end of the show we were backstage and a couple of them started off again, arguing and screaming, and it almost fell in to a punch-up and I though that's done it, that made the decision for me, fuck this I'm off. I thought I'm going up to the Rainbow. And that was funny because Ritchie was waiting for me. He said he would be at the Rainbow Bar and Grill, which was just up the road. It became symbolic then, like I'm going up to the Rainbow! Because it was literally going to the Rainbow Bar and Grill but literally joining Rainbow as well and there was Ritchie sitting at a table when I walked in, and he actually stood up and applauded and I thought wow! I was taken a back then. Ritchie Blackmore standing up and clapping. I thought that was really nice, we sat down and started a drink and I said, "count me in" and that was it. I joined the band and we started rehearsals.

You said he wanted a plectrum style bass player. Did he express the reasons why?
It was just more precise, more definite. And for that... the style of drumming that went with it so well, because Cozy used to play eighths and sixteen's on his bass drum a lot and with a pick you can really lock it in. I suppose some finger style bass players can do it but it's never as precise, it never locks in like a pick does.

Did he explain to you, that much of the album had already been done?
I was told there was an album partially recorded, and they would need the new guys, meaning David Stone and myself to finish off and record so we could at least be on the album. Ritchie had played bass on some tracks, which I thought, did leave something to be desired to be honest with you, in my opinion. Because Ritchie is a fantastic guitar player, such a great style, and he's a great musician, he's got great ears and a great mind for music, but as a bass player he doesn't think like a bass player, and he doesn't play like a bass player and it came across a bit insipid for my liking. The bass parts he did on it were sort of like reproducing the same notes the guitar had already done. I prefer more melodic bass lines; something that compliments guitar and vocals rather than just copies it.

I'm still not sure to this day, which songs he plays bass on. On some of the tracks the bass is very low in the mix.
That could be him or I think they had another bass player.

Mark Clarke.
That's right. He might be on one or two tracks on that, I'm not sure.

So were you aware of that then? They had a lot of problems making that album, Tony Carey before David Stone and so forth. I've always been under the impression that a lot of Tony Carey's stuff has been wiped off, there's very little keyboards on it as well. Did they ever talk to you about that or whether they erased any of those…
I don't know because I really didn't hear the arrangements before I joined of what had been or if there had been a difference between what had been and what was now. I wasn't aware of it. The one thing I did know was that Ritchie seemed to have a funny thing with keyboard players, they always had beer cans flying at them and cutting remarks flying at them. I don't know, but on the album there are a few tracks that are not that strong, and there are a few that really stand out as being more than strong, and one of those tracks is Gates Of Babylon: A fantastic track. The solo Ritchie did over that chord progression is one of the best solos I have ever heard him do it's just fantastic. But one thing I must add to that, that David Stone wrote that middle section, the big majestic bit and he wrote the into and they just bought it off him! He didn't get a credit and he didn't get royalties. I thought come on David you shouldn't have done that. I think he probably thought, bird in the hand… take the money and run, so they paid him a couple of grand and bought that middle section and just slapped Blackmore / Dio on the writing of it but it should have been Blackmore / Dio / Stone. It was a really important part and a big part of that song he wrote.

I've heard that wasn't the only time Ritchie had done that, and he was very clued in with the publishing side of things.
And he probably wanted control, and David Stone probably thought, well how long am I going to last in this band or how long is the band going to last. It's a section of the song; just take some dough and go.

Did he explain to you at all why he didn't want you to add bass to the tracks he had already done?
No, he didn't actually. I don't know if he kept anything that Mark Clarke just did or he had done. He probably just thought it was good enough; it's exactly what I want, so if it's not broken, why fix it, although I could have done it. In my opinion I could have done it more like a bass player rather than a guitarist playing bass. He was probably fed up with it and thought, let's get these new guys on some tracks and get the album out.

152

On the tracks you played on, were they already written, were you just adding your parts or were you developing them in the studio?
Gates Of Babylon was a new song, that Ritchie had the idea for the verses, and that's when David Stone came up with the parts for it- the into and the big middle section.

Was it a case with the others that the drum tracks were already laid down or were you working with Cozy?
Well even when we did anything that was new we weren't working alongside each other it was a matter of Cozy in another room. There was no eye contact and there was no acoustic drum sound in the room. It was with closed-circuit TV cameras so I could watch Cozy and he could probably see us. But we were playing in separate rooms, which made it a little difficult but we pulled it off. In those days there was no Pro-Tools and Soundscape and all the rest to move notes around or beats around, it was just do it and record it and that's your lot!

Was that due to limitations of space that you were in separate rooms?
No it would be a sound thing as a sort of insulated sound, so you have got a complete room drum sound without any leakage into other mic's or without any guitars or bass going into the drum mic's.

You touched on how Ritchie had problems with keyboards players, and it's been pretty well documented of the hell they gave Tony Carey. I wondered if either Ritchie or Cozy talked to you about that during those sessions.
One of the stories I heard was because Ritchie was a javelin... I think he'd been a school champion, and he was pretty good at throwing javelin and apparently he threw one and it's thirty years ago now, so it's a bit vague, but it may have gone into Tony Carey's window or something! It could have got him. Now did it hit him or stick into the wall or in his bed or something. I don't know, I can't remember that clearly but I know there was a throwing of a javelin and Tony Carey was complaining that he was trying to be murdered!

Ritchie did tell me once that he threw one at his door and it went straight through his door.
I remember it vaguely as he was out in the garden and it would have been at the Chateau where we were recording, and they had been there before I joined the band where the first part of the album was recorded. I think that's what the song LA Connection is about. That Tony Carey was trying to phone home to get himself out of there and he wanted to leave and he was saying things like they are trying to murder me with this javelin. I think it came through his window.

Ritchie told me they rigged this thing up where they turned the power of and at the same time they smashed Carey's window with the javelin, so he thought the devil was coming in!
(laughs) Ritchie was always saying that place was haunted and this being or entity that he used to contact was called Baal and that he was out to get him and make trouble and problems with the recording and we did have a few blackouts when we were recording and Ritchie would always say, "well that's Baal." That's why on the album sleeve it says no thanks to Baal.

I was actually staying at the same hotel as him a couple of years back and I left a note on his door saying Baal has returned just as a practical joke, and he didn't find out who had done it. I know how he likes practical jokes so I thought I'd play one on him.
He loves to play jokes on people.

Did he ever try any on you at the Chateau?
No, I was never a threat to anybody. I was just trying to feel my way, not rocking the boat. I was

never a yes man or a brown nose but it was my first opportunity to be in a big named band, an arena band so I just got on with it, head down and just got on with it. I knew it was a hierarchy. I knew Ritchie was at the top, then sometimes Ronnie, sometimes Cozy, and David Stone always at the very bottom because he was a keyboard player! Me- just above David Stone. I knew it was a hierarchy. I knew it was Ritchie Blackmore's band. When I joined it was just called Rainbow but the year before it was called Ritchie Blackmore's Rainbow and Cozy and Ronnie wanted to drop the Ritchie Blackmore, understandably, but in reality it was still Ritchie Blackmore's Rainbow because Ritchie Blackmore was the big name, the guy from Deep Purple, the legendary guitar player.

You were talking about this spookiness at the Chateau. I understand they were doing a lot of séances. Were you a part of that?
Oh yeah. I was always quite interested in occultism. I don't mean anything negative or dark, neither was Ritchie. He wasn't like that; he didn't like people who wore crosses upside down or anything Satanical. He was interested in spirituality and occultism but only in a positive light.

Were any of those séances scary?
I think I used to get pissed first so that they weren't. At the Chateau, there were times when we were working but there might be times when there were overdubs being done, or vocals or something else or a bit of pre-mixing being done and there was fuck all to do there. The TV was in French. In those days you didn't have satellite TV with English channels and we were miles from any town, and it was winter and we used to sit in front of the fire and drink. So by the end of the night you would end up legless and go staggering off to bed so I think we would often have the séances when I was pissed so it didn't get to me. I remember one night Cozy and I were building up the fire. There was this huge fireplace you could almost live in it, actually stand up in it, it was so big, by the side of a giant window and we used to build up the logs in it. One night we built it up so much that the big oak beam mantle around it started to smoulder! There was so much heat coming out of it, and I think I took a photo of it. We weren't pissed of course!

I interviewed Cozy and Ritchie and one of them said about that fire. It might have been before you joined and there was a big antique radio on the mantelpiece and without saying anything they just looked at each other and threw it on the fire. Colin (Hart, tour manager) came in and started trying to pull it out.
I wasn't there for that, unless I was in my room pissed! I can't remember that. I can vaguely remember it happening or being told it had happened. I can't remember if it was while I was there or if I just heard the story when I was there.

Apparently Colin was trying to pull it out and the owner walked in thinking he had done it!
Maybe it was when I was there then because they wouldn't have had the fire on in the summer. We were there for a good while. It was definitely winter, we had the fire on every night.

Do you remember the other tracks you played bass on?
Kill The King, Gates Of Babylon and Sensitive To Light.

Ritchie was living in LA at the time you joined?
He was in LA when I met him. He'd been living there for sometime, up in the Hollywood Hills overlooking West Hollywood where the Continental Hyatt House is. If you looked directly behind it, he was up on the hill up there. He moved from there in the New Year in 1978... we did the Japanese tour in January, February. Because most people tour Japan for ten days, we did about four or five weeks there. Because the band was so big and the album was doing really well. And

we did three nights at the Budokan sold out, which is a big venue. After that we had a little break because I came down to Australia and saw my folks and when we went back, probably about March we went out to Connecticut, Ritchie had just moved to Connecticut and I think Cozy was going to do a year out or something, so he was living out there to. Colin Hart was living out there. David Stone was up in Toronto still. But it was only a hop skip and a jump for him to come down from there.

That was Darian, Connecticut wasn't it?
Yeah, and I stayed there at he Holiday Inn for quite sometime, waiting for the tour to start. After we started the tour, if we had time off we'd go back to Darian and I'd stay in the holiday in there and Ritchie and Cozy were living there. So I was in a hotel by myself, which got a bit boring. I used to hang out with Cozy and say, "come and pick me up" and we'd go to the pictures or go into town. Sometimes if it was just a short break for a couple of days, David Stone would be there with me instead of going back from Toronto.

Had Ritchie split with Shoshana by then?
Who? When I joined Rainbow, Ritchie was with Sue a blonde girl from LA. Then he hooked up with...

Amy?
No, a really slim girl with dark hair: That was his new girl, and he met her in LA.

After you recorded the album, you went out on tour.
No, we went straight out on tour as soon as I joined the band. We went out in October 77. I joined the band in the beginning of August, because I remember not long after I joined the band Elvis Presley died. I was in LA and I remember us all taking about Elvis in rehearsals, and we were rehearsing that day. And then we were rehearsing in LA for at least a month, maybe four or five weeks or something. I know because I'd been on the road for like six weeks with Widowmaker and I said "God, I've been away for six weeks already" so they said "we'll fly your wife out" so they flew my wife out and we stayed at the Sunset Marquee while I rehearsed everyday, for about four or five weeks. We did the whole show and all the fine-tuning and everything. Then in September I went home to London where I was living and they all came across and we did a dress rehearsal with the full production and everything, with the lights and the rainbow and all that. Then we went across to Finland and were supposed to do a gig in Helsinki and the trucks didn't make it or there was some problem with the gear, or something happened and we didn't do that first show, so that was a day off then we went to Stockholm.

Yeah I forgot that, you toured before the album was finished.
Yeah, and that went right through to November round Europe and England until end of November, then we went to the Chateau in France to do the album. Finished the album there almost up to Christmas. We had Christmas and the New Year off, then at the beginning of January we went to Japan and did that long Japanese tour. And the album was out there because I remember seeing the artwork and the finished product for the first time in Japan.

Do you recall where that dress rehearsal took place in London?
It could have been Shepperton Film studios or something like that, I vaguely remember.

That European tour had a lot of incidents. There is obviously the one in Vienna when Ritchie got arrested for hitting a bouncer.
Apparently he was the hall manager.

What do you remember about that situation?
I remember it quite clearly actually. We went on stage. I don't know what the complaints were, whether we were too loud or something happened, and they put the house lights on and this prick stood right in front of Ritchie, being an arsehole and he stood there with his arms folded in front of Ritchie on the stage. And it wasn't a particularly high stage, and Ritchie was being provoked by him. This guy was being an arsehole, so Ritchie swung his foot out near him and he went to grab Ritchie's foot and then Ritchie kicked out and kicked him straight in the jaw! Down he went and he wanted to press charges for assault and all this shit and then... we did the whole show, and it went down great and after the show the police came back stage with sniffer dogs and wanting to arrest Ritchie for assault on this bloke. I remember him being the hall manger, who was being a dickhead.

So the incident happened before the actual gig then?
The incident happened during the gig.

So he came on stage during it?
Yeah. This was during the gig, the guy was standing in front of Ritchie being a dickhead with his arms folded, trying to provoke Ritchie. I don't know if he was saying things but I know he went to grab at Ritchie's leg and Ritchie- whack straight in the gob! (laughs) *and down he went and then they tried to arrest Ritchie. They tried to smuggle Ritchie out of the gig in drum cases but I think he got sniffed out by the dogs and the police got him. I know we had a roadie working with us called Ox, or Thee Ox* (Gerry Oxford) *his nickname was, and he went to gaol with Ritchie to keep him company and all that.*

It resulted in the following show being put back a day didn't it?
Yeah, and that was the one being filmed. By the afternoon we did the sound check and we weren't sure if Ritchie was going to show up. The gigs off, the gigs on, the gigs off, looks like we'll do it, maybe he won't make it. It was sort of on and off all the time, then by the afternoon we still didn't know. Then we went down to the gig and everybody said, "yes Ritchie's on his way, he will make the gig but he'll be late." Instead of us going on... we normally went on 8.30, 8.45, maybe nine o'clock. That night it got put back to about 11'o clock and I think some people actually had to leave because it was going past public transport hours. Because if we didn't go on until about eleven we wouldn't have finished until after one. Some people did have to leave because of busses and trains. The majority who could stay did stay, and it went down a bomb, and Ritchie broke his guitar at the end of it. Good gig.

There was definitely a lot of aggression in him there.
A lot of frustration and resentment.

That guitar demolition was really over the top.
He meant it.

The way he was swinging the guitar around he could have taken people's heads off with it!
Bits of eye hanging off the neck!

I think he did a similar one at Liverpool when you got banned from the venue. He did some damage to the balcony or something. Do you think he was an angry man at that stage or was it just because of this Vienna incident?
No that was him, that's what he was like. He was a smart bloke and an aware bloke but I suppose like all of us he definitely had a bit of anger in him. To play that sort of music properly you've got

to have a bit of a spark as far as anger goes and aggression.

He went on record two or three years after that as saying this relationship he'd had with this Shoshana was the relationship of his life and it took a long time to get over it.
Oh, did she dump him?

No I think he decided... Stuart Smith told me he had to get rid of her because she was a bit nutty at times, that she would do some crazy things, but I just get the impression that maybe that might have affected the way he played on that tour particularly.
Could have been I don't know. I didn't know about her I won't comment on that.

I believe also on that tour the electronic Rainbow was still causing some problems.
It always caused problems. When it worked it was great. It was computerised but in those days we are talking seventies, computerised things weren't reliable or sophisticated like they are now. When it worked it looked impressive but when it played up it could cause problems with noises through the amps, and sometimes in some venues it was too big to fit in and sometimes it wouldn't work properly but when it worked properly it looked brilliant.

Did one or two shows have to be cancelled because of it or cut short through interference with the back line?
That's what I'm saying, but I can't remember. There may have been times when the show got cut short.

Then obviously you talked about the huge Japanese tour you did and there was another tragic incident in Sapporo where a girl died.
That was horrible. I think she was only about sixteen or seventeen. The thing is during the gig, we walked on stage, houselights went down, our lights came on, we started playing and all the audience rushed the stage. Now during the audience rushing the stage they had those fold up aluminium chairs and she was pushed down and the chairs went on top of her and the audience over that and she was crushed. Killed by the audience trampling over her, over these metal chairs. We didn't know anything about any incident like that. We just carried on with the show. We knew the audience... and that is unusual for a Japanese audience to go barmy like that because even with the best possible acts that play they are normally quite subdued and sit and they'll clap and they'll stop. Then you'll do the next song and they'll clap and they stop. They don't normally go barmy like that. But they went nuts and rushed the stage and this young girl got killed and we didn't have a clue it had even happened. We did the show, we did encores and still nobody knew. I went back to my hotel room, and I'd left the television on because I used to leave the television on for security reasons I suppose and leave a light on and do not disturb sign so people would think you are in your room. And I walked in and I thought whoa what's that, there's us on television and it was on the news. I felt first of all that a channel had been there to report the gig or show a little bit on television of our gig. There's us on stage here in Sapporo, then they had this thing about... because it was in Japanese I couldn't make it out but I knew it wasn't good news. And later that night I found out that some girl had got killed. It was a horrible feeling. I felt so sorry for her, just someone who just goes to a concert and ends up losing her life. A horrible feeling, then I thought, what about her family and her parents, her friends, just awful. And Mr Udo, he was the promoter; he's one of the biggest promoters in Japan. He was broken hearted, because he's a very nice man and he was just disturbed by the whole things as we all were.

How did Ritchie respond then? Did you talk to him about it?
Well the one thing I remember about Ritchie is that he kind of thought... I know he was touched

by it, and it affected all of us, and it was our gig and someone had lost their life at it. Not a nice thing to happen. But after a while, after a few shows, people or either the promoters or officials or news reporters were kind of saying tone your performance down a little bit. Don't look like you are too aggressive or too rock 'n' roll because of this incident. And I remember after a few nights instead of just wearing black trousers, I came out and I had these vertically striped black and white trousers on and Ritchie came over to me and said "I like that it looks cheeky." So he didn't want to lose the rebelliousness and the attitude of the band because of this incident. He didn't want to be... he wanted to be apologetic to the press, but he didn't want it to affect the attitude of the band and the image of the band.

Did the press want to interview any of you about it?
I think most of the stuff was obviously, there would have been a public statement, probably by Ritchie and Ronnie together and I know Mr Udo talked to the press and it was really something that was no fault of the band. We didn't incite a riot or anything like that. The real fault lay with the hall manager and the promoters of that show, that didn't secure the seating. So if the seating had been secure like normally those metal chairs are chained together or bolted to the floor or whatever. But when the people rushed the stage, all the seats fell over and this girl, with the collapsible chairs, she got pushed down and crushed and the audience ran over them. So it wasn't really any fault that the band promoted or incited a riot. We just walked on stage and did our normal thing of starting to play.

And as you say, Japanese crowds are normally placid.
They are subdued and controlled and they clap between numbers and they're appreciative, and they don't normally go nuts like that but that night they went nuts.

Was that the only occasion on that tour?
Well they were keen but that one stood out.

Was it a bit like a 'Beatlemania' thing for Rainbow in Japan ?
It was because I remember some of the towns we went to we couldn't go out on the street or anything. Number one, they are all Japanese and here is us being whiteys and really obvious we are not one of them. "Oh that's them." And some of the hotels had people all around them. I never like to mention anyone in the same breath as the Beatles because that only happened once. But it was like a little taste of what Beatlemania could have been like. We couldn't go out of the hotel. We couldn't walk anywhere and the hotels were surrounded by young fans. I get sick of hearing those things like when Duran Duran came out and had a hit record and "oh we haven't seen this since Bealtemania". Then someone else and "we haven't seen this since Bealtemania". Bullshit, that happened once and that's all.

Ritchie was like a God in Japan wasn't he?
Oh yeah, anything to do with Deep Purple, that was huge there.

After that show in Sapporo you played Tokyo the night after. Was it a bit of a subdued show bearing in mind what had happened or did you just try and adopt a professional approach?
Oh yeah we had to adopt a professional approach and obviously we thought about it because it affected us but we got on with the show as normal. There would probably have been announcements on stage by Ronnie in English, and also maybe one of the promoters, Mr Udo's representatives. I can't really remember it that clearly but there would have been heartfelt sorrow for what happened because it was very sad.

Do you remember anything about the Don Kirschner show?
I remember having a t-shirt with Don Kirschner written on it.

There were three tracks done for TV.
Oh yeah I remember those.

I couldn't work out if they were promo videos or done in the studio.
I think they were done just outside of New York and I remember us doing them during the day, and I remember being half cut by the time we actually did them because we were doing run throughs over and over and sipping vodka all day and I remember being a bit pissed by the time we did them.

They were obviously done just to broadcast on this Don Kirschner TV show.
Yeah but I remember doing Don Kirschner gigs as well. And I remember there were these T-shirts and I remember making a joke Don Kirschner should have this brother Harry- Harry Kirschner!
(Hari Krishna)

Then you did two to three months touring the States. Some of those earlier shows you were second on the bill to REO Speedwagon. For a man like Ritchie with a big ego, how did that affect him?
Not good, because having been in one of the biggest bands in the world with Deep Purple and being considered a guitar god, and having done so well in Europe and Japan and you go back to America and be second on the bill to a pop rock band, but he's grown up and professional and you just got on with it and did it. And some nights we'd blow them off and some nights it was their audience. You just live with that.

Is that tough to play to someone else's audience?
Well. It's a challenge but you just get on with it and do the best you can. But there was never a night when we bombed or you just had a Speedwagon audience that yelled out their name while we were on. I think most of the time we went down really well.

And you did some with Cheap Trick as well?
Yeah and we swapped over headlining in some areas. In some areas they were bigger than us, and in some areas we were bigger than them.

Did you also see any deterioration in the break up of his relationship with Ronnie on that tour?
There were a few hints. When the drum solo came we would all go to the side of the stage, just chat to say if the gig was going well or you played good in here, and have a drink and a chat and I remember a couple of times when Bruce Payne was there. I remember Ronnie was saying to him, "I could be gone soon, Ritchie is playing weird chords." Because there was this bit in Catch The Rainbow I think it was (more likely 'Mistreated') where there would be a bit of add-libbing with only Ritchie and Ronnie and we would stop playing and it used to be different each night, and if Ritchie played weird chords and made Ronnie sing over these weird progressions he would think Ritchie was having a go at him or putting him through some weird kind of test. Sometimes you would hear Ronnie say "oh it was weird tonight that means I could be gone, he's got it in for me." And then towards the end of the tour, we had been on the road for a long fucking time. I think that tour was for about four or five months. It got to the point of "fucking hell when can I go home." But I remember towards the end of it Ronnie... It was in the afternoon and we were sitting in a hotel lobby somewhere and Ronnie said to me, "there's a strong possibility that this band could fold at the end of this tour, and if it does would you be interested in putting something together

with me?" And I said, "yes I would." I said "if this band is no longer and Ritchie is going to get another band together or things are going to change or this is going to end and you are going to continue then certainly count me in" because I liked working with Ronnie. And no one else said that. Ritchie never came to me and said this band is going to end, stick around, so Ronnie was the one who said that to me and I said "great if you want to do that count me in." But as it turned out, it was a bit of a funny story because I went back to London, Ronnie was still in Connecticut and he kept on phoning from time to time. Every couple of weeks he would phone and say "I'm looking for guitar players and I've got record companies interested and hang in there. We are going to put this together" and it went on a while and I was expecting to get a call saying well we are coming over to London or we are going to fly you over here and then one day I went out to buy NME or Melody Maker and on the front 'Ronnie James Dio joins Black Sabbath' and I thought fucking hell what happened there. Thanks Ron, thanks for telling me. But as it turned out I was not disappointed. Ozzy was out of Sabbath and put a new band together and I was in it.

When Ronnie first approached you about that was it your own gut feeling that it was coming towards the end?
When he said it then I thought there could be a possibility of it.

Did they give you any explanation or was it just a case of...
Not an official explanation. It wasn't like this went wrong or he did this or that. It was none of that, it was just... I can't remember, it wasn't like I got a phone call, you're fired, Ronnie's out and he's out, David Stone's out. It was none of that.

Well everyone bar Cozy.
But Cozy only stayed for a while. He was in the new line-up for a little while and then he was gone. So it was, I suppose in some ways to be expected but still disappointing when it did happen.

There were also some shows in America on that tour with AC/DC supporting.
Yeah Bon Scott was a mate of mine. I'd known Bon in Sydney for years and that was really enjoyable because I would see Bon after they came off stage and then Bon and I would have a drink or back at the hotel. I remember he was sharing a room with Malcolm and I went to the room one night and had a drink with him and Malcolm and they were up and coming then.

I've read on numerous occasions and Ritchie had made some disparaging remarks about them and there was some friction between him and AC/DC.
Oh I didn't know about that.

As an interesting comparison, Daisley's stint in Rainbow was alongside the band's then new keyboard player David Stone. After their joint departure in '78 Stone's career floundered and he has drifted into obscurity, whereas Daisley's career continued to bloom. He was instrumental in kick starting the solo career of former Black Sabbath vocalist Ozzy Osbourne, featuring on the first two albums 'Blizzard Of Ozz' and 'Diary Of A Madman.'

After leaving the band, alongside Ozzy drummer Lee Kerslake, Daisley joined the reformed Uriah Heep in 1982 and recorded two albums, 'Abominog' and 'Head First' with the band. However a return to Osbourne's band, once again saw him contributing to writing process on albums such as 'Bark At The Moon' and 'The Ultimate Sin', but both his and Kerslake's work was originally uncredited and a bitter legal dispute ensued. In spite of this, Daisley maintained his working relationship with Osbourne until 1991's 'No More Tears.' Daisley has also toured with Gary Moore as well as contributing to Black Sabbath's 'The Eternal Idol' album.

Since the beginning of the nineties, he has contributed to a wealth of recordings as bassist, lyricist and producer, including albums by Yngwie Malmsteen, Bill Ward and Jeff Watson. It was in 2003, following his second and unsuccessful lawsuit against Ozzy Osbourne that he teamed up with Lee Kerslake, Steve Morse and Jimmy Barnes to record 'Living Loud.'

On 7th February 2003 Daisley recorded a live show at The Basement in Sydney with Australian blues band The Hoochie Coochie Men, for a live DVD and CD. It also featured Jimmy Barnes as well as former Deep Purple organist Jon Lord. Daisley and Lord also completed an album of new Hoochie Coochie Men recordings released as Danger White Men Dancing in October 2007.

****

TONY CAREY

In the eyes of many fans, Tony Carey was the finest keyboard player Rainbow ever had. With his classically trained background, he was ideally suited for Rainbow. However despite playing an important role on arguably Rainbow's finest album (Rainbow Rising) Blackmore took a personal dislike to Carey, and like so many other musicians who were in Rainbow, his tenure was relatively short-lived.

Carey was Born in Turlock, California on16th October 1953 and after his family moved to Connecticut Carey joined his first proper band, Blessings who secured a record contract with ABC Records in 1972. Symptomatic of the American record industry at that time, Blessings spent seven months in a Hollywood studio recording an album that was never finished as Carey was then snapped up for Rainbow.

I interviewed Carey at his home via telephone on 29th December 2005 in conjunction with the Blackmore biography (Black Knight) I was researching at the time. If you have read this book from the beginning, you will be fully aware of just how hellish Carey's experiences in Rainbow were. With that in mind, as much as I wanted to get his side of events, in the back of my mind were concerns that he wouldn't want to talk about the treatment metered out to him by Blackmore and Cozy Powell. I therefore started the interview with talking about far less contentious issues. I need not have been concerned as Tony soon opened up about the events that ultimately caused his departure from the band. Admittedly events were almost thirty years ago and that may well have allowed him to have a completely different perspective on things. As a consequence, over the eighty minutes that we chatted, Tony was openly honest and forthright about his experiences, and with the benefit of age was also able to have a good laugh about it all.

I know your time in Rainbow wasn't the most pleasant of experiences…
It was all right. Actually looking back it was more of a personal problem; the music was loud, it was wonderful. I was twenty-two years old- everything was okay.

What do you recall about your audition and meeting Ritchie for the first time?
I was never really a hard rock player and Rainbow was the only hard rock, progressive band I was ever involved with. The band I had before- I was nineteen, twenty, and we got signed in Connecticut with ABC Dunhill and they sent us up to Hollywood to get high and fuck girls and maybe make a record! It was crazy times in Hollywood in the seventies. I'd heard Man On The Silver Mountain on the radio and I liked Deep Purple but Ritchie was actually looking for drummers and keyboard players- Cozy and me. We were both rehearsing. My band was rehearsing in SAR studios in Hollywood, and Ritchie was holding his auditions I guess across the hall or something and I always played a loud Hammond and somebody heard the loud Hammond and said to Ritchie "check this guy out maybe you can steal him from his band". Which was perfect timing because we would sit there in Hollywood for a couple of years and not be able to get a record finished because of various outside influences! I was fed up with the thing anyway.

We were like a country band and I was classically trained, can play anything. So Jimmy Bain came over and introduced himself and said, "Do you want to come over to Pirate Sound", which is the old CBS movie lot in Hollywood: Big sound stage, "and try out for the band?" I said "yeah I'd love to", so I went down with a buddy of mine and I was early, and I was like playing this little mini concert... about six keyboards- loud! I thought I was actually alone but Ritchie, Cozy, Ronnie and Jimmy were all in the back, seated against the back wall about fifty yards from me in the dark, so I got the job before I played with the band just by warming up.

You were the last to come in then?
Yeah Cozy was there.

Once the line-up was completed how much rehearsing did you do before the first gigs?
Astoundingly little. We liked, play a song, learn the chords a few times. I don't remember exactly, but we didn't work anything out except the structure, like you solo here, Cozy solos here. Everything was very free form, really progressive rock. We weren't The Sweet, learning all these harmonies and hooks and hit singles. We played very long songs sometimes because everybody was having fun. And that was an ass-kicking jamming band. One of the unsung heroes of that band was Jimmy Bain, a fantastic bass player who kept it going and never let up a second, and Cozy too. He was so consequent in his playing. Ritchie's idea of a drum audition was to start a fast shuffle and play off for half an hour until the drummer collapsed. Not pull a grimace, not look at him just keep playing at this thunderous volume until he had enough and the drummer went home.

But Cozy could do that?
Cozy could play all day and all night. He was a complete gentleman.

Those rehearsals at Pirate Sound, I heard that Purple were rehearsing there as well and Ritchie went to the owner and asked him how much to rent the whole building and shoved them out. Is that true?
I don't think that could be true. The owner was (Robert) Simon. These were sound stages and

Pirate sound was just an enormous room like an aircraft hanger. There weren't separate rooms in it, and next door there was another one, and another one, and I think only the one was Pirate sound first of all. I don't think he leased the whole film set. Enormous and I know that a couple of bands from Casablanca were rehearsing there. Angel, but I never heard that story. (In an interview with Pirate Sound owner Robert Simon, he did actually confirm the story was true). *We went to see Deep Purple in Los Angeles with Ritchie and we sat in the tenth row.*

I heard he got quite friendly with Tommy Bolin.
There was no problem that way. I didn't think there was a problem. I wasn't in direct competition with anybody and I worshiped Jon Lord. So he said do you want to go and see Purple tonight, so we said okay we'll go, and we sat there in a row like school kids and everybody was polite, there was no kind of vibe.

Did you go backstage afterwards and meet them?
No I didn't, maybe he did but I didn't. But I loved the band. That was the first time I saw Coverdale and Glenn Hughes together and it was unbelievable I thought they were great.

What are you memories of making the 'Rainbow Rising' album?
Well we went to Munich, and I'd never been to Germany, and I got my new passport and went. Jimmy and me we were kind of a team, we roomed in the seventeenth floor of the Arabellahaus Hotel. I lived in the Munich area for twenty-five years so I know the Hotel, in fact the same guy's on the door by the way as it was in 1976. It's amazing and he still remembers me! "Hello Mr Carey". We rehearsed in an old farmhouse and if you told me where it was today I'd know. I would say somewhere like Fürstenfeldbruck around Munich. We drove out and rehearsed with really tiny, minimal equipment. It was in December, it was freezing cold and we rehearsed the same way we always rehearsed, which was basically here's some riffs. And Ronnie would have his pad and paper and be writing lyrics and mostly we played without Ronnie singing because he would be brainstorming his demons and wizards thing. Then we went into Musicland, which at that time was a state of the art studio in the basement of the Arabellahaus Hotel. I remember they carved a drum room. This was kind of revolutionary at the time, now everybody does it. Everybody sets drum kits up in bathrooms and tiled rooms to get this crashy, banging sound. But in those days studios had rugs on the walls. This dead sound from Abba to The Beatles. Everything was this dead studio seventies sound and we wanted to definitely make a little more damage, a little more noise. I don't know if they did construction or not, I think they did. They somehow hollowed Cosy out a concrete room to put the drums in. Everybody does it these days but it was revolutionary then. Martin Birch produced and engineered... I don't know if he produced, actually I'd say Ritchie produced, he knew what he wanted but Martin engineered and was the liaison with everybody's egos, a lovely guy. Great guy. I really loved working with Martin.
I don't remember his name, the guy from Musicland, the Tonnmesiter came in, in an SS uniform one day! It was fantastic. Not the black, but the brown shirt uniform with a red and black swastika, complete Nazi uniform. Now I just thought it was funny, but being American I can just wear anything I want all the time. But being German in 1976 that's a serious crime, but he came in and the whole day his demeanour was "sieg heil" but perfectly done, really funny guy. He never cracked a smile. He would say "ve vill do it zis vay". Real German in his Nazi uniform. That stuck out from the recording. We zipped through the record. 'A Light In The Black'- basically the band cut the track without me, 'Stargazer' too and I overdubbed the keyboards. And they wanted an introduction for 'Tarot Woman' so everybody left and I sat with Martin for about an hour and a half and we did 'Tarot Woman', and on the same day we did the solos for 'A Light In The Black', the fast synthesizer solo, some stuff on 'Stargazer', the orchestra things, which I simulated and were later done with a small orchestra. Once again I'm looking back through thirty years of

whatever but compared to making records today it was effortless. It was a breeze, a piece of cake because basically what we did was what you are supposed to do when you make a record, and nobody ever does because everybody's too neurotic, is go in and play the fucking thing! The Ronnie came down with his notebook and sang "my eyes are bleeding" and all that shit! And it was done.

That writing partnership was a bit special.
There was a vibe in the air, once again there wasn't much said but there was a lot done. The melody and the track would be in the air for a couple of days and all of a sudden Ronnie would be gone with his paper and he'd come down and basically just sing the motherfucker, not spend hours doing it either. He'd just do it as if it had always been there, which is the mark of an acceptable song. It's got to sound non-contrived and I thought they had a great writing chemistry.

I guess the fact that you say it was rehearsed all beforehand...
Yeah but we never played anything twice the same way really. That's what I meant before when I said we were not The Sweet. Like any solos or anything... I mean the song has a form okay, you have to go verse chorus, verse chorus, then the intro's probably going to be similar, but not even that because Ritchie would start doodling on stage and all of a sudden it's fifteen minutes long with some kind of cue or collective telepathy to start the song.

So those recordings were fairly spontaneous?
I would say they were completely spontaneous. 'Kill The King' I know we recorded 'Kill The King' for... I wish we had recorded it for 'Rising'. I don't know why we didn't but it was the opening number on the tour for 'Rising', and that song was gigantic. That was just a jam and that went on for hours. I don't know why we didn't do it for 'Rainbow Rising'. In those days you could only put about, actually 38-39 minutes on a record before you started losing quality. And 'Rainbow Rising' actually didn't have any bass on it at all, which is the first thing to go when you have to make compromises in the length of cutting a record.

I think Ritchie had a problem with bass players as well because I find a lot of those early Rainbow albums, you can hardly hear the bass as if it's deliberately mixed down. Whether he spoke to Martin about it, but 'Rainbow Rising'- you can't here the bass.
You know one other thing, there is a physical law, turn everything up and the bass gets louder. If you listen to it really loud, you can hear the bass. Who knows what the monitors were like in Musicland really. There was a huge wall of speakers but nobody missed the bass until the record came out so I guess it was done in mastering. It's not the volume of the instrument because if the frequency was there you would hear it. The instrument is there but it's like everything from 100hz down is gone. Maybe they mastered it so it would be louder. If the record has too much bass on it, a vinyl record, the needle would jump out of the groove, so maybe that was the reason for maximum volume, before we get too deep into Ritchie's problems with bass players. Ritchie's problems would extend to most of the human race I think! Without saying bass players, or trumpet players, or flute players or whatever.

Did Ritchie strike you as a control freak?
For sure, and all the great musicians I've met since then are. Absolutely. But if he didn't like it he would be completely non-confrontational, which is a kind of maturity issue, basically sit and steam then we'll fire the guy before we sort the problem out. But yeah a control freak. Every CEO of every company in the world is a control freak. It's nothing bad to be, and if you are going to be Donald Rumsfeld or George Bush, you need to be a control freak. But very definitely.

But he didn't get involved on the business side so much, it was more on the music side.
It was only the music. Even people's personal lives, actually he was a good guy to work for in that sense. He was very passionately into the music, and not cynical about it at all, having come from Deep Purple, such a huge band and try and build up his own band, and he wanted things right.

How did that manifest itself in the studio when other guys were laying down their parts.
He'd leave. When I did all of my solos, every time, he said to Martin "I'll come back..." one time I was in Musicland and I did two different solos to 'A Light In The Black' and one of them was a low one that made the record and before that I did a high one, more your standard keyboard solo about two octaves higher. He came back and said "boy that's fast that's good, don't like it, do another one" and he left again. So I said "okay" and Martin suggested I do something completely different and we did this low one and he came back and said "that's the mark of a good musician when you do something different". When you are not written in stone from the first moment. But a control freak in the sense that had he not liked that solo I would have played a third one and hadn't liked that he would have got another guy to play it. But as far as letting people do their jobs he was great.

I guess it was tedious for him sitting in the studio listening to a guy for hours working his parts out.
Yeah. The other thing is though (he also left when Ronnie sang), *a good executive delegates. He's hired me because he thinks I'm the best he can find at the moment and he doesn't really need to sit there and tell me how to do my job. If anybody would be the one to do that it would be Martin who was ostensibly producing. He was a good guy to work for. He's gonna shit when he reads I said that. He probably thinks I hate him. I don't hate him at all.*

I assume when he did his solos the others weren't allowed to be present?
That's not true either. He'd sit there and we were in the lounge listening to everything. We were never asked to leave but it's like Ritchie doing his guitar now, you don't want to sit there and stare at his fingers. It wasn't like a rule or anything. We were mostly happy for the break. Studio time is really intense, the bottom tracks were down, keyboard solos were done, okay we're going to do some guitar solos now, he sat there with Martin and I'd pop my head in once in a while but he would sit there until five in the morning. There weren't rules like that.

That's interesting because in later line-ups other musicians would say he wouldn't like others around when he did his solos and Colin would make sure they weren't there.
In '75, '76 he was playing with good musicians. I heard all the keyboard players he used. Don Airey is a good keyboard player but everybody else I thought was garbage. That's my opinion. Ronnie Dio was a great singer but no one else could hold a candle to him I thought. Cozy was irreplaceable and bass players nobody cares about (laughs) *so there we are.*

Interesting! Your 'thing' or your sounds were vastly different to what he had with Jon Lord. Was that something that he had put upon you, that he wanted to get a way from the Jon Lord sound?
Not at all, he never said a word. Never said play this instrument instead of that instrument with the exception of maybe the Orchestron because he had this thing in mind for 'Stargazer'. Actually what I did... sounds is one thing, but playing with Ritchie is another thing and I played actually quite similar to Jon Lord in that I played like a second guitar player a lot to make this fat sound. I had my left hand- I used a clavinet with a deep bassy left hand, and the right hand on the organ, which is why when you see these old pictures I have both hands on the keyboard, one of them up and one of them down and basically I would pretty much learn his riffs and go with him, that way when he took a solo, there wasn't this big hole in the sound. I was like the second guitar, for the

heavy songs like 'Kill The King.'

So that was something you chose yourself.
We never got any instructions but he liked the way I played. That's what you want as a bandleader. Gradually nudge someone in the direction but not tell them what to play.

So you just picked up on the vibe, and if you had been doing the wrong thing he would have said so?
Yeah, exactly right or not have said so and fired me for it! On a musical level it was fabulous.

I have also read that Jimmy said when he joined the band he would also be involved with the writing. Did they ever say that to you?
Of course they did, it's all bullshit. I tried to sue them too. This is jumping ahead a little while but when we were in Australia and Japan I noticed more microphones on the stage than should have been there. I said, "We're not recording this are we?" "Oh yeah we're recording". I said, "Well I want a piece of it", "okay of course kid, you will get your contract". I never got a penny from all these Rainbow bootlegs or the official stuff that is around now.

They allegedly did the same with David Stone. He wrote part of 'Gates Of Babylon' and they actually bought the publishing from him.
Well who wrote Tarot Woman? I did! The into. Everybody left the studio and said "can you do a little mini-moog into?" And I sat there with Martin Birch, so who wrote it? Okay.

So what happened did you say I want a writing credit on this song?
No, it was the seventies and I was happy to be involved. Business didn't become… people didn't worry about publishing and song writing and things, some people still don't, until the mid eighties. We were all in Los Angeles, getting high, having a drink and we were a great band and we knew it. Everybody was cocky. I'm not sure how aware Ritchie was of everything either. In his defence actually you will notice with the Deep Purple song writing credits they were all split five ways and how much did Ian Paice write of Smoke On The Water? I would say that Ritchie's financial advisors, Bruce Payne. I tried to sue them- to litigate just about a year after I left the band because of these live recordings and everything. By the way on that 'Long Live Rock 'n' Roll' album those keyboards are mine but I didn't get credited or anything. I wanted to get something on paper. And the biggest hurdle in suing Ritchie Blackmore or Rainbow is he didn't exist as an entity on paper in the seventies. Everything was so touchy. I tried to have a lawyer serve Bruce Payne. It would have cost two years in court just to find out who was pulling the strings and it was Bruce Payne. I wish him well.
It was also completely normal business practice in the seventies. But what I have to say about Rainbow is we could have been one of the great progressive rock bands. We started off with a real bang with 'Rainbow Rising' and the live recording but on a personal level, Ritchie tends to fire everybody after about five minutes and he can't get along with anybody and never give the band chance to grow. We raged into 'Rainbow Rising' after a couple of concerts and a couple of rehearsals and imagine how good the band would have been three years later?

I think generally the fans say that band and the '76 tour was the pinnacle of Rainbow.
Yeah but okay, after that they went to these mainstream top forty attempts with Russ Ballard songs, which didn't really work. I had more chart success than Ritchie in the States; I had two top forty hits with one project and three with another. This forced pop music with Joe Lynn Turner… if that's really what he wanted to do then fine- he did it well.

I think he gets bored quickly. He says that of people. I think that's why he kept changing the line-up. But I also sense he might have changed the line-up because of an insecurity thing and didn't want people to get too well established.

He hated me personally. He was ten years older and British and I was a cocky kid from California, I still am. He didn't like me at all on a personal level. I knew that. One of the times he fired me, we were in England and we were playing somewhere and I was definitely playing too much. I know that now, but that's what a band does. So anyway, he came over in the middle of the set and said, "well why don't you just leave then". And 'problem motherfucker' that I am, I said, "okay I'm gone". Took a cab back to the hotel, called the airline and said "I'm outta here". So they said "oh no you can't do that it's the middle of the English tour". "Well he's just fired me". And I was talking to Bruce actually on a couch in the hotel lobby and not knowing Ritchie was standing right behind me and I said "I think he's just jealous because I play so fast". Ritchie of course heard this and whacked me across the back of the head. Not like... he hit me like you would hit a little kid and said, "you're nothing, you will never be anything". So it was definitely insecurity and a pride. Why should he be jealous of me? He couldn't have been, but I was a mean motherfucker organ player and I kept him on his toes musically.

That's always something throughout his career that is an anomaly. Sometimes he wants somebody of the same ability…

Well Jon Lord drove the band, that wasn't a guitar band until the seventies.

But other times he wants people to be subservient. It's like he wants it when it suits him. Do you think that's a fair observation?

I don't know. I can't figure him out. On one hand he's an absolute genius. He's got such a magnetism about him, when he walks in a room, and this was thirty years ago, he owns the room: The man in black. This is one person in fifty million, just from his charisma and what he's got. I don't really care to analyse what he is. Mozart was an arsehole, died of getting butt fucked, he was thirty-five. Ritchie's definitely an important figure. He taught me a lot. Nothing you would ever want to teach anybody, because he's way too selfish, but just observing him. I'd not like to judge his character. I'm fifty-two now and I've had bands over the years and I've always used younger musicians but I've always been nice to them. "Basically I understand where you're coming from, you want to do the best, and here's a tip". Not like "fuck you or whatever". But we all have our insecurities, but the biggest problem I had with Rainbow was the management. They were sharks. It's a shark pool. I know that, and it hasn't changed since then.

It kind of goes with the rock 'n' roll territory.

But we didn't think so we were all idealists. I was born in '53, Ritchie was born in the forties, in post war Europe, and I come from California. I was just a hippy thing, I was fourteen in the summer of love in 67. In San Francisco, so I was so blue-eyed idealistic, I still am that I was more like shocked… "oh he's lying to me?" And the other thing that followed Rainbow around was this kind of violence. He would send roadies out to beat people up. Or I heard stories about it, I don't know any details but there was always this edge of violence. One of the Deep Purple roadies was murdered that year. Shoved down an elevator shaft and that became part of the legend, breaking guitars on stage. That's okay if it's just the stage act but there's some rage going on through the whole organisation and maybe hard rock scene. As I mentioned that's the last hard rock scene I ever played with. My music is different. But it was a good gig and I jumped in and took it.

You were saying about the UK tour when Ritchie came over to you on stage and said why don't you just leave, was that the only instance or did he give you any other grief on stage.

You know what, that wasn't grief. I was definitely not playing what he expected me to play. It was his band. Now he could have come over and said will you play less or will you stick to the rulebook or some shit. But he didn't because that's not his style. I didn't know he was unhappy because he keeps it all to himself. Then he came over and said, "why don't you just leave then", like no warning. So I said, "good, I'm gone, bye! I don't need this shit". But I never got any grief at all from Ritchie on stage. He's amazing on stage; he's in his own world. And he's over there on the other side and playing, and people's mouths are hanging open in the audience. I thought the only time I could communicate with the man in fact was on stage.

I have read stories elsewhere that he said to Jimmy Bain once that he was playing in the wrong key. I guess you are not aware that when Ritchie was playing with Gene Vincent, Gene used to go up to Ritchie and tell him, he was playing the wrong chords.
I didn't know that.

I was just wondering if it was his way of getting his own back.
Now I understand. That's funny I like that story.

Apparently Gene Vincent treated him like shit.
Ah ha, thereby setting the foundation.

I think that might have had something to do with it.
Unbelievable.

Do you have any recollections of the first show you did together, it was in a big arena…
Montreal I would have to say.

Yeah, and it was by no means full.
It was a 15,000 seater, some big hockey arena and I asked how many people and it was about 7,000, which looked really empty in a 15,000 seater.

Ronnie is on record as saying it didn't matter to him because he had come from a smaller band but he thought it dented Ritchie's ego a bit, or his pride…
But you know what, here we are again, talking about things that every housewife and everybody that drives a car; normal day-to-day things in one's life. I mean okay we played a gig and it wasn't sold out, oh gee you poor guy! I don't know if it dented his ego, you have to laugh at it. I do know we played in Australia and we had two shows scheduled, a matinee and an evening show that had sold out so the scheduled this matinee for the afternoon. There was like 200 people who came into this huge hall, and I remember Bruce Payne came in behind this curtain and said, "The audience says he's ready!" We all laughed about that, the evening show was sold out and Ritchie said okay it's a rehearsal and we had fun and played. You know I never saw Ritchie Blackmore throw any ego tantrums that wasn't his style. His style was more… he disappeared into a dressing room with a bottle of scotch and keep it pretty much to himself then turn up on stage and he never played like a drunk. He played like Paganini a little bit, like he'd sold his soul to the devil or to Johnnie Walker! But I don't have much sympathy when I hear a story like that, well we didn't sell out the Montreal Ice hockey arena in the very first Canadian gig of Rainbow, gee you poor guy!

I only brought it up because Ronnie had made that comment in the press years ago. It was his feeling.
I know we were delighted and excited to play and I had a technical problem with one of my keyboards that made Ritchie mad. On 'Stargazer' we used an instrument called a polyphonic Orchestron in which you would insert a video disc like the size of a record, a big old floppy disc,

right after the mellotron, and the precursor to the digital stuff and the thing was really fiddly and at three or four shows I remember that thing being on stage in pieces before the show trying to put it back together. The roadies and this would have been Raymond's job. You had to tape the keyboards onto the volume pedals under the floor so they don't tip on their side or anything. So the polyphonic Orchestron volume pedal- I couldn't find it, it had slipped away and it wasn't taped to the floor, and the volume was down and there's this big important line in Stargazer and the sound man got as much level out of it he could so you could hear it, but technically it was all the way down. Then they found the pedal and floored the motherfucker and everybody jumped! That was one thing I remembered the most- that was really embarrassing.

It's incredible how you can remember those things because Raymond remembered that story as well.
Is that right?

Because he said Ritchie called him into his dressing room after the show and said "what went on?"
When we found it, it was fucking loud! It's funny thirty years later.

Do you recall any problems with the electronic Rainbow?
Well it was notorious; of all the places we used it I don't think we had more than three or four where it functioned. We had a grounding problem, an earth problem. Ritchie used Stratocasters with three single coil pick-ups; if he'd used a Gibson with humbugging pick-ups we wouldn't have had that problem. At times the buzz created by the reostats, the dimmers in the rainbow were louder than the band and that was the problem. Although I tell you how much of a problem it was, we were loud! We were blowing kids out of their shoes in these theatres! And I know we needed a height of some twenty odd feet to hang it, to rig it, and there were a few shows that didn't work, not technically possible.

But there were quite a few quiet moments in the show. It must have had an affect then.
Yeah, and Tony Masucci the lighting guy who built it and ran it- You could hear him searching for combinations of lighting and colours that would minimise the buzz. It's like dimmers in a recording studio. If you use the dimmers the guitar is going to buzz so you have to turn off all the reostats and the dimmers and the lighting basically. So you could hear Tony Masucci go from green to yellow and whatever, trying to minimise the guitar buzz, which was different every time.

I guess that must have pissed Ritchie off?
I don't know, depends on how drunk he was. Personally, that's the thing. If it did piss Ritchie off, back to the point, I never saw it. Ritchie wasn't a tantrum person, he was very quiet. I never heard him scream, "what's this fucking..." or anything at all. Or dress anybody down in front of other people.

He'd probably go and brood bout it.
Right. I would say that, or "I'll have a production meeting after the show" and maybe he would rant and rave but Ritchie's not a ranter and raver. He's very quiet. I'd have to wonder about his relationship with his father! Which I don't know anything about, that's just a smart-arse comment.

That's probably a fair observation. You were talking about the improvisation on stage. I assume it's kind of structured in the fact that he would say I'm going to solo or improvise for so many bars.
No, no definitely not, improvise until I do this and hold my hand up then we are done.

So it was all done on the hand signals?

Hand, head, telepathy. I mean the best way to come out of a solo is a big, huge drum fill. To go from part A to part B. That's the thing, when I say progressive rock, what this band had that made it progressive rock. I was into Miles Davies in those days an awful lot, 'Witches Brew' and twenty-five minute songs and just playing and Miles looking round and just playing with his back to the audience, and somehow the band knew where they were going. Chick Corea... he had no slouches in the band but somehow they knew where they were going and it was never, I'll solo sixteen bars and then we'll go somewhere else, it was like I'll play until I don't feel like playing anymore.

Would he use certain motifs or certain little riffs to indicate to the band to come back in?

Yeah, but over time. These things developed. That's also why I mean in three years that band would have been a motherfucker band if it had kept the line-up. You see its trial and error. You find out what works and when a solo peaks and you find the right peak and the right way to leave it then you tend to repeat it the next night. But it's not like okay I'll play D-C-D-D-C-B and that means you guys go to the bridge. If you put any good four or five musicians together and tell them to jam this number out, any in the world, and play 'Mustang Sally' it's going to be good and the solos are going to fit and it sounds like they have been rehearsing all their lives.

When it came to your solo pieces in 'Still I'm Sad' and the into to 'Stargazer' did he say to you, you have a free range to improvise or I only want you to stick to playing to a certain length of time.

No, no he said do a solo. This was the thing, it was a very democratic band, in fact what I liked about the solo on 'Still I'm Sad' is that Ritchie came down. I hate playing loud keyboard solos over a loud backing. There's no chance of any dynamics, the dynamics just go the way of anything. If I play an organ solo I'd rather have it in a Jimmy Smith vein, a small trio, where you get louder and softer. And 'Still I'm Sad' was this interplay back and forth between Ritchie and me, which I really enjoyed, because that developed almost from the first gig. Cozy came way, way down and Ritchie was noodling, and I started noodling back as it were, and we got these really fast clever little progressive rock kind of thing going on that wasn't the sound of seventies metal, it had more in common with Weather Report than Black Sabbath.

I think it shows with his knowledge of music, and yours as well with the classical background. He was into the Bach thing at that time wasn't he?

Oh he carried this stupid cello around with him. I wonder if he can play it? Because he couldn't play it then! Before he became Robin Hood, which he now is, he had a little witch's hat he put on sometimes and he had his cello. We were all into classical music, Cozy did his solo to 1812 overture, and we were very much into the 'Planets Suite' by Gustav Holst. In fact Ritchie gave me a tape of that I had for twenty-five years. We were all into this (pause)... we're better than Kiss. Not that anybody had anything against Kiss but we were the intellectual end of the scale here "although we are as loud as fuck and we'll blow you out of your socks!"

Did he play it in the studio?

No he just lugged it around and pose with it. I never heard him play a note. My quote to Ritchie Blackmore is he still can't play the fucking cello. One thing that R B taught me... he used to check in an acoustic guitar, a nylon string Spanish guitar into airlines without a case. Just like the most fragile thing you ever saw but it always came back whole because no one would ever throw it and all this equipment in flight cases would come back smashed and scratched. So if you want to send your Stratovarius in the mail don't wrap it. It always came back perfect that guitar.

On the European leg of that tour the support band was AC/DC and Ritchie had problems with them beforehand in Purple. Was there any friction on that tour?

Bon Scott was a great guy and I remember him telling me a story of how his wife farted in bed! No, but once again you're talking to the wrong guy. I never had a problem with anybody. Almost in my life on a musician level and when it's a business problem I let the lawyers work it out. Here's a story, we went to the Chateau doing 'Long Live Rock 'n' Roll', shortly before I left, and there was a French singer there like a Jacques Brell type of folk singer, kind of guy who had garlic in his pocket and a roll of salami, a real Frenchman. And I guess there were two studios there and he was using one of the rooms and Ritchie went over. It was like a scene in Animal House where John Belushi smashes the guitar. Ritchie went over to this folksinger and his whole band was sitting there in the other lounge by the fireplace and Ritchie took the guy's acoustic guitar and threw it in the fire! Went up to the guy really aggressive and took it out of his hand and threw it into the flames as it were. And in these days we had a priest from the local village who was going to exorcise somebody or something, and all this shit, and tarot cards and black magic stuff. I was more bemused by that than anything else. When you say problems with other bands that was the way they would have come about- uncalled for violence, but like childish violence. Nobody stuck a knife in anybody, and I guess he gave the guy a new Stratocaster afterwards, made it up to him, but yeah like a little kid but I was actually bemused. And later I got to know this guy and I felt fairly bad about it. He was a great guy, he couldn't help it that he was French!

I think you have reminded me of something. You were still there when Mark Clarke came in?

Yeah.

I think he said something about doing a gig in a little club in Paris or around that area and Ritchie might have done a similar thing, borrowed a guy's guitar and smashed it up.

I don't remember that, I was gone by then, but unnecessary. But you have to think how much of Ritchie Blackmore is calculated and how much is image building. I don't think very much I think that's just the guy. He is one in fifty million. He jumps out and there's no get around him, and if that's part of the guy you take the good with the bad. Until somebody gets hurt, but I don't think he had a driver's licence so at least he didn't kill anybody.

There were a lot of pranks going on then. Cozy told me something years ago about an antique radio on the mantelpiece and they threw it in the fire, and Colin walks into the room and tries to retrieve it and then the owner walks in and though that Colin had just put it in there but he was trying to take it out. Were you still there then?

Yeah that was about the week I left, I remember something about the radio.

Erik Thomsen (Scandinavian tour promoter) was a guy they always pulled pranks on.

I expect so because he was a nice guy with a family and he drove us around in his own car. He was definitely the kind of patsy for a perfect set up but not much stuff with me, road pranks.

I've heard a story of Cozy challenging him (Erik Thomsen) to a race in his Ferrari. I don't know if it was that tour or not but apparently Cozy said you can drive my Ferrari and I'll drive this old banger and I'll beat you to the end of the road and apparently the roadies had tied all the chairs from the back of the venue to this Ferrari and he didn't know about it.

Now that's a prank, that's hilarious. That's nothing to do with anyone getting hurt or traumatised.

Do you remember Shoshana?

No. Bebe Buell was around, and was together with Todd Rundgren after that. She was a playmate. She was in France. Pretty sure she was in France. I know Bebe was on the American tour, she was like a playmate of the month and a famous groupie, band groupie. She was actually a nice woman, a band follower, let's put it that way, nothing cheap about her. And she had been around in and out.

She was with Ritchie then?
Err.. yeah. Well she wasn't with me!

There was a lot of humour on that tour though wasn't there?
A lot of humour around the band anyway, but it wasn't really humour I understood, I'm an American. Ronnie's an American but he's a complete Anglophile and he was also well older than me. He was thirty-five when I was twenty-two. He'd been around the school of hard knocks and he knew the Deep Purple organisation. I was pretty much the outsider. I like British humour but I didn't understand it then. I mean there were pranks and things.

But even in the music Ritchie would throw in old Shadows tunes and stuff.
Oh yeah.

Was it also on that tour in Paris, where he and Cozy swapped instruments?
I didn't see that, we didn't play Paris. (Tony's memory clearly failed him here because the band did indeed play Paris on 13th October).

That tour also. I've read stories about in Japan when you were doing your solo the band would set chairs up on the side of the stage and read newspapers.
That happened once or twice. I think Ronnie had a monkey suit on, like a gorilla, at least a gorilla's head! I'm like completely involved with eleven keyboards on stage doing my intellectual thing and I look over and they're all there with their knees crossed, like Monty Python, reading through the newspapers and Ronnie in a Gorilla suit! Hilarious!

Goodness knows what the audience thought of that.
Permanently sealing the legend of Rainbow.

Any other funny things you remember that stick in your memory?
Not really. Australia was great, Japan was great. My first impressions of these exotic far away countries for the first time. The concerts were great. We'd be back stage and the people would be filing in and all of a sudden we'd be on stage murdering the room. It was a high intensity band. The music is pretty much what stuck in my head. There were incidents, there were women none of it notable.

In Japan was it different the way the audiences treated the band?
We came from the airport and there were like seven hundred people to meet us, it was six in the morning when the flight came in from Australia and in the Tokyo Hilton we had to go in the kitchen entrance like the Beatles or whatever but we were so full or ourselves we thought we deserved it! It didn't seem like anything special, two hundred kids in front of the hotel. And they all want to give you a little present in Japan, like a pencil box. It felt like we deserved it, and at the concerts the people just exploded and stayed exploded the whole time.

I think that was an exceptional tour.
It was great and everyone was smiling and happy when we were playing.

The thing is he gets something good and knocks it on the head, like a self-destruct mechanism kicks in.

Yeah, or he's insecure because he needs to be the big frog in the pond, but maybe he doesn't understand he is the big frog in the pond and nobody's going to take that away from him. Last year I heard there were about a million emails going around about a Rainbow reunion. I got one from Ronnie Dio's Webmaster. Had I heard about it? I said "I thought it would be a good idea, any time but it's not going to happen."

I know when Cozy was still alive they were talking about doing something. Ronnie keeps mentioning it. Somehow without Cozy I don't think it would be the same.

We'd find somebody. There are wild ass kids out there. I mean I'd use Lars Ulrich, I'd call him in a second. But you got to think Ronnie is sixty-six I don't know how he does it. Looks healthy.

You touched on the stuff in the Chateau, had he fired you a couple of times before that?

He'd fired and hired me a couple of times before that, after the 'Rising' tour. I had an apartment on sunset strip and I knew the band was rehearsing and I was waiting for them to call me but they were auditioning other keyboard players. As a matter of fact Eddie Jobson from Roxy Music had shown up at the New York show on that tour and they were obviously in contact with him. And me being naïve as I am, and being the last to know, and see how it played out. Then Colin and Ronnie showed up at my apartment. I guess I was never fired but I know that they were auditioning other people and then said to me "come on down we'll have a rehearsal". "What- you want me to play with your band or what?" Smart arse kid. "Yeah if you will" and this and that. "But I thought you had twenty-five keyboard players" or something clever, but I went down. One of the nice things, very nice... it was down at Pirate Sound again, so I said okay, all hatchets were buried but there had never been a confrontation like "you're fired". So I came into this rehearsal and they'd left this cassette tape recording of a rehearsal with this absolutely horrible Italian organ player, playing this absolutely horrible meandering terrible solo at full volume over the PA system and it was like my welcome back, and I heard this horrible organ player and I said "okay I'm back."

It's interesting you mentioned that guy because he has cropped up before.

I never met him or know anything about him, but I knew he'd been playing with the band and he sucked. If he's Italy's best B3 player I deeply apologise.

There was obviously that time in the Chateau when things got a bit too much for you with all the pranks that Ritchie and Cozy were doing...

I don't know if it was pranks it was in the guise of Satanism.

I've read stories and they've told me their side of the stories, that they did some nasty stuff and that you just had enough and packed your bags.

Yeah in the middle of the day, but it was not just like teasing but really nasty. People getting hurt kind of nasty. I was in my room in the Chateau and a big rock came through my window, shattered me with broken glass and cut the lights at the same second. I was just scared shitless, and this was after we had these séances and the 'twelve stations of the cross' and bullshit black magic stuff. And someone, I guess it was Cozy or Ritchie stood outside my room and lit tarot cards on fire and slipped them under my door and I thought the place was going to burn down. I actually called my father in California and said, "Do me a favour Dad. I can't get a travel agent here, book me the next ticket out of Paris I'm coming home". Colin tried to talk me out of it as a matter of fact and I said, "No I'm gone. This is not fun, this is not music" so I left. This is the point; I expect I'm the only guy to ever quit that band. He fired me twice, once in England and once after the 'Rising' tour but I left. Nobody fired me then. I packed and left.

You said at the beginning you tried to sue them for the royalties and stuff. I read somewhere you also tried to sue them for attempted murder.
No that's complete nonsense. In fact I never even told anybody the story until I read it on the Internet about five years ago. That's not anything I ever shared with anybody. But now since everybody seems to know it... but things were getting out of hand like that. All I could think of was this roadie that went down the elevator shaft. I'm a musician, why in the world am I getting this grief, I really didn't know, but it was what the excitement was about. I was the youngest so let's pick on someone, like this English Public School thing.

It seems that whoever is the new boy at the time has to go through this initiation, the jokes. They all suffered it.
That's just a hate thing, like ordering ten Pizzas and have them delivered to somebody's room and say sign for these Mr Carey. That's one kind of hate thing but a huge stone, three or four kilo rock come bursting through this old chateau window and glass everywhere, I cut my feet up. Then the lights went out. It's dangerous and the hate thing, well you can be nice to people or be cruel to them depending on your bent, basically depending on how you were brought up. That's why I'd liked to have met Ritchie's father! Another thing I heard years later, that nobody actually believed I'd gone. They thought I was in Paris but I was in a plane within six hours. I got a taxi all the way up to Herouville, which is about half an hour from Paris, and a taxi to the airport and I sat and waited at the airport until my plane call and I'm gone. And they thought I was in Paris hanging around like I was kidding. And it's this broody... nobody really has much to say to anybody until the explosion comes. I never talked about that with Ritchie Blackmore or anybody. They never called me up and say, "did you really quit?" I know the keyboard parts on 'Long Live Rock 'n' Roll' are basically mine.

That's something I've never been able to get to the bottom of. I don't know if you have ever actually listened to the album.
Yeah about twenty-five years ago.

There's very little keyboards you can hear on it anyway.
There's a song called 'Rainbow Eyes' that I definitely play.

I can't even hear any keyboards on it.
There you go.

Whether they just wiped them off.
I would hope so, that would be the honourable thing to do. Because I never got any money and my father went in the hole for the plane ticket from Paris to Fresno, California.

I guess when you first joined the band, some of the pranks you look back on with a laugh.
I don't remember very many. Ritchie... one of the cute things he would do is take a shit and put it in the hotel lamp, a wall lamp or he'd get somebody to do it. I don't know if it was Ritchie's shit I didn't analyse it! So what you do is you come into the hotel room, and turn the lamp on and as soon as it warmed up the room would stink and you couldn't figure out where the stink was coming from.

That's horrible.
Well it's a prank! It's humiliating. Especially when you got to call a hotel guy and say "I think there's a dead rat in the wall", and he'd say "no someone took a shit in your lamp" (laughter).

But that sort of thing, kids humour, I didn't care one way or another. Ritchie used to complain and comment that I was reading. Always had a nose in a book. He said "you're just like Ian Paice, you've always got your nose in a book". "Well what am I supposed to do, talk to you guys?" We Californians have our own sense of humour.

I've spoke to about thirty people so far and expected a lot of the ex members to say similar things but no one has really said anything bad about him.
Other than he's Ritchie!

The bad feedback tends to come from others in the business like record company executives, journalists etc who he gave a hard time to.
Ritchie Blackmore is and was a musician's musician. The bottom line is whether it's Ray Charles with his heroin problem or Miles Davies being a complete man from Mars, the bottom line is all of it is towards one end and that's the music. It's hard to dislike him for what he is because what he is is so special, that you've pretty much got to take a lot of things as part of the deal. Having said that, (raising voice) that fucking cunt shit in my lamp! (laughs)

After his departure from Rainbow, Carey set up home in Germany where he still resides to this day. In 1978 he met German producer Peter Hauke and together they worked on Carey's first solo-albums. Initially instrumental albums, but later Carey added his own vocals to his albums. He also released two albums with a band called Planet P Project, (Self Titled (1983) & 'Pink World' (1984).)

Through working with Hauke, Tony met Peter Maffay who he still performs alongside to this day. Although his career has not seen him in the spotlight, Carey has nevertheless had some American chart success in 1982 with 'I Won't Be Home Tonight', in 1983 with Planet P Project's 'Why Me?', and in 1984 with 'Fine, Fine Day' and 'First Day Of Summer' although it has to be said that his style of music is a world apart from Rainbow. As a composer he has also put his talent to use with film-music and soundtracks. As both a performer and producer Tony Carey has also worked alongside many artists such as Joe Cocker, John Mayall, Eric Burdon, David Knopfler, Jimmy Barnes and Jennifer Rush.

****

Acknowledgements

Special thanks to all those who either conducted some of the interviews within this book, as well as those who helped to make them a reality: Neil Davies, Becky Deayton, Rob Fodder, Helmut Gerlach, Rasmus Heide, Neil Jeffries, Christian Meyer zu Natrup, Peter Purnell, Jörg Schulz, Stuart Smith, Carole Stevens, Rob Walton, Sarah Watson, Mark Welch, Doogie White, Jerry Witherstone, Alan Whitman, Eileen Whitman.

Photo credits

Photo credits: MBTP, pages 8, 13, 14, 17, 22, 34, 47, 114 & 115; Rasmus Heide, p48 & 53; Frank Oheim, p18 & 21; Neil Davies, p66, 69, 77, 81 & 82; Marc Brans, p114, 115, 116, 122, 140 & 149; Roger Newport; p128; Alexander Timofeev, p145; www.truebeliever.de, p163

Every effort has been made to trace the copyright holders of the photographs in this book but one or two were unreachable. We would be grateful if the photographers concerned would contact us.

About the author

Jerry Bloom has been a life-long fan of Ritchie Blackmore and Deep Purple since he first heard Fireball back in 1971. He jointly established the *More Black than Purple* magazine with Mark Welch in 1996, and Jerry has edited the magazine since 2000.

Apart from the Deep Purple family of bands, he has a wide-ranging taste in music appreciation. His other all-time favourite artists are Bob Dylan & Frank Zappa. Having been raised on the seventies music, amongst his other favourites are Free, Genesis (up to Hackett era!), Pink Floyd and Rush. He also enjoys a diverse array of acts such as The Stranglers, J.S Bach, Abba, Enya, The Cardigans and a very personal favourite in Mostly Autumn.

As a consequence of the latter, in February 2004 Jerry also took over as editor of Autumn Leaves, the official Mostly Autumn magazine. His first full length book, *Black Knight*, the first ever Ritchie Blackmore biography was published by Omnibus Press in 2006. His other activities include freelance writing, typesetting, design and concert production. He has written sleeve notes for labels such as Polydor, Sony BMG, Angel Air & Classic Rock Productions, articles for magazines such as Record Buyer, designed the Blackmore's Night Ghost Of A Rose tour programme and was production manager for the 2004 two-day Uriah Heep convention featuring Ken Hensley.

His other interests include football (Jerry has been a life-long Chelsea fan long before the Abramovich era!), cricket, Jaguar cars, and when he finds time he enjoys travelling, particularly around Bavaria, and central Europe.

If you would like to contact Jerry regarding any proposed work, email, editor@moreblackthanpurple.co.uk or call +44 (0) 1234 326691.

Lightning Source UK Ltd.
Milton Keynes UK
UKHW011836070119

335148UK00009B/422/P

9 780955 754203